THE STORY OF
MISTLETOE
MUTUALISMS
IS ALL ABOUT
ENTANGLEMENTS OF
INTERDEPENDENCIES,
NUTRIENT CYCLES,
AND SEDUCTIONS.
IT TELLS OF AN ETHOS
OF GIVING THAT
GOES AROUND,
AND COMES BACK,
PRODUCING
ENTANGLEMENTS
THAT ARE VERITABLE
ORGIES OF
SEDUCTIVE GIFTS.
—DEBORAH BIRD ROSE

THINKING WITH

DEBORAH BIRD ROSE

THOM VAN DOOREN AND
MATTHEW CHRULEW

EDITORS

DUKE UNIVERSITY PRESS   DURHAM AND LONDON 2022

Project editor: Lisa Lawley / Designed by Aimee C. Harrison
Typeset in Arno Pro and Scala Sans by Westchester Publishing
Services

Library of Congress Cataloging-in-Publication Data
Names: Van Dooren, Thom, [date] editor. |
Chrulew, Matthew, editor.
Title: Kin : thinking with Deborah Bird Rose /
Thom van Dooren and Matthew Chrulew.
Description: Durham : Duke University Press, 2022. |
Includes bibliographical references and index.
Identifiers: LCCN 2021034592 (print)
LCCN 2021034593 (ebook)
ISBN 9781478015420 (hardcover)
ISBN 9781478018056 (paperback)
ISBN 9781478022664 (ebook)
Subjects: LCSH: Rose, Deborah Bird, 1946- | Nature—Effect of
human beings on. Ethnoecology. | Ethnology—Methodology. |
Human-animal relationships. | Human geography. | Environ-
mental ethics. | BISAC: SOCIAL SCIENCE / Indigenous Studies |
SOCIAL SCIENCE / Gender Studies
Classification: LCC GF75 .K55 2022 (print) | LCC GF75 (ebook) |
DDC 304.2/8—dc23/eng/20211008
LC record available at https://lccn.loc.gov/2021034592
LC ebook record available at https://lccn.loc.gov/2021034593

Chapter 4, "Speculative Fabulations for Technoculture's Generations: Taking Care of Unexpected Country," by Donna J. Haraway,
was previously published in the Artium exhibit catalog, Vitoria,
Spain, October 2007.

Cover art: Orange-flowered mistletoe (*Dendropthoe glabrescens*),
Sundown National Park, Queensland, Australia. Photo by
Robert Ashdown.

FOR DEBORAH BIRD ROSE

CONTENTS

WORLDS OF KIN

An Introduction

THOM VAN DOOREN AND MATTHEW CHRULEW

This entangled quality of life on Earth depends on and supports connectivity. There are numerous ways into thinking about these matters. I offer one way: the kinship mode. It situates us here on Earth, and asserts that we are not alone in time or place: we are at home where our kind of life (Earth life) came into being, and we are members of entangled generations of Earth life, generations that succeed each other in time and place. . . . Ethical questions within the world of connectivity start with how to appreciate the differences between humankind and others, while at the same time also understanding that we are all interdependent. How to engage in world making across species? How to work toward world making that enhances the lives of others? And how to do all this in the time of extinctions, knowing, as we must, that we are living amidst the ruination of others?

—DEBORAH BIRD ROSE, *Wild Dog Dreaming* (2011)

THE LIFE AND WORK OF Deborah Bird Rose were grounded in and animated by a world of kin. This is a world of interwoven, intergenerational, more-than-human connectivity that both sustains and obligates, calling out for care and responsibility. Kinship is reciprocal, situated, tying human beings to other kinds of animals and plants, vulnerable and creative bodies all, and to the wider seasons and patterns of Earth and the cosmos. While such an understanding always carries great significance, the particular challenge of Debbie's work—the question that she returned to relentlessly—is how we are to keep faith with such a world in the midst of ongoing processes of colonization and extinction, of ecocide and genocide.

This book takes this expansive and generative notion of kin as its title and its watchword. Importantly, this is a mode of thinking and living that is thoroughly rooted in the insights of Debbie's Indigenous friends and teachers, especially those of the Aboriginal communities of Yarralin and Lingara in northern Australia. As Debbie put it in the monograph that grew out of her doctoral research in the 1980s, *Dingo Makes Us Human*, "Yarralin people tell us that the earth is alive and constantly giving life, the mother of us all. The fact of one mother makes us all kin of a sort" (Rose 1992, 220). Over the decades that followed, this fundamental notion of a more-than-human kinship took on an increasingly central role in Debbie's thinking, drawing the insights of her Aboriginal teachers into dialogue with both relational Western philosophies and the emerging ecological sciences. In this way, she sought to articulate and advocate for a world of kin, grounded in a profound sense of the connectivities and relationships that hold us together, vulnerable and responsible to one another.

Inspired by and in conversation with the remarkable body of research and writing that Debbie produced during her life, this collection seeks to make a distinctive contribution to the environmental humanities. It features contributions on decolonial and multispecies cosmopolitics, more-than-human sociality, speculative fabulation, ecological totemism, Anthropocene extinctions, and a range of other topics. Engaging with the central concepts of Debbie's work—from Year Zero and ethical time to ecological existentialism and world-crazy love, from double death and wild country to responsive attentiveness and generative care—the contributors to this volume work to face up to the social and ecological inheritances of settler colonialism and industrial modernity, searching for effective and ethical modes of address, storytelling, and practice in the wake of dispossession and destruction.

2

THOM VAN DOOREN & MATTHEW CHRULEW

Deborah Bird Rose (1946–2018) was one of the founding and most original thinkers in the emergence of the environmental humanities, both in Australia and internationally. Over the course of a career spanning almost forty years, she published many widely read, cited, and often-reprinted books: *Hidden Histories, Dingo Makes Us Human, Nourishing Terrains, Country of the Heart, Reports from a Wild Country, Wild Dog Dreaming*, and, finally, *Shimmer* (Rose 1991, 1992, 1996; Rose et al. 2002; Rose 2004, 2011, 2021); edited numerous volumes, such as *Aboriginal Australians and Christian Missions, Manifesto for Living in the Anthropocene*, and *Extinction Studies* (Swain and Rose 1988; Gibson, Rose, and Fincher 2015; Rose, van Dooren, and Chrulew 2017); and cofounded the journal section Ecological Humanities in the *Australian Humanities Review* and the international journal *Environmental Humanities*. Through this work Debbie made major contributions in a range of fields: from the environmental humanities and the anthropology of Indigenous Australia, to extinction studies, animal and multispecies studies, and philosophies of ethics, justice, religion, environment, temporality, and place. At the same time, Debbie also inspired the development of new modes of scholarship. Hers was a scholarly practice of paying close attention, of drawing together disparate voices from within and far beyond the academy, a practice grounded in a skilled refinement of the crafts of writing and storytelling, and a deep commitment to and creative intervention toward better possibilities for life and death.

Debbie was initially trained as an anthropologist, and her writing and thinking were characterized by a profoundly dialogical approach. Her great art and skill was to bring diverse stories, ideas, and concepts into generative conversation, not to create harmony or synergy but rather to stretch them beyond their comfort zones, rubbing them together to see what sparks might be produced—an approach that she named "firestick wisdom" (Rose 2011, 13–16). In this way, she drew on Indigenous knowledges, philosophy, literature, theology, ecology, and the broader natural sciences. But all of her work retained a strong grounding in the ethnographic methods of her anthropological training.

Born and raised in the United States, Debbie came to Australia in 1980 to carry out PhD research.[1] She began her academic career living and learning with Aboriginal communities of the Victoria River District in northern Australia. This was to be a lifelong relationship. Over the next forty years, she continued to visit these communities and work and think with them. In addition to them being her friends and adopted family, Debbie worked with

3

the community—as she did with numerous others around the country—on their claims to have the lands stolen through colonization returned to them (see Ford, this volume). In 2016, just a couple of years before her death, these Traditional Owners of the Yarralin area were finally awarded an Aboriginal Freehold title on their lands.

Again and again throughout her life, Debbie returned in her writing to the stories and insights shared with her by her Aboriginal teachers, people like the clever man Old Tim Yilngayarri, Daly Pulkara, Hobbles Danaiyarri, and Jessie Wirrpa. In some cases, for example, in her first published article (Rose 1984) and in the collaborative, coauthored book *Country of the Heart* (Rose et al. 2002), she worked to create spaces for Indigenous people to tell their own stories, in their own words. In much of her writing, however, she took up the careful work of weaving these voices and stories into her own accounts, of thinking with their shared wisdom. While never a substitute for their testimony or for the powerful Indigenous scholarship now gaining place within and beyond the academy, for many decades she sought to make her writing a means by which otherwise-silenced voices could be heard. As these elders passed away, one by one, she continued their conversations, working to keep them moving in the world. As Debbie put it in an interview shortly before her death: "When I go back to my notebooks, or to stories that I've told in one context that I want to return to in another context, they just keep *unfolding*. It hasn't reached bottom; it never would reach bottom—there just isn't a bottom."[2]

These are stories that describe and perform a world of kin, of significant connectivities, reciprocities, and responsibilities. While Debbie had come to Australia with the same kinds of environmental sensibilities as many people of her generation, in Yarralin she learned to see a world in which the social and cultural did not stop at the edges of the human, in which "the environment" took on a whole different set of meanings. During her first few years in Australia, Debbie spent a great deal of time on Country with these communities. She also spent time with Aboriginal people and natural scientists working and learning together. She recounted her initial amazement as the same knowledgeable elders worked with botanists, geologists, hydrologists, and other specialized scientists, possessing a depth of knowledge across each of these domains and drawing connections between what Western disciplines separated.[3] This knowledge arose out of kinship relations, interactions of attention and care. It was at this point that she realized that to really understand this world, she needed to look beyond the conventional approaches of anthropology. As she put it, "If I'm going to understand the questions I want

THOM VAN DOOREN & MATTHEW CHRULEW

answered I can't just stop at the edge of the cultural or the edge of the social, I have to keep going. . . . Especially in a kin-based society, where what's happening is in your Country, to and with your nonhuman kin, anthropology just isn't going to take you there. You really have to have a different suite of skills, of questions, and a different paradigm as to what counts as society."[4] Debbie began to take up these questions in a serious way in *Dingo Makes Us Human* (1992). This book is, in a sense, her most conventional ethnographic piece of writing—an effort to give an account of the way of life of the communities of Yarralin, for whom "kinship is all about the matrix of country, Dreamings, flesh, and people" (117). Her ethnography listens carefully to accounts of frontier violence and resistance as well as to stories of sustaining lifeways and of ongoing care for Country.

Debbie's account in this book did not neutrally reconstruct a foreign worldview or reduce Indigenous cosmologies and practices to curious artifacts but aimed instead to explore their cultural context, to articulate their status as situated knowledge, and to find ways to draw connections with comparable Western concepts and to elaborate their significance for contemporary problems.[5] To this end, for example, she drew tentative comparisons between Yarralin knowledge and cosmology and the emerging sciences of ecology and Earth systems theory, both of which challenge theological and metaphysical notions of human separation and control: "Lovelock notes that his understanding of Gaia as a living organism is not new. When Yarralin people speak of mother Earth they speak to a similar understanding. They are the inheritors of a theory and practice of participating in living systems. They understand these systems scientifically, through observations and hypotheses developed and tested through time. They also understand them metaphysically. Dreaming Law tells the story, often obliquely, frequently in bits that people have to put together for themselves. Dreaming and ecology intersect constantly, providing a rich understanding of universal and local life" (Rose 1992, 218). The depth and significance of these intercultural translations between systems of knowledge and practice in her work only grew as, at the turn of the millennium, interdisciplinary dialogues gained in sophistication alongside growing recognition of the urgency of ecological crisis and its irreducible social complexities.

Particularly from the late 1990s, Debbie's work took on a more explicitly philosophical and speculative approach and delved forthrightly—while equally carefully—into the task of building bridges between Indigenous and European concepts, understandings, and ethics. *Reports from a Wild Country* (2004) focused on histories and ongoing realities of colonization in Australia, working to imagine possibilities for decolonization and genuine reconciliation. Comparing Western and Aboriginal understandings of time and land, life and death, she indicts the specious colonial narrative of progress enacted on the frontier at such devastating social and ecological cost, articulating against it the resilient and creative intergenerational work of Dreaming: "Memory, place, dead bodies and genealogies hold the stories that tell the histories that are not erased, and that refuse erasure. Painful as they are, they also constitute relationships of moral responsibility, binding people into the country and the generations of their lives" (57).

Reports was also one of the first books to bring Levinasian ethics into efforts to think about the challenges of life for contemporary Indigenous communities. As Debbie later reflected on the ethical challenges of her ethnographic work:

> It was talking to those dingo dreaming guys, [talking] with Old Tim, that I realized, he has been through slaughter and he's a survivor of genocide. He's a survivor in a really particular and peculiar way, and he is sitting here witnessing the war against dingoes. He is seeing another round of extinctions. He knows the white guys would just like to get rid of dingoes forever more, so he is seeing it happen now to his nonhuman kin. That, I think, was what drove me to the understanding that you can't sit and listen to this stuff in an innocent way, you can't be detached from it, you can't be overinvolved with it either (it's not your story); and so you have to listen in a really different, attentive way.[6]

To help think through these difficulties and obligations, Debbie turned to the work of scholars of genocide, especially of the Shoah. Emmanuel Levinas was foremost among them, but so, too, was the work of others such as James Hatley, Lev Shestov, Emil Fackenheim, and Edith Wyschogrod.

Wild Dog Dreaming (2011), the last book Debbie published before her death, continued in this vein. This is a disparate, mongrel collection of stories from some of Debbie's Aboriginal teachers, brought into conversation with biblical narratives and novels and poems from J. M. Coetzee, Peter Boyle, and others, alongside the insights of the natural sciences, from evolutionary theory and microbiology to ecology and biosemiotics, and the work of philosophers from Jacques Derrida to Val Plumwood. But, most of all, this is a book in which dogs guide the way. Among many other canine presences, we encounter Bobby, the dog that adopted Levinas and others during their internment in a Nazi prison camp; the fictitious Youngfella of Coetzee's novel *Disgrace*; the black dogs that guard King Solomon's tomb; and countless

THOM VAN DOOREN & MATTHEW CHRULEW

1.1 Debbie with her two dogs, Kelly and Jay Jay, in 1998. PHOTO BY DARRELL LEWIS.

dingoes and wild dogs of outback Australia, variously cherished as kin and marked for extermination as vermin. In weaving together these diverse stories, this book is an invitation into a world of kin: a world of connectivities, of beauty and mystery that exceeds us in every way, and yet one that we find ourselves inescapably bound to, at stake in, and accountable for.

In the chapter titled "Job's Grief," Debbie tells the Aboriginal story of the dingo and the moon in dialogue with Job's biblical struggle with God. Each story helps us to see the other differently, to draw out possibilities for relationship and responsibility. In this case, the dialogue becomes a site for reimagining the conclusion to Job's story, a reimagining that inserts a canine presence: Blackie, a dog who befriends Job in his time of greatest need. "Being a dog, she would not be fussy about open sores and flaking skin, bad breath or loathsome odors. More than that, she would see him not as a sickly shell but as a full human" (Rose 2011, 78). In other chapters, a host of living and dead, philosophical and literary, canines guide the way. In each case they become vital figures for new ethical possibilities. More than simply embodying the good, they interrupt and reorient, transforming the status

WORLDS OF KIN: AN INTRODUCTION

quo through the provision of comfort, connection, recognition, guidance, and loyalty.

At the time of her death, Debbie had just completed work on a final book, *Shimmer* (2021), which explores the entangled lives and deaths of humans and flying foxes in Australia. Combining her research in multispecies studies, extinction studies, anthropology, and environmental philosophy, this book paints a vivid portrait of flying fox life and death in the Anthropocene that has important wider lessons for ecological and decolonial ontologies and ethics. Drawing on ethnographic fieldwork both with Aboriginal Australians and with wildlife carers rescuing flying foxes from heat stress, tick paralysis, and managerial harassment, she bears witness to cruel practices and other anthropogenic and "natural" perils to coexistence. Building from sources such as Jesper Hoffmeyer's biosemiotics, Lucien Lévy-Bruhl's philosophical anthropology, Levinas's post-Holocaust ethics, Shestov's existentialism and Isabelle Stengers's cosmopolitics, and the many insights of her Aboriginal friends and teachers, she articulates her own uniquely situated testament to the intergenerational gifts of ancestral power, ever more threatened, yet preciously shared and affirmed. As she put it:

> I was called to flying-foxes. My research questions led me into multispecies ethnographic work involving wildlife carers and academically trained scientists in eastern Australia. The people I met were at the front line in the work of holding flying-foxes back from the edge of extinction. I continued to visit the north, and I revisited my notebooks from several decades of research with Aboriginal people. The research was exhilarating, and then again at times deeply disheartening. I was to encounter more passion, intimacy, cruelty, horror, complexity, generosity and wild beauty than I could ever have imagined. Living with flying-foxes, I came to understand, takes us straight to the heart of every big question facing earth life in the 21st century. (Rose 2021, 2–3)

Flying foxes were one of Debbie's core passions. She was captivated by their silhouettes and gentle wingbeats across the sky at dusk, by their multifaceted social relationships and fidelity to one another and to particular places, by their ecological roles as pollinators and seed dispersers for increasingly fragmented forests: beings who dip their faces into blossoms in search of nectar and in so doing carry forest futures on their furry little bodies (228). *Shimmer* takes us into the fascinating lives and worlds of these remarkable creatures.

It does so, however, in a way that is equally captivated by the diverse human communities that flying foxes find themselves and their futures tangled up with in contemporary Australia. Around this vast continent, flying foxes are simultaneously cherished and despised. As such, the book explores the long and ongoing history of flying foxes' violent persecution by orchardists and others, the loss of their key habitat, and the emerging impacts of climate change. Debbie tells the story of how "cruelty and its allies" have rendered flying foxes disposable, setting up ongoing, self-perpetuating processes of mass killing: vortexes of death in which connectivities unravel and mutualities falter (150). These threats have together imperiled the lives of countless individual flying foxes and are today pushing their species ever further toward the edge of extinction. But the human–flying fox relationships that most captivated Debbie, and that are the central focus of this book, are those that seek to intervene in, to challenge and resist, all this death. Ultimately, it is a set of stories told *against* mass death, in fidelity with life, in celebration of the waves of ancestral power that are our living world.

From *Dingo Makes Us Human* to *Shimmer*, Debbie's writing retained the character of a careful meditation that is both celebration and lamentation. In different ways and in company with different voices and creatures, her work is a cry of love, passion, and outrage in the face of the ongoing death work of our times, a period that Debbie recognized as characterized by entwined processes of colonization and environmental destruction, of genocide and ecocide. But it is also an effort to imagine, honor, and enact other possibilities for living and dying well. These are the issues that animated Debbie's life and writing. Drawn into a world of more-than-human kinship right at the outset of her career, she spent the remainder of her life working to understand, acknowledge, and keep faith with such a world.

AT THE HEART OF DEBBIE'S OWN EFFORT to inhabit this world of kin was her understanding of the work of storytelling. She insisted that stories do not just recount connectivities; they also weave new ones. They are about forging relationships, about learning to see and understand, and, as a result, about being drawn into new obligations and responsibilities. There are no abstract ethical systems here; instead, as Debbie put it: "Stories themselves have the potential to promote understandings of embodied, relational, contingent ethics," to "pull readers into ethical proximity" (Rose 2013, 9). Through the slow, careful work of paying attention to the world—in our own or others' stories—we come to understand, to be connected, to be redone, in ways that just might enable better possibilities for living.

But she also knew that the power of stories is very far from being absolute. She argued that even if there is only death, even if nothing is to be gained through "writing into the great unmaking" (Rose 2013, 8), there is still an obligation to take up this work. In another aspect of her work profoundly indebted to philosophers and writers of the Shoah, she insisted on the importance of storytelling in the mode of witnessing, of refusing to turn away from suffering, from violence, from injustice, an act of "keeping faith" (Rose 2011). To refuse to turn away, she argued, was "to remain true to the lives within which ours are entangled, whether or not we can accomplish great change" (Rose 2013, 9). To turn away, to disavow, to forget: all are modes of abandonment that must be resisted in times of colonization and extinctions when living beings and their ways of life are under threat en masse.

These senses of the ethical importance of storytelling—as a mode of connection and avowal—ground much of Debbie's later work. In this way, her writings are not simply *about* ethics; they are in themselves ethical acts, efforts to interrupt the relentless momentum of death work to make a space for something else. They are efforts to relay the witness of massacres and land theft, to summon a pack of dogs into this difficult space, to evoke the fragile beauty of flying fox camps and flights.

In no small way, Debbie's work provided the foundation for the interdisciplinary environmental humanities in Australia and has in turn been profoundly influential in shaping the field around the world. She articulated a vision of the environmental humanities as a passionate and engaged space of scholarship. She did this in her own writing but also in her stewardship of the field as a founding editor of the journal *Environmental Humanities*, as a convenor of early conferences and workshops, and as a supervisor of numerous PhD students and postdocs and a collaborator with junior and senior colleagues.

Through her body of work, Debbie modeled a scholarship that was committed to life: to exploring the living world in its beauty and its challenges and to making a stand for flourishing, for inclusive possibilities. She opened up space for the next generation to write, think, and research in new ways. Put simply, her work was animated by and aimed to draw us all into a kind of "world-craziness." Adopting and adapting Shestov's thinking, she called for us to turn toward the earth: "to cherish birth and growth, and to love that which is perilous. . . . World-craziness immerses us in the power, resilience, connectivity, and uncertainty of the living Earth" (Rose 2011, 118).

THOM VAN DOOREN & MATTHEW CHRULEW

1.2 Debbie camping at Jasper Gorge near Yarralin and Lingarra in 2012. PHOTO BY DARRELL LEWIS.

This passionate scholarship is grounded in the insights and commitments of Indigenous and decolonial thought, of feminist philosophy, of multispecies and more-than-human perspectives. In short, it is a scholarship that insists that "the environment" is from the outset relational and, so, ethical. The task, as Debbie often put it, quoting Val Plumwood, was "to resituate the human in ecological terms, and . . . to resituate the non-human in ethical terms" (Rose 2015, 3). This is an understanding of connectivity that works against the clichéd notion that everything is connected to everything and that instead insists on attention to the specificity of the multispecies kinships that hold us together: dependent on, vulnerable to, and responsible to one another. At the heart of her philosophy is an insistence that there is no outside to connectivity—only the arrogant delusion of attempts to occupy such a position of detachment and control.

She modeled this engaged attachment with a generative and imaginative philosophical style. There is a deliberate generosity in her scholarship as she invites diverse thinkers, understandings, and stories into company with each other. Sometimes these encounters are staged by her in the text, perhaps as a gathering around a campfire. At other times they take place less explicitly. Always, however, she is interested to see what sparks of creativity and possibility might be struck. In this way, her writing is an effort to both tell and dwell with stories in a way that works against closure, "keeping the wisdom rolling, allowing it to accumulate, and refraining from declaring final meanings" (Rose 2011, 15).

This collection seeks to continue and extend this generous and generative dimension of Debbie's character and approach. Instead of writing *about* Debbie and her work, the chapters in this book think *with* her and her many powerful contributions; they are pieces of original scholarship rather than summaries or discussions of her work. In practice, this means that the chapters draw on or are guided by Debbie's writing in a substantial way but equally draw it into conversation with new places and themes. In this way, this book both celebrates Debbie's existing body of work and opens up the scope for her remarkable thought and writing to reach out into the world and continue to transform understandings and practices. Whatever the path by which its contributors have emerged from or engaged with the many fields that Debbie worked within and between, they—like her—seek to think across and athwart disciplines. Their work coheres in its grounding in a relatively consistent set of methods and styles, each of them drawing on a combination of ethnographic, philosophical, literary, and historical approaches. Perhaps most important, the contributors all share Debbie's commitment to scholarly writing as an ethical praxis grounded in careful attention to the particular, to a world of diverse human and other-than-human lives bound up in relationships of interdependence and obligation. In short, they are writing within and for a world of kin.

NOTES

1. For more information on Debbie's biography, see van Dooren (2020); Muecke (2020).
2. Deborah Bird Rose, unpublished interview conducted by Thom van Dooren, September 26, 2018.
3. Rose, unpublished interview.
4. Rose, unpublished interview.
5. On the traps, challenges, and necessity of such dialogue, see Rose (1988).
6. Rose, unpublished interview.

REFERENCES

Gibson, Katherine, Deborah Bird Rose, and Ruth Fincher, eds. 2015. *Manifesto for Living in the Anthropocene*. Brooklyn, NY: Punctum Books.

Muecke, Stephen. 2020. "Her Biography: Deborah Bird Rose." *a/b: Auto/Biography Studies* 35 (1): 273–277.

Rose, Deborah Bird. 1984. "The Saga of Captain Cook: Morality in Aboriginal and European Law." *Australian Aboriginal Studies* 2: 24–39.

Rose, Deborah Bird. 1988. "Exploring an Aboriginal Land Ethic." *Meanjin* 47 (3): 378–387.

Rose, Deborah Bird. 1991. *Hidden Histories: Black Stories from Victoria River Downs, Humbert River and Wave Hill Stations*. Canberra: Aboriginal Studies Press.

Rose, Deborah Bird. 1992. *Dingo Makes Us Human: Life and Land in an Aboriginal Australian Culture*. Cambridge: Cambridge University Press.

Rose, Deborah Bird. 1996. *Nourishing Terrains: Australian Aboriginal Views of Landscape and Wilderness*. Canberra: Australian Heritage Commission.

Rose, Deborah Bird. 2004. *Reports from a Wild Country: Ethics for Decolonisation*. Sydney: University of New South Wales Press.

Rose, Deborah Bird. 2011. *Wild Dog Dreaming: Love and Extinction*. Charlottesville: University of Virginia Press.

Rose, Deborah Bird. 2013. "Slowly ~ Writing into the Anthropocene." In "Writing Creates Ecology and Ecology Creates Writing." Special issue, TEXT, no. 20, 1–14.

Rose, Deborah Bird. 2015. "The Ecological Humanities." In *Manifesto for Living in the Anthropocene*, edited by Katherine Gibson, Deborah Bird Rose, and Ruth Fincher, 1–5. Brooklyn, NY: Punctum Books.

Rose, Deborah Bird. 2022. *Shimmer: Flying Fox Exuberance in Worlds of Peril*. Edinburgh: Edinburgh University Press.

13

Rose, Deborah Bird, Sharon D'Amico, Nancy Daiyi, Kathy Deveraux, Margy Daiyi, Linda Ford, and April Bright. 2002. *Country of the Heart: An Indigenous Australian Homeland.* Canberra: Aboriginal Studies Press.

Rose, Deborah Bird, Thom van Dooren, and Matthew Chrulew, eds. 2017. *Extinction Studies: Stories of Time, Death, and Generations.* New York: Columbia University Press.

Swain, Tony, and Deborah Bird Rose, eds. 1988. *Aboriginal Australians and Christian Missions: Ethnographic and Historical Studies.* Bedford Park: Australian Association for the Study of Religions.

van Dooren, Thom. 2020. "Deborah Bird Rose (1946–2018)." *American Anthropologist* 122 (1): 192–195.

THE SOCIALITY OF BIRDS

Reflections on Ontological Edge Effects

ANNA LOWENHAUPT TSING

ON THE ISLAND OF WAIGEO, off the coast of West Papua, Indonesia, I've been interacting with a community currently fascinated by birds. Birds, people figure, might be the path to the future: they might attract international tourists who could fund village enterprises. And yet relationships between people and birds seem to me filled with ambivalence. Only the pagans of the past, local residents assured me, had special relations with birds and other animals. Today everyone is a Christian, and the terms of Christianity, they told me, require a disavowal of connections with other beings. This seemed to me a puzzle worth attention. Given this disavowal, why do so many men notice birds, and with such precision? Why are Waigeo men such good field guides for international bird-watchers? Earlier anthropologies of bird-watching, including in Papua (West 2006), have stressed the cosmological gulfs dividing Indigenous residents and Euro-American experts. How is it, then, that they can talk to each other at all?[1]

To answer this question requires bringing the sociality of birds into the conversation. In doing so I draw on the pioneering work of Deborah Bird Rose. Rose changed how practitioners get to do anthropology. She urged ethnographers into multispecies *attention* (Rose 2011). She showed us how animals participate in the social and ethical lives of human beings and that human responsibilities and modes of empathy stretch beyond humans to include the social responses of other beings. Despite the challenge of even greater communicative gulfs, my questions cannot be limited to interactions between one kind of human and another kind of human. Varied kinds of birds respond to varied kinds of humans, and vice versa (van Dooren 2014). Indeed, including the birds might allow analysts to glimpse overlapping strategies for empathetic attunement, despite cosmological gulfs, not only between one bird and another but also between expert and vernacular and between Euro-American and Papuan. I do not deny the colonial heritage of European bird science (e.g., McGhie 2017), but I do not stop with its reaffirmation. In dialogue with Rose (2004), I follow call-and-response as it refuses to stop at the lip of ontological ravines.

One of the most memorable sections, for me, of Rose's book *Reports from a Wild Country* is her exploration of Australian Aboriginal relations to the cattle brought by white settlers. On the one hand, Rose is clear about the colonizing role of cattle; cattle are "four legged soldiers in the army of conquest" (2004, 86). Furthermore, the celebration of cattle in white Australia is a performance of Man's triumph over Nature. On the other hand, Aboriginal cattle handlers manage to do something surprising with cattle. "Cattle events, rather than performing triumph, actually perform uncertainty, and thus contribute to the ongoing life of the Year Zero as a manifold of possibilities [i.e., Aboriginal ways of understanding time and community, with their contrast to white progress narratives]" (89). In rodeos, cattle respond to both settler and Aboriginal cultural logics. Rather than stopping with ontological differences, Rose brings us into performance events that sponsor multiple forms of relation, human and not human. This practice inspired me to open the study of birds in Waigeo beyond the otherness of international bird-watchers, as established in anthropological literature. How might local residents and international bird-watchers each, respectively but also in dialogue, respond to birds—and birds to them?

To begin to answer this question, I enlisted the help of ornithologist Kristof Zyskowski of the Yale Peabody Museum and bird photographer Yulia Bereshpolova. They showed me birds I would otherwise never have seen or heard. Kristof's and Yulia's patience and ability to notice, in turn, allowed me a much richer conversation with local residents who also saw and heard these birds, although not always on the same terms. Between these various interlocutors, the birds started to come to life for me as interlocutors on their own. Let me begin again, then, with birds.

Red bird of paradise (*Paradisaea rubra*): At dusk, they gather at the lek, a great tree the birds have designated as the place for performance.[2] This is not the place they eat, nor a place to make nests; this is the place for dancing. The males are superb in their maroon mantles, as saturated with color as velvet, with short golden capes and emerald face masks. This evening no females show, and the males entertain each other, working out their dance steps. First they shiver, shaking their feathers and then opening their wings, which turn crimson and translucent in the slanting light. Then they "moonwalk," shifting forward but pushing back in a shuffle. If the day is overcast, local people tell us, they don't perform. Yes, says our ornithologist, a study has been done showing that the birds recognize those bright days in which their colors glow. Now three males have lined up along a diagonal branch. First they shiver and shimmy; then they moonwalk. They approach the synchrony of a Motown trio. For me, this is the lasting image, those three, moving together through their steps. In the morning, there are females, and the action is less coordination among males and more competition for females' attention. And yet—we pay too much attention to functional goals. The three males dancing in the evening light still haunts me as an image of masculine beauty and coordination.

Across much of Papua and New Guinea, men adorn themselves with feathers to take on the beauty of birds. Post-Enlightenment Europeans, in thrall to the imagined force of masculine rationality, forgot about male beauty; it takes a visit with Renaissance paintings of saints to remember the celebration of male bodies in Europe. But in New Guinea, masculine beauty is paramount. When I saw red birds of paradise, I thought I sensed why: the birds astonish and amaze. In some New Guinea villages, male dancers wear birds of paradise on their heads (Kirk and Strathern 1993). In some, dancers evoke birds, at the edge of becoming them (Schieffelin 2005). In myths, birds become people, and people become birds (West 2006). Alas, none of this is true on the island of Waigeo, the home of red birds of paradise and the place I had gone to study people and birds. In the villages I visited, Christianity had plowed a great furrow separating the people who could change into birds and animals from the people of faith. The former are the "lost people," pagans now transformed into invisible cannibal witches. Christian conversion did not wipe out the pagan past, but it transformed what it means to be human so that animal transformations are signs only of malevo-lent, satanic powers. The beauty of birds exists across an unreachable divide. And yet: even in this echoing rift, there is an opening. Local men have not forgotten birds, since they encounter them every day in the forest. Most men know dozens of birds' sounds, characteristics, and habits. When ornitholo-gists and bird-watchers showed up in the area to make their bird lists, locals were intrigued—and ready to become facilitators and guides.

This chapter explores the strange spaces of partial contact among birds, Waigeo islanders, and traveling bird-watchers. To understand these spaces, I've borrowed the ecological term *edge effect*, which refers to what happens in the boundary zone between habitats. My habitats here are world-making projects, the distinctive features of which some anthropologists call *onto-logical* (Holbraad and Pedersen 2017). At the edges of these world-making projects, contact can create unexpected effects. While we may not be able to transform ourselves into radically different others, we can learn about them from immersion in these edge effects. I'm interested in contacts among different kinds of human projects—as when missionaries and villagers to-gether manage to call up cannibal witches. I'm also interested in the contacts between human world making and bird world making. To emphasize that element, I've divided what follows into three parts: birds watching humans, birds and humans watching each other, and humans watching birds. Designs for living together should take all three seriously.

BIRDS WATCHING HUMANS

Watching is a shorthand here by which I really mean "attending to works and lives." Birds pay lots of attention to human projects, although not nec-essarily in the ways we might first imagine. Perhaps the really important thing, for birds, is human infrastructure, the landscape-modification projects through which we make our living space, with major implications for all life. Many human infrastructures have been harmful for birds, as when pesticide-laced agriculture destroys their ability to hatch eggs (Carson 1962). Indus-trial infrastructures have been especially deadly, in part because investors do not stick around to see the results of their landscape interventions. Such infrastructures destroy not just individual birds but the very possibility of life. I think it's important, however, to distinguish industrial projects from all human existence. Thus, I begin more gently with the possibilities of humans, from birds' perspectives, by situating birds in the small villages and gardens beside Mayalibit Bay, Waigeo.

ANNA LOWENHAUPT TSING

Radjah shelducks (*Radjah radjah*) are big black-and-white ducks often seen waddling around in pairs or small groups; they forage for mollusks, algae, insects, and sedges. I started this project because, on a previous research trip to Waigeo, I was surprised to see Radjah shelducks walking confidently about a village, vocalizing loudly to each other—and then again in another village. Why weren't people eating them, I wondered—or at least scaring them away? On this trip, they were in every village we visited, sometimes foraging together with village chickens and dogs. To answer my original question, however, I had to learn something about the meaning of *village*. It turns out that most of the villages of Mayalibit Bay are very recent enactments of government and missionary dreams. These are not spaces for pursuing livelihoods but rather for being civilized, worshipping God, and receiving government development aid. Not eating the local ducks is part of a new way of being human, which does not depend much on local resources. This is a story worth telling for understanding the relation between local people and birds. But, first, two more things about ducks.

First, village children enjoy feeding Radjah shelducks. Children sometimes offer the ducks the leftover rice from meals. The birds learn to haunt human living places.

Second, Radjah shelducks cannot take commercial logging. The watershed around our village was logged by an Ambonese company between 2002 and 2008. A huge swath around the village is still essentially deforested, although an aggressive species of weedy vine covers everything in green. Village people explained that the ducks were gone until the past few years; without trees, they abandoned the village. This is probably because the ducks nest in trees near where they forage. Kill the trees, lose the ducks.

All this matters for thinking about the concept of village. Until the 1950s, one elder explained, this village hardly existed on the bay shore, where it is now. Most people lived inland, in groups attuned to their sago orchards and vegetable gardens. Sago was the staple, and it was eaten along with garden foods such as taro, sweet potatoes, sugarcane, bananas, papayas, and green vegetables, as well as hunted meat, avian and otherwise. Freshwater fish and shrimp were an important part of the diet, but foods from the bay were less convenient. Historically, the bay was a dangerous place, full of slaving and fighting vessels. He mimed how people approached the shore—looking right and left and creeping carefully—on those occasions they dared to search for the bay's resources. He was born in 1968 in the shore village, but his father was born in the interior. As a child, he recalls, he could not ignore a great pile of human bones, left from the wars, near the shore. Only with the coming of

19

THE SOCIALITY OF BIRDS

Christianity, he says, were the people pulled out of the forest to the bay-shore village sites.

But even this did not last long. In the 1970s, as part of New Order Indonesia's development plan for rural areas, villages were asked to consolidate to form supervillages where the government could control the populace and locate schools. People chafed at the consolidation, which left them far from their sago orchards and vegetable gardens, and in 2001 they mobilized to move back to their previous shore-edge places. The New Order had ended, and the new government was open to decentralization. By then, their old coastal village had become a forest, the elder recalled. Following coastal fashion in this region, they built houses right into the water, on high stilts so the tide ran underneath. But this was not the current government model of civilization, and by 2004 they had conceded the necessity to move away from the shore and to build flat on the ground with cement platforms and metal roofs. This planned-looking community is the development style to which "villages" are asked to aspire. (Meanwhile, old ironwood posts, set out in the tidal mud in front of the village, have become nesting sites for singing starlings [*Aplonis cantoroides*], who line the cavities made for crossbars with fresh insecticidal leaves to protect their eggs. The nesting starlings are the first sight as a visitor enters the village from the bay.) In 2008 the logging company built a church as payment for the watershed's forest. In 2015 a cement seawall was built to keep back the tide and transform the village's shoreline from mud into dry ground. Now this is a model village: neat, modern, and well ordered. It was one of two areas chosen by Flora and Fauna International, for example, to receive aid in developing ecotourism. It is hardly a scene of "traditional culture."

Some people, the elder recalled, did not convert and move to the coast. They became the orang Gi, "Gi people," the "lost people." They became invisible (gaib); they became witches (swanggi). Gi can turn into birds and animals, but they are also cannibals and sorcerers. That kind of power is not available to modern people on the coast, who are churchgoing men and women of faith. Even though the church front is painted with enormous men with wings (the Javanese finisher copied these angels from a pattern book, people said), there is no tie between humans and birds, even in stories, they told me. The only exception my interlocutor could think of was the possibility of reading the flights of brown-headed crows (*Corvus fuscicapillus*). If a crow flies from the west and gives a special call, it means someone in the family has died or, alternatively, that someone unexpected and unwanted will come. Of the animal relations once possible, there has been a bifurcation into prophecy—legitimate and respected—and satanic force. The latter is identified with the lost people, who retain the animal relations of the region's pre-Christian heritage. Today's village dancing and drumming (with no feathers involved) were learned from Ambonese Christian missionaries and schoolteachers.

Villagers are subsidized by a variety of government handouts, including rice supplies from the "Rice for the Poor" program. Rice handouts supply most families with a staple food for two to three months, after which cash incomes become necessary to keep the family eating rice, which is imported from western Indonesia. While older people still like sago, the elder explained, the children cry for rice. Thus, everyone scrambles to pick up a little cash here and there, from working on construction projects or selling betel in the regency capital to, in everyone's dreams, opening a homestay for bird-watchers. While the village does not yet have successful facilities, it's on everyone's minds.

Villages, then, are government and missionary infrastructures—with good results for a few birds, such as the starlings who lay their eggs in abandoned posts and the ducks that wander around the village collecting scraps. Those birds who do not thrive in the midst of such infrastructures are missing; they do not participate in this contact zone. They should not be forgotten. Still, it's worth paying homage to those who have found some use for human things. For them, new affordances are gained as infrastructure is put to new uses. In villages at the edge of mangrove swamps, government-subsidized piers form landing places for migrating sandpipers, stints, and sand plovers, who rest on the wooden surface between food-gathering expeditions in the mud. Without the pier, they might not visit this place. Human things are not useful just for humans.

In gardens, the shared use of human landscape modification is even more evident. As Rose's approach allows us to see, these are storied-places for birds as well as humans, emerging out of histories of interaction and meaning making. They are places of significance and attachment, as they are for humans, even if each of us comes to know and inhabit them differently. As Thom van Dooren and Rose (2012, 2) explain, "places are co-constituted in processes of overlapping and entangled 'storying' in which different participants may have very different ideas about where we have come from and where we are going. What would it mean, in a multispecies context, to negotiate 'across and among difference the implacable spatial fact of shared turf' [Massey 2004, 3] . . . ? What would it mean to really share a place?" (van Dooren and Rose, 2).

Most gardens here are inland, several hours' hike from the bayside villages, and because of the history I've just described, they tend to be visited too rarely for careful tending. The gardens I knew were overgrown and weedy, blending in and out of the forest. What a haven for birds! The edge of the gardens is a noisy place, full of bird vocalization. In contrast, walking through the surrounding forest was often quiet; birds were less concentrated there. Birds cluster in the trees at the edges of gardens, making use of both forest and garden habitats. Brahminy kites (*Haliastur indus*) find hunting viewpoints on high trees overlooking the bright gap. Glossy-mantled manucodes (*Manucodia ater*) display their dipping flights over the open space. These birds don't care much about the garden as a garden; it's just a gap in the forest. But other birds find the garden a good place to eat, and this might introduce the conflicting perspectives—humans versus birds—that I am calling "looking both ways."

LOOKING BOTH WAYS

Eclectus parrots (*Eclectus roratus*) are the most sexually dimorphic of all parrots; eclectus males are a brilliant green, while the females are scarlet red with blue and purple. Once, Western birders thought them to be different species. Now, however, everyone seemed to know their sexual morphs, including all my companions from Waigeo, some of whom also knew the English name *eclectus*. They were so common around gardens that my birder companions stopped caring when they flew overhead or perched nearby. Indeed, they are one of the worst garden pests in the area, along with wild boar. Flying foxes, which also haunt gardens, eat only ripe fruits; eclectus parrots eat everything. Sulphur-crested cockatoos (*Cacatua galerita*) perch on high trees around gardens, but they specialize in forest—not garden—fruits. In contrast, eclectus parrots are there to eat the food raised by gardeners, and especially bananas and papayas, green or ripe.

Our host had put a nylon net around a big bunch of ripening bananas, still on the plant, to protect it from the birds, and a bright scarlet female had caught herself in its mesh. She was screaming fiercely when we moved into the shelters by the garden, and eventually our party asked that she be released. Our host did it in our honor, and Yulia gently rinsed her plumage from the feces with which she had soiled herself during her captivity. But our host grumbled. "If it was up to me," he said, "I would sentence that bird to death." As long as the bird was there screaming, other eclectus parrots stayed away, he said, so, held fast by the nylon net, she protected his field. "I would give that bird the punishment [setrap] of standing there until death," he added. Setrap, he explained, is the punishment schoolteachers give their pupils for disobedience, handed down from Dutch colonial discipline: you might be ordered to stand on one foot or stare at the sun for an hour. The violence brings orderly, civilized behavior, and the bird, he thought, deserved it. With other garden birds, however, our host was surprisingly tolerant. Eclectus seemed to him out of bounds.

Eclectus parrots get in the way of people; other birds work hard to stay *out* of the way, and for them, too, the clash of modes of watching is particularly evident.

The Waigeo brush-turkey (*Aepypodius bruijnii*) is Waigeo's most internationally famous bird, at this moment, but it is described by villagers with the banal name of *forest chicken* (*ayam hutan*); as a result, most foreign birders conclude that villagers don't know a thing about the species. (Indonesian birders, more attuned to the excitement of international guests, call the bird *maleo Waigeo*.) The bird is famous because international confirmation is new. A bird specialist from Belgium, Iwein Mauro, reported its existence based on field observations in 2002 (Mauro 2004, 2007). He found the mounds built by males to incubate eggs in the stunted cloud forest that grows at altitudes over 620 meters, that is, on the higher mountains south and east of Mayalibit Bay. This opened a bit of a mystery for him. Historical specimens were found in the lowlands, but now, it seemed, the birds' populations were limited to a few high places. After some consideration, however, he dismissed those lowland birds, which local people knew, as "vagrants." Meanwhile, his reports spread the dogma of local ignorance; based on the local name, he figured that locals mistook the bird for an ordinary village fowl.

The villagers I spoke to had different ideas. Although everyone admitted that the bird was hard to find today except in remote high places, men said that not so long ago, in the lifetimes of their fathers, the bird had been quite common in the lowlands. They thought it had moved to high country to get out of the way of increased human activity—especially after the consolidation of human settlements along the coast in the middle of the twentieth century. Before that, it had been a regular part of hunters' diets, but that was when people were still scattered in gardens inland, or so my informants said.

One of the previous lowland specimens Mauro (2007, 108) reports involved the head and the bones left from a hunters' meal. That part of the local story finds agreement on both sides. As to the historical ecology of the species, it seems important to note that Mauro invokes a strange timeline, which appears sensible only because of the political cosmology that produced it.

Mauro imagines a past in which "nature" was untouched by human effects; meanwhile, he yokes this past to a future in which villagers are likely to destroy everything immediately. Thus, the birds' distribution in the past has nothing to do with human histories. In contrast, the future is human: Mauro's first conservation suggestion is to stop local villagers from destroying the birds. (While he admits that industrial mining and logging are key problems, he never suggests that corporations be contained.) He wants to outlaw hunting (even pig hunting—and pigs are the birds' worst egg predators); only trained scientists should have access to the areas where one might find birds (Mauro 2007, 114). Nature comes to scientists pure, and yet it arrives immediately vulnerable to native depredation. This is an exotic mythology in which scientists inherit the colonial burden of saving the land from its people.

To balance out the strangeness of this cosmology, it seems sensible to attend to the stories of local hunters, whether mythical or otherwise. For this, it doesn't matter where the core nesting areas of brush-turkeys lay historically. Let's say lowland birds are vagrants. It seems likely that they have sometimes, perhaps sporadically, been frequent visitors. It also seems likely that they have paid attention to humans in a different way than the smaller, less inviting (as food) dusky megapodes (*Megapodius freycinet*), which merely melt into the bushes when humans make an appearance, returning later. The bigger, more delicious brush-turkeys, it seems, got out of the way more firmly, finding refuge in high places. Brush-turkeys no longer visit the lowlands because there are too many people there. Ontological edge effects: brush-turkeys, too, may be capable of skilled practice on the borders between world-making projects.

Mauro's recommendations for restricting villagers' access to their highland forests resonate with common parlance among international bird-watchers, who are worried about the ways local people treat birds.[3] This reaction allows me to take some distance from bird-watchers. Surely capitalists have developed more powerful ways to kill birds, mostly involving toxicity and habitat destruction. The strangeness of bird-watchers' focus on local ignorance and destruction, then, is a reminder that bird-watching as a world-making project is as parochial and exotic as that of Waigeo islanders using colonial punishments on parrots. When every cosmology is strange, we might notice edge effects—a way into others' lifeways that does not erase the effect of observation itself.

In this section of the chapter, I've tried to show the distinctiveness of world-making projects—of birds, bird-watchers, and Waigeo island residents. This is necessary but not sufficient to understand the ontological edge effects I've promised. Let me turn to the most taken-for-granted part of bird-

ANNA LOWENHAUPT TSING

human relations (to Western readers): bird-watching. I hope I've already made it richer by suggesting bird-watching's interplay with many projects, human and not human. Now I'll identify some dynamics at play in the intersections across those projects.

HUMANS WATCHING BIRDS

What is bird-watching all about? One element is finding empathetic attunement with another being. This is a matter of working through edge effects, that is, tentative sites of touching. In this section I'll focus on three kinds of edge effects: copying, negotiating differences, and finding overlapping curiosities. Each takes me a little further into thinking through how varied kinds of humans and birds do and do not create common worlds together. Let me clarify: I'm not longing for the unification of all worlds. But I also refuse to assume that all these worlds are autonomous and nonoverlapping. We need to see where and how touching occurs, that is, what happens in edges.

COPYING: Birds and humans each copy the other. This is really clear among the pet sulphur-crested cockatoos (*Cacatua galerita*) that people keep in Waigeo's regency capital. Cockatoos were chained to perches in front of people's houses. One woman I met had nursed hers from the bedraggled state she bought it in to a healthy shine by feeding it a human baby food of milk and rice porridge; the bird, she said, would not eat her domestic fruit. But it could call motorcycle taxis (ojek) by crying, "Ojek," and wake the children for school by calling, "Sekolah" (school). She copied its high nasal voice, and, in turn, its voice copied her copy. Copying each other's copies: here is one edge effect.

Mimicry is not limited to the relationship of pets and owners. All the Waigeo men with whom we traveled used bird sounds to call birds. Kristof used his recorder in the same way: he would record a birdsong (or, if necessary, call it up from his library) and play it back to see if the bird would come to investigate. And the birds, too, copied. The first reaction to hearing a version of their song was often to sing it out again. One of the most impressive was the hooded butcherbird (*Cracticus cassicus*), which has a complex song and mimics the sounds of other birds around it. As we walked through a forest grove thick with butcherbirds, the songs kept morphing, drawing new elements into the melody. Like mockingbirds, butcherbirds are alert to sounds around them, copying and reweaving. Copying is one kind of attunement.

Just as biologist Scott Gilbert (2012, 336) says, "We are all lichens," to highlight our symbiotic natures, when it comes to copying and reweaving, we are all butcherbirds.

NEGOTIATING DIFFERENCES: It's easy to accept new information as long as it fits easily into the framework we already know. But it's really hard to even notice something from outside one's own world-making project.

After some years of attention to contact zones and hybridities, anthropologists have become obsessed with just how difficult it is to get outside one's own world and with how people just reinterpret what they experience—however divergent—into their own frames (Viveiros de Castro 2004). This is especially true, my colleagues say, for scientists and conservationists (e.g., Blaser 2009). I'm investigating edges because I think anthropologists have gone too far now in ignoring them, and yet the new scholarship is a helpful reminder: both disconnections and connections matter. Deborah Bird Rose motivates just this remembrance by attending to multiple ways of knowing and being while insisting on overlaps, dialogues, and cross-pollinations.[4] Paying attention to what happens at the edges of discrepant world-making projects requires noticing refusals to hear each other as well as unexpected forays into each other's worlds.

I thought about this problem a lot in my interactions with villagers, birdwatchers, and a tiny, bright bird, the yellow-capped pygmy parrot (*Micropsitta keiensis*). It was one of my most breathtaking glimpses of bird life. The tiny birds were clutching an arboreal termites' nest, near the lip of a hole near the bottom. At first I saw one, then two, then three. They glowed green, and the male had a red chest. They moved to a branch. He sat between two females exchanging overtures and glances back and forth, seemingly courting both. It felt intimate to see this, so near through my binoculars. Kristof checked his book, which said they are communal breeders who excavate in the termites' arboreal nest to lay their group's eggs.

Kristof asked Pak Noh, the village man who was with us, to climb the tree to see if there were any eggs in the hole. There were not, and besides, Pak Noh claimed, the hole was not a nest. The birds were eating there, he said. But Kristof said that parrots only eat fruit; the hole was a nest. We were at an impasse. Later, looking at another source, I read that pygmy parrots are eaters of lichen and fungi, not fruit. (Some sources said the sexes look the same, which was not true for ours; not everything one reads is true.) But might termites' nests be a good source for fungi? I don't know and can't make a judgment. But, as an anthropologist, I was interested in the conflict. Pak Noh said that parrots and kingfishers do make nests in termite constructions, but not this parrot. Kristof said Pak Noh lacked the experience to know.

Where does certainty come from? Birders come to the field expecting to identify a known series of birds. Birders do not expect to see any birds that are not cataloged in their books, and they trust the book's knowledge. Having more experience with fungi, I expect many organisms to be unclassifiable by eye at the species level as well as sometimes to lack names or classifications at all. Birds are different. Kristof and Yulia thought the lizards and butterflies they photographed might be "new to science." But not birds. Because of the international birding community, this is well-trodden territory. At least for birders, the classification of birds and the general outline of their habits are considered well known and stable. Birders add information from local people but only where it fits known gaps in their already established knowledge base.

When Kristof and Yulia, who have been around the world watching birds, explained to me that everywhere they went, local guides showed them birds, I found this a great mystery. Why would local people necessarily be interested in birds at all—and when they were, why would it be on close-enough terms to those of Western bird-watchers to allow communication? I don't know the answer for the world, but from working with villagers and bird-watchers in Mayalibit Bay, I have a few ideas about that place.

Consider the ambitious young villager I'll call Yosep. Yosep aspires to open a homestay for international bird-watchers, and he has already built a toilet and a gazebo in an auspicious place, close to the water so tourists won't need to hike. To augment his skills, Yosep—who knows no English at all—sat down with a booklet on Waigeo birds produced by a nongovernmental organization (NGO) and memorized eighty-two English bird names in one week. For me, who before this project knew almost no bird names, this seemed astounding. But without more training in English, Yosep was unable to say the names in a way that an English speaker might understand without a whole lot of work. Kristof and Yulia were annoyed by his attempts to say bird names in English. They were particularly disdainful of his attempt to pronounce *yellow-capped pygmy parrot*, which came out as a slurred single sound arranged around a two-syllable *cap-ped*. And yet—Yosep knew the sounds and habits of every single bird we heard calling while we walked together. His detailed knowledge of bird life in the forest will make him an ideal guide.

Two cultural legacies come together here. First, there is the strangeness of scientific ornithology, which is much influenced by the lay practice of bird-watching: as a result, and in contrast to the science of fungi, for example, cryptic species and traits not picked up by human eyes and ears are not particularly important in discussions of birds across the lay-scholarly line. This makes it easier to find resonance between villagers and international birders. Both international birders and Waigeo villagers know birds through sounds and appearances.

Second, there is the strangeness of Mayalibit Bay village life, which is torn between the earnest adoption of an evangelical Christianity and the still-necessary practices of a forest and bay-edge livelihood. Village men see and hear birds every day, and they continue to attend to the details of bird lives. But they are cut off from bird worlds by Christian dogma, which demonizes human-animal boundary crossing. The vehemence with which villagers denied speaking to animals was impressive; it is this refusal that makes one civilized and, indeed, now, properly human. And yet the men *know* birds. In the midst of this tension, along come international bird-watchers and a potential source of new income. The eagerness with which village men embraced this possibility is not just about the money. They have skills and experiences that keep birds important—but difficult to fit into current cosmological practice. Yosep's eagerness to learn English names is exemplary here. In the gap between Christian faith and forest practice, local language is inadequate. English names and international bird-watching practices jump in as a promising alternative. Here, both refusing and grasping the framework of others gain traction—creating unexpected edge effects. This is a difficult and risky road to navigate.

FINDING OVERLAPPING CURIOSITIES: Let me end this section with something gentler—and one more bird story, for the Raja Ampat pitohui (*Pitohui cerviniventris*). Kristof had wanted to see this endemic bird, which is special because, at least if it is like its relatives on the mainland, its feathers and skin are poisonous, discouraging predators. Because we had not encountered these birds in the villages of Mayalibit Bay, he asked Yakub, a local and self-trained bird guide who worked out of an ecotourist-oriented coastal village. Kristof told us the story of how the poison became known to Western science, itself a story of overlapping curiosities. A researcher studying Papuan birds of paradise netted a pitohui by mistake. As he tried to free the bird, it clipped him. Instinctively, he put his finger to his mouth—and his lips and tongue instantly lost feeling. He realized the bird had poisoned him. He asked the local people, who told him of course it was poisonous. Following a curiosity nourished in common space, he switched his dissertation research to study pitohui, documenting several kinds. Very few birds carry poisons.

ANNA LOWENHAUPT TSING

These birds eat a poisonous beetle, he found, and are able to transfer the beetle's poisons to their skins. Incubating eggs in the nest transfers enough of the poison to protect the eggs.

Yakub knew a lot about pitohui, and before long, he caught the bird's song. We stopped on the trail (a former logging road wide enough to offer good visibility), and because Yakub did not have it on his phone, Kristof played a library recording of the male's call. He put the speaker by the side of the road, and we stepped back, hoping the birds would come to the speaker. They did. Not just one male but several males gathered to find out about this interloper. We admired their burnished breasts, took photographs, and let them go about their business. Kristof offered Yakub a copy of his song recording.

Conventional wisdom has it that male pitohui come to a call to drive invaders from their territory. We attracted at least five, and if they were all on their own territories, those territories would have had to have a rather strange shape. It does not seem so far out of bounds to offer a simpler explanation: they were curious. Just as humans remake our skills for the socialities of different kinds of humans as well as birds, birds remake their skills for the socialities of humans. If we each—birds and humans—satisfied our curiosities a little that morning, it was because our respective skills were extended into the opportunities at the edges of others' worlds.

SOME FINAL THOUGHTS

Research is always a series of edge effects across human and nonhuman world-making projects. As researchers, what we learn is what our research subjects allow us to notice through the edges we mutually create with each other. This is why it is important to keep observers in the stories we tell; otherwise, we build our prejudices into our research without realizing what we are doing. Watching pitohui together with a local self-trained professional geared toward foreign tourists and their pocketbooks on the side of a former logging road built to fund a regional government geared toward ecotourist "protection" of the very biodiversity that the logging kills is so full of contradictions I can hardly begin to unpack them. Clearly, however, the pitohui's willingness to hang out in logged-over forest and come to bird-watchers' calls shapes the possibilities of interaction.

Yet pitohui responses to bird-watchers and logging roads are still an odd-looking element of analysis coming from the humanities and social sciences.

29

Even social and cultural analysis that highlights the importance of other living beings continues to privilege human relations with other humans. We learn that there are varied ways people make sense of and live with other organisms. We learn that human-nonhuman relations form part of human systems of power and knowledge. We learn that other cosmologies challenge the tools of Western science. Too often, the active responses of other beings are not part of the analysis—even when the whole point is to move beyond the Enlightenment-sponsored nature-culture dichotomy. Indeed, social and cultural analysts have been wary of attention to the active practices of other organisms for fear of subsumption into hegemonic scientific logics. In contrast, I argue that allowing bird responses to human projects, as well as the other way around, into social and cultural analysis opens more avenues to consider how science and its alternatives variously shape bird-watching practices.

Making a sharp contrast between local, Indigenous, and vernacular, on the one hand, and expert, scientific, and colonial, on the other, has been an important move in questioning the hegemony of colonial science. Mary Pratt's *Imperial Eyes* (1992) pioneered scholarly attention to the ways that European natural history ignored Indigenous land rights and advanced colonial knowledge and power; a host of scholarly exposés of natural history followed. Bird-watching has been closely tied to imperial expansion; this continues in contemporary imperial conquest, as when NGOs send their bird-watchers to the Iraq marshes to support the American occupation (Guarasci, n.d.). It is important to keep a critical eye on the dangerous alliances and imperial institutions that ornithologists and bird-watchers build (Lewis 2004). At the same time, merely reiterating the contrasts between local and scientific, or vernacular and expert, is not enough. Instead, I have argued that we need attention to edge effects, where touching and overlap occur even across varied projects of world making, whether those of Waigeo residents, foreign bird-watchers, or birds themselves.

To bring nonhuman responses into social and cultural analysis also opens possibilities for collaboration between anthropologists and natural scientists in moving beyond human exceptionalism—even as we continue the work of decolonizing public knowledge. I do not believe this means giving up attention to violent histories of dispossession and exclusion, but I have devoted this essay, instead, to the spirit of possibility. In the events described here, some Waigeo villagers, Western bird-watchers, a local NGO representative, and two anthropologists, one Indonesian and one not, got a little closer to appreciating more-than-human sociality, which we will need to build better alliances together.

ANNA LOWENHAUPT TSING

NOTES

1. This chapter—an early missive from a continuing project—reports on material gathered in December 2017. The fieldwork also included Salmon Weyei, at the time a local representative of Flora and Fauna International, and anthropologist Hatib Abdul Kadir of Universitas Brawijaya. Each made this research possible. I am grateful to them, my ornithology colleagues (who taught me all the science here concerning birds), and the local people who facilitated the research (and taught me everything else here concerning birds). Nils Bubandt of Aarhus University got me started in Raja Ampat and shared invaluable insights. The research was supported by the Danish National Research Foundation as part of a Niels Bohr Professorship and the Aarhus University Research on the Anthropocene project it supported (https://anthropocene.au.dk).

2. About names: No naming gets at the essence of a being; at best, it can gesture in a useful direction. In the ontological ecotones that form the subject of this chapter, naming is particularly fraught, and no choice covers enough territory. To make the chapter readable by ordinary English speakers, I privilege English common names here. I supplement those names with current Latin binomials to honor the ornithology and bird-watching community that forms part of my discussion here. In the summer of 2018, I worked with Waigeo men to put about seventy-five Ambel bird names in dialogue with international bird-watcher identifications; however, an accident of the US Postal Service seems to have deprived me of that material. Those names do not form part of this chapter as originally planned. I will have to redo that research.

3. To his credit, Mauro (2007, 113) states that human predation is not currently a major threat. Many bird-watchers, in contrast, jump to the assumption that local hunting is the first concern for any bird, even where major infrastructural disturbances seem likely to be more deadly.

4. In discussing the philosophy of Val Plumwood, Rose (2013, 103) considers how insects and other beings communicate with humans, both Indigenous and settler. She argues for attentiveness: "March flies, for example, start biting across a wide area, but the meaning of that bite varies from one locale to the next. The system opens the human sensorium, extending it through attentiveness to others: jangarla trees tell what is going on under water where humans cannot stay for long; swifts tell what is happening in the upper atmosphere; march flies tell what is happening along the banks of billabongs and rivers, whether people are there or not. For humans and others to gain knowledge from tellers, therefore, they must pay active attention."

REFERENCES

Blaser, Mario. 2009. "The Threat of the Yrmo: The Political Ontology of a Sustainable Hunting Program." *American Anthropologist* 111 (1): 10–20.

Carson, Rachel. 1962. *Silent Spring*. New York: Houghton Mifflin.

31

Gilbert, Scott. 2012. "A Symbiotic View of Life: We Have Never Been Individuals." *Quarterly Review of Biology* 87 (4): 325–341.

Guarasci, Bridget. n.d. "Birding under Fire: The Violence of Environment in Iraq." Unpublished manuscript.

Holbraad, Martin, and Morten Axel Pedersen. 2017. *The Ontological Turn: An Anthropological Exposition*. Cambridge: Cambridge University Press.

Kirk, Malcolm, and Andrew Strathern. 1993. *Man as Art in New Guinea*. San Francisco: Chronicle Books.

Lewis, Michael. 2004. *Inventing Global Ecology: Tracking the Biodiversity Ideal in India, 1947–1997*. Athens: Ohio University Press.

Massey, Doreen. 2004. "Geographies of Responsibility." *Geografiska Annaler: Series B* (Human Geography) 86 (1): 5–18

Mauro, Iwein. 2004. "Field Discovery, Mound Characteristics, Bare Parts, Vocalisations and Behaviour of Bruijn's Brush-Turkey (*Aepypodius bruijnii*)." *Emu* 105 (4): 273–281.

Mauro, Iwein. 2007. "Bruijn's Brush-Turkey *Aepypodius bruijni*: Field Discovery, Monitoring, and Conservation of an Enigma." In *Katanning National Malleefowl Forum 2007: Proceedings*, edited by S. J. J. F. Davies, 107–119. Melbourne: Victorian Malleefowl Recovery Group. https://www.malleefowlvictoria.org.au/s/2007ForumProceedings.pdf.

McGhie, Henry A. 2017. *Henry Dresser and Victorian Ornithology: Birds, Books and Business*. Oxford: Oxford University Press.

Pratt, Mary. 2007. *Imperial Eyes: Travel Writing and Transculturation*. 2nd ed. New York: Routledge.

Rose, Deborah Bird. 2004. *Reports from a Wild Country: Ethics for Decolonisation*. Sydney: University of New South Wales Press.

Rose, Deborah Bird. 2011. *Wild Dog Dreaming: Love and Extinction*. Charlottesville: University of Virginia Press.

Rose, Deborah Bird. 2013. "Val Plumwood's Philosophical Animism: Attentive Inter-actions in the Sentient World." *Environmental Humanities* 3 (1): 93–109.

Schieffelin, Edward. 2005. *The Sorrow of the Lonely and the Burning of the Dancers*. London: Palgrave Macmillan.

van Dooren, Thom. 2014. *Flight Ways: Life and Loss at the Edge of Extinction*. New York: Columbia University Press.

van Dooren, Thom, and Deborah Bird Rose. 2012. "Storied-Places in a Multispecies City." *Humanimalia* 3 (2): 1–27.

Viveiros de Castro, Eduardo. 2004. "Perspectival Anthropology and the Method of Controlled Equivocation." *Tipití: Journal of the Society for the Anthropology of Lowland South America* 2 (1): 3–22.

West, Paige. 2006. *Conservation Is Our Government Now*. Durham, NC: Duke University Press.

LOVING THE DIFFICULT

Scotch Broom

CATRIONA SANDILANDS

SCOTCH BROOM: GALIANO ISLAND

the long slope of the hill
is logged burned gouged
shattered
and alight with
delicate leguminous
          yellow flowers
                              awaiting bees

even new spring branches draw blood
resinous old bushes invite summer fires
elaborate root chemistries give rise only to grass
          and even the deer won't eat it

extreme drought and rapid change
    favor global opportunists
(like other travelers who wear
    prophylactic layers of gore-tex
            and bring their own freeze-dried food
scotch broom is an individualist with a sense of entitlement
and little interest in friendly relations)

wet winter dry summer
heat popping earlier blooming longer seeding accelerating timespace
changing climates assemble new neighborhoods
and we must learn

eyes pods hands branches blood resin sweat mingling

to live in them.[1]

IT IS A BRIGHT, blue-skied morning in late May on Galiano Island. Galiano
is one of the Southern Gulf Islands of British Columbia (BC), located in the
Salish Sea between the mainland and Vancouver Island.[2] If you look at it on a
map, it is the long, skinny one northeast of the biggest one, Salt Spring. I am
standing about two-thirds of the way up a fair-sized hill on the northeast side
of the island, looking northeast toward the mainland. There is a slight chop
on the water; I am glad that I am wearing long sleeves, long pants, and boots.
I can see the coastal mountains across the water: there is still some snow on
the peaks. I can also see the Roberts Bank Superport, which includes the
busiest single coal export terminal in North America as well as a major international container shipping facility. Especially on winter nights, the lights of
Roberts Bank dominate the northeastern view from Galiano; this horizon is
a well-lit reminder that I am never far from everything the Superport does.

    Today I am in the Galiano Heritage Forest, and I am here to attend to the
hillside, not the view. The term *forest* is largely aspirational for this devastated
landscape. The area has been repeatedly logged in the past 140 years, including
extensive use of industrial machinery that clear-cut the trees, gashed the land
with roads, and heavily compacted the soil. In 2005 the 312-acre parcel that
includes this hillside was donated by private landowners to the Galiano Club
as a "Heritage Forest," including some space for social housing, in exchange
for development rights in an adjacent area. In July 2006 the largest wildfire
in recorded settler history in the Southern Gulf Islands swept through the
area, and firefighters clawed new roads and sprayed any number of chemical
fire retardants to bring the blaze under control. In the years immediately after

the fire, foragers were warned against eating mushrooms from these lands because of their toxic load. In the years since, a carpet of foxgloves has given way to a thick, shrubby mass of scotch broom (*Cytisus scoparius*), and the hillside has been targeted by the Galiano Club for organized "broom busting" to help the forest move toward some version of restoration.

I am on the hill today, gloves on and loppers in hand, to help with this effort. Scotch broom is considered one of the most pernicious exotic-invasive species in the BC south coastal region. According to the Centre for Agriculture and Bioscience International's Invasive Species Compendium, it is "an aggressive fast-growing invader with the capability to grow forming dense impenetrable monospecific stands that degrade native grasslands, forests, rangelands, and agricultural lands; prevent the regeneration of natural forests and prairies; and create fire hazards" (2019). According to the Invasive Species Council of BC (ISCBC), scotch broom is also "a serious competitor to conifer seedlings" (it is blamed for Douglas-fir plantation failures in both Canada and the United States), and its dense thickets "obstruct sight lines on roads," "limit movement of large animals," and "displace native plant species," especially but not only in endangered Garry oak ecosystems (2019, 2). Not surprisingly, a lot of public attention is devoted to the best strategies for killing it. At one end of the spectrum, the ISCBC (a multipartner NGO partially funded by the BC Ministry of the Environment) recommends a strategy of "integrated pest management" that includes any pragmatically necessary combination of mechanical, biological, and chemical controls (e.g., cutting or using seed weevils or 2,4-D; 2019); at the other end of the spectrum, the grassroots community organization BroomBusters (Qualicum, BC) has an online tutorial "How to Cut Broom" (n.d.) that includes videos demonstrating the precise way to "cut broom in bloom": while the plant is in flower, sever the main trunk at or below ground level and *don't disturb the soil*.

Despite my loppers, I have mixed feelings about my participation in broom busting (aka bashing, blasting, or blitzing). Part of me is uncomfortable with the ease with which the often-connected concepts of "alien" and "invasive" are applied to plants that, for the most part, *white settlers* don't want to have around *at this historical moment*. Plants like scotch broom are, in my experience, largely categorized as invasive because they interrupt current colonial economic and aesthetic interests and not only (or even mostly) because they are *non-native* (exotic) or *ecologically intrusive* (invasive), although they may also be both. The very definition of an invasive plant as a foreign, unruly species that exceeds the interspecies dependency of anthropogenic cultivation—that is, it has naturalized and continues to thrive and expand without human assistance—makes it clear that the concept of invasiveness is as much about *control* as anything else. Most industrial food-plant crops in North America are not indigenous, yet one seldom hears the term *invasive* applied, say, to wheat, despite the large amount of space wheat has taken over from indigenous grasses, not to mention the vast resources it requires, at the expense of indigenous plant species, to thrive. It seems that if a plant takes up a lot of space with people or an industry as ongoing enablers, it is a crop, an ornamental, or a commodity; if it does so of its own weedy volition, it becomes an invasive. Kentucky bluegrass, *Poa pratensis*, is an instructive example of the jagged line between the two categories: in some places, it is cultivated and carefully nurtured on an industrial (and personal) scale for lawns and golf courses, but in other, geographically quite proximate spaces, it is subject to intentional destruction by burning and grazing to restore native prairie ecosystems.[3]

A larger part of me is uncomfortable with the zeal of broom busting, however, because of the political and emotional work that invasive species "eradication" does to forestall a more comprehensive conversation about ecological *decolonization*. How easy it is, it seems, to focus on blitzing broom in order to make a niche for indigenous *plants*, when the larger question of repairing relations with Indigenous *peoples*—and with the multispecies reciprocities that bloomed (and continue to bloom) between plants, nonhuman animals, and peoples and that colonization has severely disrupted—is not a matter of nearly as much conversation, at least in the anti–scotch broom universe. Not surprisingly, neither the ISCBC page nor BroomBusters mentions the lives and relationships that were disrupted in the process of broom's arrival in this landscape; neither mentions partnering with local Indigenous organizations to engage in the much more complicated conversation about the relationship between restoration and reconciliation that this land offers up. It is not that nobody on Galiano is doing this work (e.g., Salish Harvest, the Galiano Conservancy).[4] But if you were to create a Venn diagram of the community of settlers seriously working, in partnership with Indigenous organizations, toward reconciliation or decolonization of this unceded land and the community of people involved in broom busting, the area of overlap between the two would be pretty small.

Even a casual settler conversation about broom on this island brings to the fore remarkably strong expressions of hatred toward the species: stories about how prolifically it seeds, about how it is taking over spaces in which more desirable plants might grow, about how very hard it is to kill, about how constant vigilance is needed. Given that I have publicly confessed the

CATRIONA SANDILANDS

loppers, I have to underline that I think there is a real place, in the thoughtful work of caring for the land, for practices like speeding up processes of ecological succession by taking out some of the broom so that other species might have a bit more room to flourish, like the little Douglas-fir seedlings that are starting to pop up among the yellow bushes on the hill and that will, eventually, shade out and diminish the sun-loving broom. (Contrast this practice to the fact that invasive species "management" is a multibillion-dollar venture for companies like Monsanto, which manufactures the popular glyphosate herbicide Roundup, used in many invasive plant eradication campaigns; see Cockburn 2015.) The problem is not the intervention itself but, rather, the larger set of practices and understandings in which the intervention takes place, including questions of scale, technology, intention, relationship, attentiveness, respect, and—crucially, I think—*context*, both historical and ecological. Without underestimating the serious global role of invasive species in biodiversity loss, and without pretending that broom is just another plant in some kind of happily cosmopolitan local ecology, I ask, inspired by Deborah Bird Rose: What difference might it make to think about scotch broom as a species with which we are—like it or not—rather literally *entangled*, rather than as a plant whose primary cultural existence is as an enemy to be eradicated as effectively as possible?

In their article "Anishnaabe Aki: An Indigenous Perspective on the Global Threat of Invasive Species" (2018), Nicholas Reo and Laura Ogden, drawing on the extensive collective wisdom of Anishnaabe traditional doctors and plant helpers (their terms) in what is now Michigan, point out that despite the serious negative impact of plants like common reed (*Phragmites australis*) on important Anishnaabe plant-human relationships in the region, such as those with broadleaf cattail, the Eurowestern managerial focus on invasive species control is not aligned with traditional ecological understandings and practices. Beginning with the central Anishnaabe ethical concept of aki, "typically translated as 'Earth' in English . . . [and] encompass[ing] a broader cosmological sense of the sacredness of place" (1446), they argue that three key elements of Anishnaabe ecological understanding provide an alternative perspective on plants and animals that are typically deemed invasive. First, *all* plants and animals are persons, kin, and members of extended families that include human people: as such, our relations with them are steeped in ethical obligation, even if we do not fully understand the kinship relations in which they are enmeshed in their ecologies of origin and even though we may not yet know how they will establish kin relations in their new situations. Second, all plants and animals have a *purpose*, and a key ethical imperative for

37

human persons in "novel" ecologies involves developing, patiently, an understanding of the complex purposes that migrant animals and plants bring with them: there are fast and instrumental uses (e.g., cash crops grown in new locations without heed to local ecologies), and then there are generous and attentive relations, which involve developing a longer-term, reflexive understanding of how new species might come to play an ongoing, sustainable role in local ecologies. Finally, and perhaps most important, Reo and Ogden note that their Anishnaabe interlocutors are more concerned with invasive *land ethics* than they are with any one invasive *species*. As they write, "Elements of this invasive land ethic include the imposition of Euro-American property ownership regimes, 'command and control' forms of environmental management, and a worldview predicated on the separation of people from nature" (1449). In this view, it is much more important to think about the ways in which plant-human relationships have been organized according to settler-capitalist imperatives than it is to focus on the behavior of a given species within these ongoing colonial regimes. To use Eve Tuck and K. Wayne Yang's (2012) language, exclusive focus on the *plant's* "colonizing" behavior is a kind of "settler move to innocence," in which the key problems—disruptive and dispossessive settler-colonial property relations and accompanying Eurowestern environmental understandings—are ignored as settlers focus on trying to make the land look as if it were never disturbed, primarily by taking away a symptom rather than addressing the larger cause.

To develop a noninnocent response to scotch broom, I think it is crucial for white settlers to come to terms with the fact that the plant is a *companion species* in settler colonialism and that the entangled agencies of plant and human colonization are ongoing (Neale 2016). Undoing colonialism, in this case, is not just a matter of "cutting broom in bloom" (it is *definitely* not a matter of buying and applying Roundup); it is a matter of telling a more truthful story about broom's particular involvement in the ongoing unfolding of settler colonialism in the region and, even more, of developing a relationship to broom that holds me accountable to the Indigenous communities who may be more concerned about the cascade of land devastations, expropriations, purchases, and deals that created what is now the Heritage Forest than about the plants that currently inhabit it. As a settler scholar, I think that one of the most important things I can do is to help to remember *how* settler colonialism has brought scotch broom to the BC South Coast as part of the imposition of an "invasive land ethic" on this place and to thus develop an understanding of the very particular entanglements in which we find ourselves with this plant at this moment. In addition, however, I think it is important to think about how to have a *relationship* with scotch broom that, following Rose, is not focused on eradicating it out of "western eagerness to remake everything in the name of progress" (2013a, 7) but that instead acknowledges, with humility, that "taking care of country doesn't mean engineering it. It means doing your part as a human-being while others do their part, and country's own life-giving capacities have the chance to flourish" (9). I see scotch broom—following Rose, Reo and Ogden, and others such as Robin Wall Kimmerer (2013)—as a being with whom we have little choice but to coexist on this island, at this historical moment. In the spirit of exploring new forms of conviviality, I then ask, What would it mean to engage *with* the plant *against* an invasive land ethic, rather than *against* the plant as if settlers could situate themselves apart from the invasion?

SCOTCH BROOM: BOTANICAL COLONIALISM

They say James Douglas himself in the 1840s carried in his pockets
seeds of scotch broom to sow along the streets of Fort Victoria:
his vision of pastoral British paradise, built overtop
spacious Lekwungen-tended camas beds beneath the oak trees at
    Meeqan.

Eden secured by any means:
military or political, architectural, botanical.

The settlers around him, too, clothed their naked acquisitions
in bright-flowering Scots sentimentalities of thistle, broom, gorse.
Those less romantic (or less rich) saw in broom cures for dropsy,
for bleeding after labor. A source of dyers' yellows, greens and browns.
It was a brewer's fix in a place without hops,
that heightened both the bitter and the strength. And of course,
one could make a broom.

Broom came in the ballasts of the ships, cradled whisky
bound for single-minded prospectors,
spread through streams and rivers. It was deliberately planted
on roadsides, under power lines, to right catastrophes of soil.
It was a keystone in the building of a colony. It held together
    infrastructural dreams.

But broom has its own desires.

Its thousands of ripe, ballistic pods shoot seeds metres away,
summer after summer. (They can live, dormant, more than fifty years.)
Its waxy stems devour light even when it drops its leaves in drought.
It draws nitrogen from the air and roots in whatever scant soil.

They now say broom is aggressive, an invasive,
a competitor in the often dry, thin micro-regions of its flourishing.
That it is a fire hazard, that it is toxic and impenetrable,
that its roots are too tenacious, that it is (most ironically) an eyesore.

I have taken to saying that broom is a companion species
in settler colonial dispossession. It has also done its own settling
more successfully than anyone could have dreamed.

SCORES OF FACT SHEETS, lists of tips, and other easily accessed sources of
official and semiofficial information on scotch broom are available online.
Perhaps because almost all of these sources are primarily geared to dissemi-
nating best killing practices, there is a striking similarity in the rhetoric they
employ to describe the plant's impact on local ecosystems: it is an "escaped"
garden ornamental that invades exposed, disturbed soil by prolifically producing long-lived seeds, photosynthesizing even in the absence of leaves (i.e.,
even in drought), growing in extremely high density, fixing its own nitrogen,
being toxic to browsers, and changing the chemical composition of the soil
to its own advantage (allelopathy). As is so often the case in discussions of
invasive species, the agency of the *plant* is very much foregrounded. As in the
following example from the Islands Trust Conservancy (a federation of local
governments that includes Galiano), broom is consistently depicted as active
and creative, making its own history at the expense of other species, ecologies, and relationships: "Broom *changes* the chemistry of the soil around it so
that other plants can't grow there. It *spreads* and *grows* quickly, creating dense
monocultures" (2018, my emphasis). If there is any hint that people may be
directly involved in enabling broom's liveliness, the relationship tends to be
buried in the past tense: that the plant escaped from cultivation, that it favors
already-disturbed soils, that it was once commercialized. The Islands Trust
provides one of the rarer glimpses of the ongoing particularities of broom-
human entanglement in BC, but even then the references are oblique: broom
"was first *introduced* to southern Vancouver Island in the 1850s and now grows
prolifically throughout southwestern British Columbia. Broom is most often

found in open areas such as meadows, *forest clearings, roadsides* and *hydro corridors*" (2018, my emphasis).

The introduction story to which the trust refers is the most common, shared public acknowledgment of settler agency in broom's regional proliferation. Environmental historian Troy Lee, in what may be the only detailed consideration of scotch broom's social and historical emergence in BC, notes that there are actually at least two stories about the plant's specific introduction to Vancouver Island, both reported in the local Victoria press (the *Daily Colonist*!) some years after the fact. In one account, Captain Walter Colquhoun Grant brought broom seeds to a property in Sooke, BC, in 1851, having been given them by the British consul of the Sandwich Islands the previous year. Grant's property consisted of approximately forty hectares that he had purchased from the Hudson's Bay Company (HBC), which had, in turn, leased the land from the British Colonial Office after the Colony of Vancouver Island was declared in 1849. In the other account, HBC chief factor James Douglas obtained broom seeds from Oregon City and brought them to Fort Victoria in 1849, carrying them in his pocket and "scattering them as he drove throughout the city" (Lee 2010, 45). Douglas became the governor of the colony in 1851—a position that he held, problematically, while also formally overseeing the HBC's interests in the region—and was responsible for negotiating the fourteen highly controversial "Douglas Treaties" with local First Nations on Vancouver Island, as well as for engaging in ongoing acts of violent dispossession on the island and beyond as the colony expanded (see Arnett 1999).[5]

What should be clear here is that the specific vector of broom's move to Vancouver Island is far less important than the colonial relations in which its arrival took place. Whether Douglas scattered or Grant planted (most likely, many colonists did both), the soil was thoroughly prepared—both metaphorically and literally—for broom's establishment by British colonial expropriation policies and practices, by existing economic and political networks facilitating the plant's global movement, and by Douglas's mandate to encourage settlement in the colony, meaning also, of course, the expansion of land-disturbing practices such as agriculture and logging (Grant quickly established a farm and built a sawmill, and he noted in his correspondence that the land produced particularly excellent wheat [1857, 283, 274]). In addition, broom rapidly insinuated itself into ongoing relations of botanical colonialism that were not as species-specific. As the ISCBC (n.d.-a.) acknowledges, "The progression of invasive plants into BC began

41

with the fur trade of the early 1800s. For instance, fur-trade gardens were established at Stuart Lake in 1811, Fort Langley in 1827, and Fort Thompson in 1842. These gardens may have contributed to the transfer of invasive plants and seeds to new areas of the province, either unintentionally in hay and other livestock feed products, or sold deliberately as ornamentals for flower gardens." Broom was not part of these fur-trade gardens (another species, common burdock, likely was because of its widely acknowledged medicinal qualities), but it rapidly came to be a garden staple. For some combination of aesthetic, utilitarian, and sentimental reasons, British colonists liked to have it around, and scotch broom thus became a desirable botanical commodity. Lee (2010, 45–46) notes that it was widely available both globally and locally; it was advertised for sale in Upper Canada's first nursery catalog, Kew Gardens in London sold seeds on order to select individuals, and local Victoria nurseries probably stocked it as well. By the end of the nineteenth century, broom was an established part of the colonial infrastructure of British Columbia. Knowledge of its practical uses—as medicine, as ingredient, as craft material, as bakers' broom—accompanied the plant's material travels. More important, however, broom's aesthetic presence naturalized the British colony. The city of Victoria, ablaze in European yellows every spring, could appear as organic as the broom lining its roads, an observation often made by turn-of-the-century observers. Charles St. Barbe, in a wide-ranging 1911 commentary on the city's Beacon Hill Park—a designation superimposed on important Lekwungen-owned and fire-cultivated camas meadows—noted that the park should focus on acquiring a "collection of all the animals and birds indigenous to British Columbia" and also, without a hint of irony, commented that the park's eponymous hill was "the glory of the place . . . acres and acres of broom that in spring and early summer are a blaze of gold" (quoted in Ringuette n.d., ch. 9).

Scotch broom is not, however, simply an escaped ornamental. Lee (2010, 48) suggests that its seeds may have been carried to the region in ships' ballast, and the ISCBC (n.d.-b) notes that "it was also used in fresh cut bundles to package cases of imported whiskey for gold camps across California and northward into BC." Although these introductions are not confirmed, the evidence is incontrovertible that one of broom's other, more practical uses further amplified its role in colonial development: it is an excellent ground stabilizer, precisely *because* it grows so enthusiastically in disturbed, loose, open soils such as sand dunes, road embankments, and

42

utility corridors. The ISCBC (n.d.-a) suggests that this was the reason for Grant's experimentation with the plant, not sentimentality; as a matter of more certainty, as late as 1991 the US Department of Agriculture listed scotch broom as a *recommended* woody shrub for sand-dune stabilization along the Pacific Northwest Coast (Carlson, Reckendorf, and Ternyik 1991, 50). Most important for this chapter, however, broom was actively planted, starting in the late 1940s, "in several BC Hydro and Ministry of Transportation and Highways slope stabilization projects on the south coast" (Zielke et al. 1992, 3), where the shrubs simultaneously held together industrially disturbed soils and "beautified" roads and utility corridors (see also Lee 2010, 53). Even long after broom was no longer the plant of choice for infrastructural expansion projects (it is now considered a "vegetative pest" by BC Hydro), "the Ministry of Transportation and Highways . . . avoided mowing or removing broom where it ha[d] become established naturally along highways and roads on the south coast" (Zielke et al. 1992, 3). Like many plants that are now considered invasive because they thrive in disturbed areas, broom was a favored botanical ally for capitalist extractive and development projects at an earlier stage in the province's colonial history precisely because of this quality. Scotch broom very literally helped to solidify the expansion and resourcing of colonial modernity; moreover, it continues to do so.

Every pair of loppers currently in use on Galiano is, then, more or less directly enabled by precisely the broom that the loppers are wielded to cut. I think this insight is important, not just because it reinforces the knowledge that settler colonialism has always been, and is still, a matter of multispecies entanglement, and not just because it makes it more difficult for me and my settler neighbors to "cut the blooming broom" without getting a small but sharp reminder of our complex and ongoing implication in the plant's flourishing. I think it is also important to take this insight and pause with the loppers to think more carefully: What am I doing, and how am I doing it? Are there ways to turn my attention to broom toward an ecological project that is not predicated on a settler move to innocence but that instead makes space for new kinds of relationship? As Timothy Neale (2016) suggests, how do I develop a practice "in which invasive species are made *otherwise* rather than eradicated; targets of both hostility and hopefulness," in which I live "*with and against*" them in an agonistic project of restoration that does not take settler futurity for granted, including the economics and ecologies enabled by an invasive land ethic?

43

damage has created novel ecosystems and the plants are slowly adapting

scotch broom can be controlled mechanically
with a chainsaw
at the point its main trunk appears above the soil

how we approach restoration of land depends on what we believe that
land means
land as sustainer land as identity land as grocery store and pharmacy
land as moral obligation land as sacred land as self

the plant will often not die on the first attempt and vigilant shearing
is necessary

restoration is imperative for healing the earth but
reciprocity is imperative
for long-lasting successful restoration

glyphosate herbicides are successful in killing broom
but the treatment must be applied before the flowers emerge

we restore the land and the land restores us

experiments are underway with biological controls
such as certain species of seed weevils whose larvae
enter the pods and eat the seeds before they disperse

especially in an era of rapid climate change
species composition may change
but relationship endures

cut broom in bloom
buy your Extractigator™ today!

restoring the land without restoring relationship is an empty exercise[6]

CATRIONA SANDILANDS

PERHAPS APPROPRIATELY FOR a work that is located on Galiano Island, my title, "Loving the Difficult," is taken from a posthumously published essay by Jane Rule (2008), one of the island's most famous settlers. In her essay Rule writes about loving the difficult as a matter of learning to engage well with the things that one most fears: "to practice, however hard it is, however frightening, however dubious the worldly rewards" the things that allow us to *love*, no matter what the "silencing odds" (3). As Kimmerer (2013) reminds us, although invasive plants are signs of relations gone very wrong (she singles out European buckthorn, *Rhamnus cathartica*, for both its "botanical imperialism" and its powerfully purgative berries), it is still important to approach the practice of restoration with love at the forefront, not with a predefined idea of what the land should look like that should be pursued by any means necessary: "We're not in control. What we *are* in control of is our relationship to the earth. . . . It is the most authentic facet of the restoration. Here is where our most challenging and rewarding work lies, in restoring a relationship of respect, responsibility, and reciprocity. And love" (336). And as Rose has argued in so many ways, love, however "tangled up in trouble" it may be (2013a, 1), is "exactly what is called for in the death zone": a "crazy love that is directed toward earth life" (2013b, 1).

I am neither arguing that settler-colonial ecologies and economies can be dismantled by love, nor suggesting that the work of decolonization can proceed without concretely addressing the fact that some lands may be deeply loved by the settlers who live on them but are nonetheless stolen: some forms of love are enabled by settler-capitalist private property relations, whereas other forms of love are violently expunged (see TallBear 2018). Instead, I want to suggest that "loving the difficult" might be a way for settlers like me to approach the practice of caring for the land in a way that unsettles colonial land ethics in a *noninnocent* way. This noninnocence begins in a place of reciprocity and respect rather than control and erasure and understands the restoration of relationship to lands, plants, and animals as an element of the larger and more difficult work of "relinquishing settler futurity" (Tuck and Yang 2012, 36) that decolonization requires, including both direct repatriation of lands and large-scale disruption of the narratives in which settlers continue to imagine that our inhabitation of places like Galiano is something that can be "made right" without the primary leadership of Indigenous peoples.

Scotch broom is a powerful accomplice in the work of botanical colonialism, to be sure. But rather than focus on eradicating the plant (trying to erase its history), I wonder what would it mean to work *with* broom as a way of beginning to practice relations that acknowledge its role in ongoing colonialism but that also—in the spirit of the Indigenous environmental ethics articulated by Kimmerer, Reo and Ogden, and others—try to turn its unwanted presence toward an ecological futurity that focuses on displacing invasive land ethics rather than only on displacing broom? In thinking through this kind of project, Rose's work is exceptionally important: What would happen if we were to think about broom in terms of its *life* rather than always with an eye to its death? When a plant like broom is "declared a pest, death becomes its destiny. Suddenly, whatever it does is wrong in the eyes of those who are determined to get rid of it. And suddenly, wherever it is, that is where it must not be" (Rose 2013b, 15). What would happen if we imagined scotch broom as, instead, a "fragment of creation, a chip off the great block of earth life" (15): perhaps even a creature with a lively *purpose* that we may simply not yet understand in our rush to eliminate it?

Rose's philosophical commitment to thinking and feeling with multispecies life in the necrophilia that characterizes the Anthropocene—and to truly appreciating the delicate lived lives of fleshy creatures in concrete historical relationships—is one of the things that I have always found most powerful in her work. Living an ethical life in these times of fragmentation involves the slow and often-painful work of developing connection: not unity, not transparent certainty, but "embodied and emplaced ethics" that involve listening and responding, with genuine respect, to the lively voices of others in a project of dialogical world creation (Rose 2013c, 5). For Rose, guided by her long-term work with Australian Aboriginal people in Country, this listening and response take place in the context of *encounters* with others: others who have senses, worlds, and purposes that intersect with human ones and that may or may not align with them at any given moment. "Encounter, in any fundamental sense of the term, does not preclude conflict" (6). However, "the more important point is that an ethics of mutual becoming starts with the presupposition of relationality and potential mutuality, not a presupposition of isolation and inevitable hostility" (6).

Perhaps, in relation to scotch broom, Rose would ask for a more *open dialogue*: with the Indigenous peoples whose traditional relationships with lands, animals, and plants have been disrupted by the settler colonization that occurs in and with broom, and also with the plants themselves now that they are so clearly part of the universe of multispecies encounter in this place. As she writes, "Openness is risky because you do not know the outcome in advance" (2013c, 7). Many people are not interested in risking the time it would take to listen to broom or even to listen to the Indigenous knowledge keepers who might (or might not) advocate a more patient approach to it. But I think doing so is important. Broom's *story* in this place gives us a vector of understanding the multispecies networks involved in colonization; busting it, without thought to this story, does little to dislodge the larger relations that give the plant so very much space to grow. Perhaps even more important, broom's potential to contribute to the *life* of this place is foreclosed in the overwhelmingly managerial approach to its current existence, an approach that works as hard as possible *to extinguish the story that broom is telling about the land*. As Rose writes, a slow, situated, dialogical approach to ecological conversation with and about broom may be a way of bringing together settler and Indigenous ethical traditions in a manner that "requires that [settlers] acknowledge and understand our particular and harshly situated presence" on the land at the same time as we explore shared possibilities for "tak[ing] care of all that we can in this time of crisis" (2015, 129, 130).

Might scotch broom, understood away from settler fantasies of harmony, be part of these multispecies dialogues, contributing to futurities that do not reinforce narratives of settler naturalization? Might *the plant* be part of unsettling futurities for the place, against settler desires for a particular "native" botanical pantheon? This is a complicated question, but it deserves to be asked: Is it possible for broom to participate in a healing, decolonizing futurity? Although broom has not, perhaps, been around in this region for long enough to make known its longer-term ecological effects (it will, in all likelihood, eventually be shaded out by the Douglas-firs in many places), even its detractors acknowledge that one of its great short-term abilities is its capacity to fix nitrogen in very poor soils. Even as this capacity *changes* the soil and changes the ecological and cultural relations that grow in the soil—which may not be desirable in places that, for example, continue to support Indigenous plant-human relationships such as camas meadows—it may offer a clue to its potential contribution to devastated places like the Heritage Forest. One study from New Zealand suggests that broom may play a constructive role in emerging dryland ecologies: here, indigenous species planted underneath the existing canopy of broom bushes did *better* than ones planted in places where broom had been mechanically or chemically managed (Burrows, Cieraad, and Head 2015); although this may be mostly about soil disturbance (which hand-cutting is intended to minimize), the result does indicate that killing broom by any means necessary may do more harm than good. Another study goes even further: mulched broom (presumably cut before seeding) subjected to six weeks of vermicomposting produced high-quality, nitrogen-rich organic fertilizer in which broom's phytotoxicity was almost entirely degraded (Domínguez et al. 2018).[7] Again, making use of this entangled broom-worm-human technology may not be a great idea everywhere, but the study does suggest that broom may be able, if we turn to it with a more loving desire to hear what it has to contribute, to play a role in healing some of the highly disturbed landscapes that it favors.

I think about this as I work in the Heritage Forest, carefully cutting and trying not to pull or otherwise disturb the soil any more than it already has been. I have told a lot of people my thoughts about our complicit entanglements with broom and my hopes for a longer, slower conversation that includes the possibility of loving the difficult; this practice has been met with a variety of responses, ranging from overt hostility to genuine interest. There are people on Galiano who are looking at the cultures of the places of broom's origins to guide experiments into potential medicinal uses for the plant; there are people who graze goats on it (I am in awe of hircine digestive powers); and then there are probably people who furtively apply Roundup to the stumps of the shrubs they have just cut by chainsaw. I think the ubiquity, agency, and visibility of broom nominate it as a superlative species with which to begin a dialogue about botanical colonialism and about multispecies futurities, led by the Indigenous peoples whose unceded territories are the lands about which we are all talking. This conversation will, however, require a willingness on the part of settlers to displace the invasive land ethic that currently animates and organizes so much broom busting—property, separation, control, killing—in favor of a generous and respectful multispecies openness.

NOTES

1. The sections of poetry opening each of the three sections of this essay are slightly revised excerpts from my triptych "Concerto for Scotch Broom," in Sandilands (2019, 142–146).

2. Galiano Island is part of the unceded, traditional, ongoing territories of the Puneluxutth', Lamulchi/Hwlitsum, and Tsawwassen peoples and other Coast Salish peoples. Although the Tsawwassen First Nation signed a tripartite comprehensive agreement (modern treaty) with Canada and BC in 2009, the island is still in dispute. The Puneluxutth' First Nation is part of the Hul'qumi'num Treaty Group and has claim to the entire island, not just the small reserve it currently holds at the north end. The Hwlitsum (with a complex relation to the former Lamulchi) First Nation also claims the entire island, but as the Lamulchi Nation was not recognized by Britain or the United States during the drawing of the international border in 1846, the Hwlitsum Nation is currently negotiating with Canada and BC for the legal recognition it requires to proceed with the formal treaty process. This version of the story is not the only one.

CATRIONA SANDILANDS

3. There is, of course, a large body of philosophical, ethical, and political debate about invasive plants, including concerns with the militarized, adversarial, often-xenophobic rhetoric employed in invasive species biology and management (e.g., Atchison and Head 2013; Larson 2011); concerns about the definition, history, possibility, and even desirability of the idea of "original" landscapes without anthropogenic intervention (e.g., Boivin et al. 2016; Hobbs, Higgs, and Hall 2013); and concerns with the ethics and political/experiential usefulness of categorical distinctions between native (good) and exotic-invasive (bad) plants, especially in and for Anthropocenic landscapes (e.g., Head et al. 2015; Hill and Hadley 2018). I have engaged directly with this body of work in several different ways in other venues (e.g., Sandilands 2013, 2016), so will not do so here.

4. For more information on Salish Harvest, an intercultural wild-food knowledge partnership between Galiano and Penelakut Islands (spearheaded by the Access to Media Education Society and the Puneluxutth' Nation), see the organization's website: https://www.salishharvest.com/. For more information on the Galiano Conservancy, including its steps toward creating the Nuts'a'maat forage forest in (complex) partnership with Indigenous participants (and the Access to Media Education Society), see Galiano Conservancy Association, n.d.

5. The Douglas Treaties, or Fort Victoria Treaties, were signed between 1850 and 1854 and cover about 930 square kilometers of territory on Vancouver Island. There are ongoing disputes about the terms of the treaties: where the English text of the treaties refers to "the land itself" becoming "the entire property of the white people forever" (Crown-Indigenous Relations and Northern Affairs Canada 2013), Salish signatories understood that the treaties were an attempt by Douglas to "keep the peace" in the midst of rapidly escalating violence (e.g., Claxton 2007; Elliott 1983). Douglas did not even hold to the treaties' promises that Indigenous "village sites and enclosed fields are to be kept for our own use, for the use of our children, and for those who may follow after us" or that First Nations "are at liberty to hunt over the unoccupied lands, and to carry on our fisheries as formerly" (Crown-Indigenous Relations and Northern Affairs Canada 2013). Galiano Island is not part of the Douglas Treaties: as Chris Arnett (1999) describes in detail, Douglas's bad-faith negotiations were well known to Indigenous leaders by the time he turned his attention to the Gulf Islands.

6. Right-justified text in the poem is excerpted from Kimmerer (2013, 333, 328, 336, 337, 338).

7. Although many species of earthworm are considered invasive in northern North America (they have a dramatic impact on the ecologies of forests that have largely evolved since the last Ice Age without the presence of worms), the red wigglers used in vermicomposting (the study used *Eisenia andrei*) are considered unlikely to survive outside of compost piles and manure heaps. There are what researchers call "ancient earthworms" in parts of BC that were not subject to glaciation but not on southeastern Vancouver Island or in the Southern Gulf Islands ("Earthworms of British Columbia" 2021). The use of one exotic species (worm) to enable the potential benefits of another (broom) is an interesting entanglement to think with. Slowly.

REFERENCES

Arnett, Chris. 1999. *The Terror of the Coast: Land Alienation and Colonial War on Vancouver Island and the Gulf Islands, 1849–1863*. Vancouver, BC: Talonbooks.

Atchison, Jennifer, and Lesley Head. 2013. "Eradicating Bodies in Invasive Plant Management." *Environment and Planning D: Society and Space* 31 (6): 951–968.

Boivin, Nicole L., Melinda A. Zeder, Dorian Q. Fuller, Alison Crowther, Greger Larson, Jon M. Erlandson, Tim Denham, and Michael D. Petraglia. 2016. "Ecological Consequences of Human Niche Construction: Examining Long-Term Anthropogenic Shaping of Global Species Distributions." *Proceedings of the National Academy of Sciences of the United States of America* 113 (23): 6388–6396.

BroomBusters. n.d. "How to Cut Broom." Accessed June 12, 2021. http://www.broombusters.org/how-to-cut-broom/.

Burrows, Larry, Ellen Cieraad, and Nicholas Head. 2015. "Scotch Broom Facilitates Indigenous Tree and Shrub Germination and Establishment in Dryland New Zealand." *New Zealand Journal of Ecology* 39 (1): 61–70.

Carlson, Jack, Frank Fred Reckendorf, and Wilbur Ternyik. 1991. *Stabilizing Coastal Sand Dunes in the Pacific Northwest*. USDA Soil Conservation Service Agriculture Handbook 687. https://naldc.nal.usda.gov/download/CAT92981355/PDF.

Centre for Agriculture and Bioscience International. 2019. "Invasive Species Compendium: *Cytisus scoparius* (Scotch Broom)." Last modified November 22, 2019. https://www.cabi.org/ISC/datasheet/17610.

Claxton, Nick. 2007. "Douglas Treaty." In "About SȾÁUTW̱ First Nation," Tsawout First Nation website, accessed May 4, 2021, https://tsawout.ca/about-tsawout/.

Cockburn, Andrew. 2015. "Weed Whackers: Monsanto, Glyphosate, and the War on Invasive Species." *Harper's Magazine*, September 2015. https://harpers.org/archive/2015/09/weed-whackers/.

Crown-Indigenous Relations and Northern Affairs Canada. 2013. *Treaty Texts—Douglas Treaties*. Accessed June 16, 2021. https://www.rcaanc-cirnac.gc.ca/eng/1370373165583/1581292088522.

Domínguez, Jorge, María Gómez-Brandón, Hugo Martínez-Cordeiro, and Marta Lores. 2018. "Bioconversion of Scotch Broom into a High-Quality Organic Fertiliser: Vermicomposting as a Sustainable Option." *Waste Management and Research* 36 (11): 1092–1099.

"Earthworms of British Columbia." 2021. In *E-Fauna BC: Electronic Atlas of the Fauna of British Columbia* (www.efauna.bc.ca), edited by Brian Klinkenberg. Accessed June 12, 2021. Vancouver: Lab for Advanced Spatial Analysis, Department of Geography, University of British Columbia.

Elliott, Dave, Sr. 1983. *Saltwater People*. Edited by Janet Poth. Saanichton, BC: School District No. 63.

Galiano Conservancy Association. n.d. "Nuts'a'maat Forage Forest." Accessed June 12, 2021. https://galianoconservancy.ca/nutsamaat-forage-forest/.

Grant, Walter Colquhoun. 1857. "Description of Vancouver Island." *Journal of the Royal Geographic Society of London* 27:268–320.

Head, Lesley, Brendon Larson, Richard Hobbs, Jennifer Atchison, Nick Gill, Christian Kull, and Haripriya Rangan. 2015. "Living with Invasive Plants in the Anthropocene." *Conservation and Society* 13 (3): 311–318.

Hill, Avery, and Elizabeth Hadley. 2018. "Rethinking 'Native' in the Anthropocene." *Frontiers in Earth Science*, July 16, 2018. https://doi.org/10.3389/feart.2018.00096.

Hobbs, Richard, Eric Higgs, and Carol Hall, eds. 2013. *Novel Ecosystems: Intervening in the New Ecological World Order.* Oxford: WileyBlackwell.

Invasive Species Council of BC (ISCBC). 2019. "Scotch Broom: *Cytisus scoparius*." April 2019. https://bcinvasives.ca/wp-content/uploads/2021/01/Scotch _Broom_FINAL_10_04_2019.pdf

Invasive Species Council of BC (ISCBC). n.d.-a. "The History of Invasive Plants in BC: How Did They Get Here?" Accessed June 30, 2019. https://bcinvasives .ca/news-events/media/articles/the-history-of-invasive-plants-in-bc-how -did-they-get-here. (No longer available.)

Invasive Species Council of BC (ISCBC). n.d.-b. "Weed of the Week: Scotch Broom." Accessed June 30, 2019. https://bcinvasives.ca/news-events/media /articles/weed-of-the-week-scotch-broom. (No longer available.)

Islands Trust Conservancy. 2018. "Protect against Invasive Species: Scotch Broom." Accessed June 30, 2021. https://islandstrust.bc.ca/conservancy/protect -nature/care-for-your-land/protect-against-invasives/scotch-broom/.

Kimmerer, Robin Wall. 2013. *Braiding Sweetgrass: Indigenous Wisdom, Scientific Knowledge and the Teachings of Plants.* Minneapolis: Milkweed.

Larson, Brendon. 2011. *Metaphors for Environmental Sustainability: Redefining Our Relationship with Nature.* New Haven, CT: Yale University Press.

Lee, Troy V. 2010. "'Glistening Patches of Gold': The Environmental History of Scotch Broom (*Cytisus scoparius*) on Southern Vancouver Island, 1848–1950." *BC Studies*, no. 166, 39–54.

Neale, Timothy. 2016. "Settler Colonialism and Weed Ecology." *Engagement: A Blog Published by the Anthropology and Environment Society*, November 2, 2016. https://aesengagement.wordpress.com/2016/11/02/settler-colonialism-and -weed-ecology/.

Reo, Nicholas J., and Laura A. Ogden. 2018. "Anishnaabe Aki: An Indigenous Perspective on the Global Threat of Invasive Species." *Sustainability Science* 13 (5): 1443–1452.

Ringuette, Janis. n.d.. *Beacon Hill Park History, 1842–2009.* Accessed June 12, 2021. https://beaconhillparkhistory.org/contents/contents.htm.

Rose, Deborah Bird. 2013a. "Anthropocene Noir." In *People and the Planet Conference Proceedings*, edited by Paul James, Chris Hudson, Sam Carroll-Bell, and Alyssa Taing, 1–11. Melbourne: Global Cities Research Institute, RMIT University.

Rose, Deborah Bird. 2013b. "In the Shadow of All This Death." In *Animal Death*, edited by Jay Johnston and Fiona Probyn-Rapsey, 1–20. Sydney: Sydney University Press.

Rose, Deborah Bird. 2013c. "Slowly ~ Writing into the Anthropocene." In "Writing Creates Ecology and Ecology Creates Writing." Special issue, TEXT, no. 20, 1–14. http://www.textjournal.com.au/speciss/issue20/Rose.pdf.

Rose, Deborah Bird. 2015. "Dialogue." In *Manifesto for Living in the Anthropocene*, edited by Katherine Gibson, Deborah Bird Rose, and Ruth Fincher, 127–131. Brooklyn, NY: Punctum Books.

Rule, Jane. 2008. *Loving the Difficult*. Sidney, BC: Hedgerow.

Sandilands, Catriona. 2013. "Dog Stranglers in the Park? National and Vegetal Politics in Ontario's Rouge Valley." *Journal of Canadian Studies* 47 (3): 93–122.

Sandilands, Catriona. 2016. "Some 'F' Words for the Environmental Humanities: Feralities, Feminisms, Futurities." In *The Routledge Companion to the Environmental Humanities*, edited by Ursula Heise, Jon Christensen, and Michelle Niemann, 427–435. London: Routledge.

Sandilands, Catriona, ed. 2019. *Rising Tides: Reflections for Climate Changing Times*. Halfmoon Bay, BC: Caitlin.

TallBear, Kim. 2018. "Making Love and Relations beyond Settler Sex and Family." In *Making Kin, Not Population: Reconceiving Generations*, edited by Adele Clarke and Donna Haraway, 145–164. Chicago: Prickly Paradigm.

Tuck, Eve, and K. Wayne Yang. 2012. "Decolonization Is Not a Metaphor." *Decolonization: Indigeneity, Education and Society* 1 (1): 1–40.

Zielke, Ken, Jacob O. Boateng, Norm Caldicott, and Heather Williams. 1992. *Broom and Gorse in British Columbia: A Forestry Perspective Problem Analysis*. Victoria: Province of British Columbia, Ministry of Forests.

AWAKENING TO
THE CALL OF OTHERS

THREE

What I Learned from Existential Ecology

ISABELLE STENGERS

I STILL REMEMBER MY EXPERIENCE when first reading Deborah Bird Rose's *Wild Dog Dreaming* (2011). At that time I had still to discover the environmental humanities field. But I was immediately caught by something deeply unusual and important in the very style of this book and associated it with the fact that a woman was the author. I vividly remember addressing the ghost of Virginia Woolf, telling her, "Maybe you were wrong after all, in your *Three Guineas*, maybe women can actually make a difference that matters in the academy!"

This was a very partial reaction indeed—so many voices inhabit Rose and enter into the composition of her essay, so many torments get co-intensified when she takes it upon herself to feel with the death work, daring to weave together the anguish of the survivors of the Nazi holocaust and the revolt and shame she experiences confronting the torture and extermination of the Australian dingo. I still believe that the acute sensitivity of her text is that of a woman—echoing those innumerable women who have cried and wept over the mutilated bodies of senselessly killed people, whatever the words and reasons justifying their "sacrifice." But it is also the echo of the teaching of the Aboriginal clever man Daly Pulkara, who entrusted her with a task: "We have listened to your stories. You, you Whitefella, you can listen to stories too" (D. Rose 2011, 4). She makes us listen; she enables us to listen—not to understand, in the sense of "OK, I get it," but, as she writes, to feel drawn into an encounter. Her writing penetrates our defenses and awakens layers of feelings and questions that connect us with a frailty we had learned to forget.

Rose practices what she presents in this book as "ecological existentialism," and this does not amount to presenting a relational conception of existence. She captures the dramatic character of philosophical existentialism but crucially transforms the sense of the drama, centering it not on the loneliness of Man in an indifferent world but on the "call of others," a call that, she writes, brings us to our own selfhood. Responsibility is no longer a crushing abstraction, the correlate of the sovereign freedom that would differentiate the human subject from all other inhabitants of this earth. It requires learning to listen in order to make oneself able to hear and respond.

The silence of God made Job the father of existentialism, refusing to admit that some unknown divine reasons must explain the destruction of everything that gave meaning to his life. From Søren Kierkegaard to Fyodor Dostoyevsky and Jean-Paul Sartre, existentialism has posited sheer existence against "essence," essence being whatever would explain why things are as they are. In contrast to what may be called "critical existentialism," ecological existentialism, together with the environmental humanities, does not reject explanations, be they storytelling or scientific, so-called objective ones. They side with the Aboriginal clever men and all those who do not silence explanations but weave them into stories telling of a meaningful existential situation. Taking any explanatory power as situated within history, place, and relationship, they demand that this power be accountable for its impact and repercussions. And their stories then shape our capacity to respond, to feel with the world. This is indeed what my encounter with Rose's writing made me experience, enriching my understanding of my own attempt to enter into an accountable relation with what scientists call "objectivity."

Not all explanations can be shaped into existentially meaningful stories. It can hardly be denied that as soon as we speak of Science, capitalized and

54

in the singular, we deal with a power hostile to existential accountability: the right to not take into account is justified if it is the price for muting calls that would impede the advance of Reason and Objectivity. But ecological existentialism will not for all that refuse to hear the call of those others who try to resist the pseudo-objective facts that colonize their own fields, scientists who care for a difference to be made between "good" (relevant) and "bad" (abusive) sciences.

In her *Wild Dog Dreaming* (2011), Rose listens to imaginative scientists who, she imagines, could accept being gathered around a campfire, listening to calls exchanged in the night, feeling called to listen to each other. Maybe this campfire could also welcome the tales of wounded ones who felt betrayed by critical thinkers deriding their struggle against the abuse of power committed in the name of Science. For instance, another Rose, Hilary, would tell how the enemies of her enemies had proved no friend to her as she struggled against the objectification of intelligence: for the critics, there was no "bad" science since it would imply that some are "good" (H. Rose 1996). Feminist biologists would tell how they were not helped either when an iron curtain came to separate biological sex, abandoned to its mistreatment by sociobiologists, from sociocultural gender.

I will certainly not claim that critical thinking is responsible for the domination of Science. I intend to make explicit where I am coming from, as Stephen Muecke proposes we do (this collection). I come from the academic land, where critical thinkers and objectivist scientists oppose as warring brothers, both parties mobilized by antagonistic versions of the human exception, unable to escape the commanding abstractions that mobilize them against each other. And both parties act as do mobilized armies, destroying, in the name of either imperative objectivity or irreducible subjectivity, situations that might have slowed them down, forced them to listen to the call of other voices protesting against the way their judgment dismembers what matters for them.

This is why I so deeply appreciate the way Deborah Rose refuses to participate in this mobilization, that is, refuses to linger over epistemological questions or to pass judgment against scientific work, as expressing the fateful, modern opposition established between humans and nature. Why do sixteenth- and seventeenth-century texts still sound relevant today? Does it testify to a continuity that would give to the "birth of modern science" the power to explain what followed, or is this continuity itself to be explained? This question matters because it communicates with the idea that a "rebirth" would open to a "new," successor science.

The thesis that scientists would be doomed to privilege isolatable objects and the general laws that explain how they behave is clearly part of the past. Today the concerns of Aldo Leopold's "Thinking like a Mountain" or of Rachel Carson's *Silent Spring* belong, if not to mainstream scientific ecology, at least to a vigorous part of it. Lynn Margulis and Dorion Sagan's story about the network of cross-kingdom alliances that "help keep the entire planetary surface brimming with life" (D. Rose 2011, 50) might be the motto of a new generation of biologists for whom mutualisms—partnering, symbiotic relationships—begin to impose themselves like the very definition of life. The point is not, however, to embrace such interesting sciences as innocent or as reliable allies. In fact, the discovery of the extraordinarily complex diversity of the human gut microbiome, and of its impoverishment in industrialized countries, has already resulted in campaigns to collect and preserve the microbes for future use, a campaign that concentrates on Indigenous people, who must contribute before a change of diet or the use of antibiotics destroys the resource (Dominguez Bello et al. 2018). Extractive practices are able to follow sciences whatever the path they take.

The point, then, is to escape the grip of the idea that Science has an identity of its own, to be blessed or damned, and it does not demand only escaping the pseudo-evolutionist story of Man as the one who rose up on His own two feet and challenged a world to be conquered. If evolving comes to be understood primordially as "evolving together," or, better, as an ongoing creation of ways to co-involve, to get involved in each other, each giving and owing to others capacities to make a living, the stories we need to tell might be not about a "new" science, gifted with a new ideal of rationality, but about the possibility of "another" science, co-involving with other species of protagonists (Stengers 2018a).

Again, thinking in terms of co-involvement is not thinking in terms of some kind of innocent harmony. To characterize such entanglements, Donna Haraway (2008, 216) borrowed the term *contact zone* from colonial and postcolonial studies—Haraway quotes Mary Louise Pratt's *Imperial Eyes* (1992)—in full awareness that radically asymmetrical relations of power might be at play. Evolution as co-involution may be stories of subjects becoming what they are in and by their relation to each other, but those subjects are also at risk with respect to each other. Symbiotic co-involution may mean the existential risk that interdependence becomes sheer dependence.

When I derived from Lynn Margulis's emphasis on the crucial role of symbiosis in the history of Life (see, for instance, 1998) the idea of the creation of symbiotic relations as key events in the shaping of modern sciences, it was not to exonerate but to hold open the ecological question of what such sciences could become capable of if they were to enter into different interconnections and alliances. It was at a time when the existential risk of sheer dependence was becoming fully actual. In fact, as early as the end of the nineteenth century, scientists working in those sciences most closely associated with the so-called development of productive forces, physics and chemistry, had perceived the risk involved in the situation they had attained, that of precious partners symbiotically associated with modern states and industry. They felt the precariousness of symbiosis, the possibility that their allies would take direct control and demand that scientists stop posing "idle" questions and dedicate their work only to solving really interesting ones. Their claim that, in order to be generative and fruitful, research requires autonomy reflects this anxiety.

Today the theme of the autonomy required for reliable knowledge to advance and of the correlative need for its allies, in their very best interests, to respect the ways scientists proceed has become a sad and reproachful lament as the socio-ecological network on which modern sciences depended is being destroyed. To contemplate the present-day academic landscape—the inability of its inhabitants to learn how to resist together—is to contemplate desolation, an ecologically devastated landscape. Again, critical academic colleagues will not help. They have their own lament, complaining that all the resources go to objective Science while they themselves are left to die away. But, further, they cannot take seriously their colleagues' complaint since, from their critical standpoint, the very idea of an objective disinterested science was always a sham. What they denounced has just shown its true color. Intervening as a tentative peacemaker between those protagonists would have been pointless. Indeed, none of them desired peace, each rather accusing the other for their own beleaguered situation, each dreaming of a better world from which the other would have disappeared.

Listening to these endangered but belligerent academic species, it may be important to consider the way each feels threatened. On the one side, that of critique, the question is that of their material (that is, professional) survival, and this question only confirms that their stance is justified—those in power have no reason to feed whoever sees through their game and makes it public. In contrast, on the other side, the menace is really existential. They feel they are in danger of betraying their own reason for existing if they accept subordination. They discover that they are expendable as providers of "reliable knowledge"—blind objectification and unilateral imposition never needed reliable knowledge. Science, in the singular, can do without sciences as "practices."

It is at this point that Deborah Rose's existential ecology is crucial. Hearing the calls of others on the brink of extinction demands that we do not indulge in the so very tempting feeling that their fate is well justified. This would be aligning with those who justify the killing of dingoes by the depredations they are accused of—they are pests, and our world would be better without them. Certainly, it is not a question of "killing" people here but of destroying practitioners and their worlds. My entry into political ecology was through an understanding of "practice" as not simply a human activity in general but a manner of activity that may be destroyed if it is redefined through chains of dependency.

Initially, I came to use the term *practice* in order to complicate the critical claim that "sciences are human practices like the others," a war motto the concerned scientists understood perfectly well: their practices would be explained (away) like any others, in purely human terms, meaning that their claim to entertain a relation with "reality as it is" would be critically explained away. I simply proposed to substitute *like* with *among*. But this substitution has a double consequence that has since become crucial. First, *among others* means no special privilege, no exceptionality—"reality as it is" may be at stake for scientific practices, but it will not serve as a standard to disqualify other ways to relate with reality. Second, other practices must be addressed in a similar way. What is existentially at stake for each of them? What do they need to affirm, maintain, and nurture in order to exist? Or else, what makes their vulnerability? If scientific practices are no exception, the scientific practitioners' feeling that they might be destroyed is no exception either. Many others are also threatened. And Rose proposed another correlative version of this commonality: Would learning to listen to the "call of others" bring sciences to their own selfhood?

Indeed, modernity, from the beginning to the present day, resounds with practitioners' anxious calls: if you demand this from us, or if you impose this on us, you will destroy us! These calls are usually addressed to those who present themselves as rational reformers, clearing the path for the advance of whatever they will call progress. It was the case at the time of the enclosure and after, with the eradication of commoning practices all over the planet. It is the case today wherever neoliberal production and management redefine tasks and imperatives in such a way that those who are forced to comply feel abased, forced to do what they know to be a "bad" job—including scientists when told to directly serve the economy and provide profitable innovations. In all those cases, resistance against "reform" is characterized as a lack of flexibility, a remainder of outdated attachments and privileges. It is the great sadness of Karl Marx's modernism—to ask us not to hear the calls of the many whose world was destroyed and to accept these destructions as paving the way to socialism.

In a sense, critical thinkers need, then, to learn what naturalists know: the loss of a living species may be explained but never explained away, never characterized as well deserved, never justified in the name of something higher (see D. Rose 2011, 89). It is the loss of something that participated in the web of life in its own right, valuing it in its own way, affirming its connection with others in its own mode. And what is lost is also its future, what it might have come to connect with and become with. If sciences as practices are destroyed, their memory will be appropriated by their sneering namesakes, for whom these stories of relating to "reality as it is" will be a matter of outdated metaphysics.

It can certainly be objected that scientists do not think of themselves as practitioners in the sense I use. Further, they have been active in the destruction of many practices, against which they have used "reality" as a weapon, as if they were its authorized spokespersons. They have accepted that Science is the key to human progress, identified as the inexorable advance of objective knowledge. None of that can be denied. The proposition to address sciences as practices is not a proposition to address a "pure" or "innocent" victim to be defended but an enterprise that has actively demonstrated its loyalty to those who now betray it. It is, rather, betting on the possibility of dissolving this loyalty, as an acid dissolves an amalgam, to free some of its components for other associations, other co-involvements.

This is why it is important to complicate, that is, demobilize, the relation of sciences with reality, to understand it not as a privilege but as a commitment. To put it in a nutshell, I came to propose that the claim for realism of (some) modern sciences means that they are committed to give to what they address the power to make a crucial difference for what concerns the way they are addressed. The only interpretation that they value is the one that will be "endorsed" as relevant by what it addresses, not unilaterally imposed on it. This value marks a specific and selective kind of achievement—the possibility for something to receive multiple interpretations is unexceptional, and many of these interpretations escape the "either endorsed or imposed on" alternative. The kind of achievement valued by sciences may thus easily turn into an abuse of power if it is presented as rational or objective. But this achievement also marks scientific practices as generative collective enterprises. The question a new claim activates for the concerned collective is typically: Is it possible to interpret what this colleague has obtained in another way than the one she or he proposes? Is it reliable; that is, can we rely on it? Such a question is not skeptical or hostile but expresses a concern shared by all those for whom the achievement matters for their own work: Does it hold? We might think of spiders that would weave a collective web: each of them is vitally interested in testing the claim produced by a colleague before using it as a support for the one they envisage. It is because experimenters understand experimental endorsement as an event, not as a methodological result, that, since the end of the nineteenth century, when their sciences were systematically associated with industrial development, they have claimed that they vitally need what they call autonomy. Indeed, if other values come to prevail in the definition of what is an achievement for experimenters—innovations or patentable promises of innovation, for instance—the testing web of interdependent concerned colleagues on which depends the authentication of the event would unravel. However, what they did not emphasize is that this event together with their own practice is strongly situated and can in no way serve as a general model for reliable scientific knowledge.

To characterize what scientists are accustomed to celebrating as objective or rational as the achievement of an endorsement is a manner of thinking sciences as practices among others—or more precisely as a positive plurality of practices: endorsement as an achievement is not unifying scientific practices but rather dramatizing their problematic and fragile kinship. What experimenters achieve is situated by the kind of environment in which what they address can effectively get the power to eventually endorse the relevance of the way it is addressed, that is, the laboratory. This is why reliability may be lost when experimentally well-identified beings leave the lab and the web of colleagues who tested the reliability of their identification. How, for instance, to address genetically modified organisms when they enter into a world of multiple interdependencies? This also means that the experimental achievement is conditioned by the fact that what is addressed may effectively be transplanted into a lab, that is, separated from its world, without being altered or even wrecked. This is indeed the case for electrons, molecules, and some bacteria but not for rats. As for humans, their all-too-easy endorsement of interpretations about themselves keeps pseudolabs and other objective social-psychological fact-producing methods busy. Recalcitrant ones who would question the presupposition implicated in the way they are addressed are quickly excluded from the sample. One way or another, when experimental practices are promoted as a general model, interdependency and co-becoming are considered pests, thwarting the progress of scientific rationality.[1]

Dissolving the amalgam that makes objectivity a general attribute of Science activates a wealth of questions that challenge the idea that Science would reflect and express an ontological commitment. Ontology emphasizes an a priori framing that would be shared by a culture and dramatized by its ways of knowing. In contrast, those questions draw attention toward the web of powers that are symbiotically associated with Science and enjoy a capacity to impose objectivity that scientists may dream of but do not have. They demand a speculative, not a critical, stance.

Speculation does not occur in the void. It attempts to hear and answer the voices of many scientists, past and present, who have remained true to the commitment of having what they address make a crucial difference and have been caught in the crossfire of critiques and of defenders of methods blindly warranting objectivity (remember Hilary Rose!). For the critiques, they were legitimate targets as those critics would not be impressed by the idea that objectivity could be divorced from blind objectification, that it could mean that those scientists had learned *from* what they addressed which kinds of questions are relevant, that is, also, which kind of relation generates a knowledge that does not reflect an abuse of power. For the defenders of objectivity, those "relevant questions" have an unforgivable weakness. As they do not derive from a command-and-control relation like the experimental one but rather from a "learn how to connect" one, they could not confirm the image of Science as the advance of knowledge, as an advancing mobilized army. Worse, they could not enter into a symbiotic relation with the powers that thrive on objectivity as giving the right to define what should be taken into account and what may, even must, be ignored.

My speculative attempt is to associate those scientists with the claim that only a strong, positive pluralism can allow scientific practices to cultivate what it means to relate objectivity with the power of the object to have a voice in the way it will be understood, that is, indeed, to "object." Some would say that such a pluralism means a regress from science to empiricism. And indeed it does not comply with Immanuel Kant's famous definition of what makes Science rational in his *Critique of Pure Reason*: "Reason must take the lead with principles for its judgments according to constant laws and compel nature to answer its questions, rather than letting nature guide its movements by keeping reason, as it were, in leading-strings" (1998, 109). But empiricism is a catchall category and usually a pejorative one, emphasizing the arbitrariness, unreliability, and anecdotal character of "empirical" observations. As such it is usually used to disqualify any "nonscientific" knowledge. In our case, it willfully ignores that scientists who endeavor to be true to the specific achievement that I associate with scientific practices are committed to a demanding "adventure of relevance" (Savransky 2016). Let us take the example of anthropologist Helen Verran's (2013) claim that in order to learn *from* those she and her colleagues encounter, they have to resist "bad faith," which she associates with tolerant, good-willed anthropologists listening to others in a way that refuses them authority over their existential and experiential commitments. So doing, she knows that no easy so-called relativist, "anything goes" position will help them, because they are there to learn, not to dream the dreams of others: they have to situate *their own* knowledge practice and commitment (Who knows? What do we know? How do we know?) in order to make room for the others.

We should be careful, however, not to go from reductive, objectifying Science to generally agreeable scientific practices, not to accept Kant's contrast and celebrate, as a successor to the figure of the judge, that of gentle scientists listening to what they address as one listens to a master (whatever this might mean). A term like *claim* should put us on the alert: Verran claims to bring back relevant knowledge and anticipates that it is up to her colleagues to discuss its relevance. I would dare to characterize what I called the adventure of relevance as an "entrepreneurial" adventure.

I do not take *entrepreneurial* in a disqualifying sense but in the generic sense of associating achievement with commitment to the possible. For "adventurous" scientists, it means commitment to the possibility of creating situations that empower what they address in such a way that they can claim that their question was relevant for the addressee, not imposed on it. Such a commitment is very specific and indeed leads to subversive engagement against Science and what it imposes in the name of objectivity. But it is also vulnerable, liable to turn the adventure of relevance into a disqualification of other ways of knowing, entertaining different values. We can think, for instance, of the constellation of technical practices that aim at obtaining from some nonhuman or other-than-human that it contributes to the fulfillment of a human intention. A typical scientific concern is to understand what technicians "empirically" succeed in doing, and as we know, scientifically understanding technical practices typically results in disentangling such practices from what is deemed superfluous, traditional, or even superstitious. And this opens the path to so-called rationalizations, which neglect the thick question of their artful efficacy. As we know very well for therapeutic practices, such rationalizations, even if they sound benevolent, open them to a redefinition by other entrepreneurial powers, that of the pharmaceutical industry, for instance, which substitutes pills for the arts of healing.

The way I address scientific practitioners is crucially related to Deborah Rose's existential ecology because it demands that we speculatively envisage what they might existentially become capable of in a different ecological environment, an environment offering different possibilities of symbiosis. An environment demanding "entrepreneurial accountability," or response-ability in Haraway's sense. The notion of an "ecology of practice" was born from this perspective. It is not a knowledge-oriented notion but a notion speculating on the specific existential relation a scientist entertains with knowledge as an achievement. Could scientists in an accountability-demanding environment come to perceive as an abuse and an offense the transformation of what is for them an achievement into an instrument of judgment and disqualification? Could the full awareness of the partial character of the connection they have to craft in order to obtain such an achievement result in an active concern for the way it could be (mis)used?

Such an awareness is not a matter of intellectual lucidity. Most scientists are quite aware of the difference between our messy world and their clean schematization of it. What they often lack is the vivid experience of the mess their own propositions may create. The storying of resounding failures to anticipate consequences is not part of scientific culture and education, and when it is, the lessons are few and optimistic—we now know better. But mostly, seeing only a mess, they do not perceive the interdependent web that their propositions may endanger. Such a perception might be generated, however, if they were confronted with those who know the danger and if they were constrained to really listen in order to make themselves able to hear and respond. This means an ecology of situations in which people practically concerned by an issue are recognized as practitioners in their own right, empowered by their practice to assess propositions regarding this issue—that is, are considered experts about aspects of the situation that matter for them.

Thinking of such situations, I often associate them with procedures like the palaver, and its constraint, that each protagonist should intervene and be listened to as an "ancient," someone who "knows things." This prohibits any implication of tolerance, of dealing with what a protagonist knows as a mere matter of belief or of habit. Instead, scientists might experience the partial character of the knowledge they claim. The collective assessment would not concern the reliability of what they know, as is the case with their colleagues, but the effects of their proposition, the way it would affect those concerned. And such effects, through the contrast they might display with what they, as scientists, were equipped to perceive, would situate their own perception—neither objective nor subjective, intrinsically correlated with the specificity of their own relation-making practice.

If some middle ground could be obtained through such procedures, it would be an ecological event, a composition obtained through interdependent affective modifications of the participants' perception of their own existential relations with what matters for them, of what they need in order to go on existing. I understand such composition events as generated through the power given to the issue to make them all think and imagine together, and to learn to feel what others cannot accept. They demand a moderate measure of initial trust, which may build up along with the power obtained by the issue but will be broken if any protagonist entertains a judgmental position about others' reasons and demands. And they may generate what they vitally need: a practical culture of trust in the possibility of composition. Scientists sharing this culture would then consider, as part of their practice, that they are committed to resist any authoritarian use of the reference to Science because they need recalcitrant others if their proposition is to keep some reliable relevance in the situation that concerns them all.

However, even as a speculation, one does not innocuously transplant procedures like the palaver into a world that has taken entrepreneurship as a quasi-normative human existential attribute. Again, the point is not to reduce entrepreneurship to its neoliberal caricature, a mobilization of the means to maximize one's advantages in a competitive market, but to emphasize the high value entrepreneurs associate with the question of the possible, their refusal to consent and give authority to what they see as settled states of affairs. I myself, refusing the settled fate of sciences, am part of this entrepreneurial world. And, as such, I have to be cautious. The perspective of an ecology of practices, with the demanding relations it implies between concerned practitioners, be they scientists or not, may well be a well-meaning speculation, but it presupposes that those who engage in those relations care for the possibility of the event, the generation of a shared middle ground. What about those who are not interested in this event? Or who have nothing to contribute? Would Deborah Rose's teacher, Old Tim, be interested?

The ecology-of-practices proposition belongs to the political register. Politics here is understood as an issue-centered practice, and its proposed achievement corresponds to the unfolding of an issue against its possible dismemberment into preset conflictual positions. It is not privileging consensus over conflict, or else it activates a meaning of consensus that refers to an ecology of affects (Hustak and Myers 2012), not to the transformation of many voices into one unanimous voice. Consensus may mean feeling the reasons of others and allowing them to affect or inflect the relation entertained with one's own reasons. Not in general but around "this" issue, which has then received the power to "make sense in common." But, again, what about those who situate themselves as not concerned by the issue but as potentially endangered by some consequences of the consensus in the making?

We should not forget here that our usual conception of politics is itself entrepreneurial when each participant gives voice to reasons, that is, arguments aiming at a possible conclusion—which is not the case with palavers. The ecology of practices does not denounce this conception but tries to complicate it. It does not dream of turning entrepreneurs into "wise ancients" but trusts in their awareness that, as practitioners, their sense of what might be possible is not self-reliant but derives from a practice that, like any other, might be destroyed. The actualization of this existential risk is issue dependent, but no practice is safe regarding all issues. This is why, when the cry resounds, "This way of addressing the issue will destroy us!," practitioners would listen and pay attention. What I called *cosmopolitics* marks the involvement of diplomacy, the art of negotiating on the brink of confrontation, of rendering present those whose very existence is at stake in the issue.

However, reading Rose and some others, I have come to understand that the involvement of diplomats is not sufficient. Diplomats can function only between parties who have a voice, who are able to agree or disagree, a restriction that de facto excludes many beings involved and put at risk in collective deliberations. I had already understood that the cosmopolitical proposition demanded that "making sense in common" take place in the haunting presence of the voiceless ones who nevertheless are implicated by the deliberation (Stengers 2011, 397–399), but I was thinking this presence not for its own sake but as a way to cool down the passion that may lead entrepreneurs to conflate what might be possible with what has to be possible, that is, to consider deliberation in terms of obstacles to be overcome. I have been made to realize that this marked me as a European philosopher and that for others an actively decolonial cosmopolitics demanded that other-than-humans be included in their own right in my conception of politics (for this realization, see Stengers 2018b).

As we know, so-called traditional ways of achieving collective thinking often implied convoking other-than-human beings, beings that no participant could appropriate, or claim to represent, but whose presence has to be given the power to be felt, exposing the way in which the issue is debated to the test of their presence, enacting Harawayan response-ability. The Great Binding Law of the Iroquois required that all deliberations include the consideration of the impact of any decision on the seven coming generations. It goes without saying that these unborn generations were present not under the guise of demanding from the participants a planification of the future but as making reasons rooted in the present accountable to a future that they cannot appropriate. In those cases, as in many others, it can be said that the question of accepting to "let oneself be affected by" is not implicit, as it is when listening to the others' reasons or protest, but is openly enacted in the existential experience that it does not belong to the assembled humans to define the issue alone. It must be pondered in the presence of others who share our world in their own enigmatic way.

When I first envisaged what could be a cosmopolitical procedure in our world where the entrepreneurial reference to the possible has become the norm, I thought of this affect in terms of fright. The source of my inspiration was what philosopher Alfred North Whitehead called Oliver Cromwell's cry, which, he wrote, "echoes down the ages": "My Brethren, by the bowels of Christ I beseech you, bethink that you may be mistaken!" (Stengers 2011, 368; Whitehead 1967, 16). Even if it was addressed to the Church of Scotland, which had pledged allegiance to the royalist cause, by Cromwell, as the head of an army about to defeat the Scottish, this call has indeed echoed as if carrying no such memory, its efficacy fully in the now of each of its moments of reception. "Think it possible that you may be mistaken" is, for instance, a quasi-ritual motto widely used in Quaker meetings.

The call is not an argument. The invocation of Christ brings no authority. It may induce a fright or, rather, maybe more adequately, a certain solemnity in the act of reaching a decision—more is in balance with our decisions than we are able to grasp. Quoting Whitehead again: "The full solemnity of the world arises from the sense of positive achievement within the finite, combined with the sense of modes of infinitude stretching beyond each finite fact. This infinitude is required by each fact to express its necessary relevance beyond its own limitations" (1968, 78–79).

The feeling that the "infinitude" of the world—or cosmos—is involved in, and concerned by, the manner of the stand we take is not a matter of belief. It may be at the very heart of the pragmatism of William James, who intensely inspired Whitehead. James formulated what he called "the great question," which gives its solemnity to the relations we entertain with what we take as true. Our truths, he wrote, whatever they are, break the flux of sensible reality, and, in so doing, they add to this flux. "We build the flux out inevitably. The great question is: does it, with our additions, *rise or fall in values*? Are the additions *worthy* or *unworthy*?" (James 1907, 98). This question is not looking for an answer; it aims at inducing, against any self-supporting feeling of legitimacy, against our ability to rationalize them away, an opening to voices that do not argue but call to be heard.

If I have chosen to quote Whitehead and James at the end of this text, it is because they were my guides and teachers and might be welcome around Deborah Rose's campfire. I learned from them that philosophy was not about knowing the world or ourselves but about inducing an existential change in our relation with what we take for granted. Decisions, feeling responsible about the consequences of our decisions, or awakening to the calls of others who bear these consequences, were not to be reduced to, or exalted as, human additions to the blind functioning of the world. If they matter to us, they matter, period. And they saw as their job, as philosophers, to turn the fact that they matter into a witness for the very texture of reality. What we may feel when taking a stand—that this stand is not only our decision but a decision for a world—would then correspond to an existential intensification of the way this world is woven.[2]

James and Whitehead inhabit the cosmopolitical proposal. I dearly hope that they would recognize my speculation as worthy. But I am sure that they would welcome Rose's existential ecology as a powerful, vibrant, and intensely transformative rendering of what made them feel and think. And a rendering that demonstrates that we do not know what scientific practices might make their practitioners capable of.

At the time when I invoked fright as the affect that might open practitioners to the call of those who might bear the consequences without participating in the negotiation, I was still in an entrepreneurial-centered perspective. When I understood the need for the practitioners to slow down and let themselves be affected by the cry of the absent or mute ones, which requires witnesses rather than diplomats, I thought of artists as those who might convey something like Whitehead's "solemnity of the world" or the test of James's "great question." But reading Rose, I discovered that researchers themselves could become such witnesses, conveying the power of love, of grief, of rage, of anguish.

Rose has documented the fact of human blind cruelty at work in the dingo persecution, but she has also made this cruelty felt, together with the existential and cosmic drama this persecution constitutes for the Aboriginal inhabitants of Australia she loves, but not only for them. The way she

AWAKENING TO THE CALL OF OTHERS

has answered the call of her teacher tasking her with listening to Aboriginal stories has enabled her to become a witness that cuts through our defenses, generating a contact zone that makes it impossible to enclose and neutralize the Aboriginal drama as a matter of cultural belief. And she has also cut through the divide between science and philosophy. Contrary to philosophy, scientific research is collective, and she has taught others not to refer to facts as support for an argumentation but to become-with facts, to become their vehicle for a generative bequeathing. Since I got acquainted with the environmental humanities, I became aware that this scientific field indeed fosters a becoming-witnesses of its researchers, and that for the best of reasons: because what they address calls them to do so. They work with facts but follow the facts wherever relevance demands it, and to do so, they have to learn from others, human and nonhuman, who experience these facts quite differently.

The practice of the logic of "both-and" (D. Rose 2011, 111), or of connection between heterogeneous ways of being and feeling, is a hard one. It intensifies what we intellectually know, that worlds are at stake in our decisions. For me, it created a contact zone that has turned cosmopolitics, a speculative proposition, into a living and lived one, one that has found what it needs and mutely cried for. Cosmopolitics was born with the question of what entrepreneurial practitioners might be capable of, but it is now in the hands of those for whom this question is vital because they have taken it upon themselves to live with, and try to relay, the calls of the so many others whose worlds are unraveling.

NOTES

1. Anna Lowenhaupt Tsing's important proposition in *The Mushroom at the End of the World* (2015) about *scalability*, an engineering term, is precious because the transversal contrast she proposes between "scalable" and "nonscalable" is then explicitly relative to a *practical* concern—how to *make* scalable, or how to *retain* scalability—not to a matter of fact. As such this concern prevails not only in the lab (reproducibility) but also in the factory (processes and workers), in the fields (monocultures), and in the rule of law (attribution of legal personhood), without even speaking of objective evaluation, clinical tests, technical or hygiene specifications, and so on.

2. Whitehead's formula for this weaving, "the many become one, and are increased by one" may be developed in many ways, among which, rather strikingly, is Rose's proposition about our participation in three lives, "that which is given, that which is lived, and that which will be bequeathed" (2011, 89).

ISABELLE STENGERS

REFERENCES

Carson, Rachel. 1962. *Silent Spring*. New York: Houghton and Mifflin.

Dominguez Bello, Maria G., Rob Knight, Jack A. Gilbert, and Martin J. Blaser. 2018. "Preserving Microbial Diversity." *Science* 362 (6410): 33–34.

Haraway, Donna. 2008. *When Species Meet*. Minneapolis: University of Minnesota Press.

Hustak, Carla, and Natasha Myers. 2012. "Involutionary Momentum: Affective Ecologies and the Sciences of Plant/Insect Encounters." *differences* 23 (3): 74–118.

James, William. 1907. *Pragmatism: A New Name for Some Old Ways of Thinking*. New York: Longman Green.

Kant, Immanuel. 1998. *Critique of Pure Reason*. Cambridge: Cambridge University Press.

Leopold, Aldo. 1949. *A Sand County Almanac*. London: Oxford University Press.

Margulis, Lynn. 1998. *Symbiotic Planet: A New Look at Evolution*. New York: Basic.

Margulis, Lynn, and Dorion Sagan. 2000. *What Is Life?* Berkeley: University of California Press.

Pratt, Mary Louise. 1992. *Imperial Eyes: Travel Writing and Transculturation*. New York: Routledge.

Rose, Deborah Bird. 2011. *Wild Dog Dreaming: Love and Extinction*. Charlottesville: University of Virginia Press.

Rose, Hilary. 1996. "Science Wars: My Enemy's Enemy Is—Only Perhaps—My Friend." *Social Text* 45–46:61–80.

Savransky, Martin. 2016. *The Adventure of Relevance: An Ethics of Social Inquiry*. London: Palgrave Macmillan.

Stengers, Isabelle. 2011. *Cosmopolitics II*. Minneapolis: University of Minnesota Press.

Stengers, Isabelle. 2018a. *Another Science Is Possible: A Manifesto for Slow Science*. Cambridge, UK: Polity.

Stengers, Isabelle. 2018b. "The Challenge of Ontological Politics." In *A World of Many Worlds*, edited by Marisol de la Cadena and Mario Blaser, 83–111. Durham, NC: Duke University Press.

Tsing, Anna Lowenhaupt. 2015. *The Mushroom at the End of the World: On the Possibility of Life in Capitalist Ruins*. Princeton, NJ: Princeton University Press.

Verran, Helen. 2013. "Engagements between Disparate Knowledge Traditions: Toward Doing Difference Generatively and in Good Faith." In *Contested Ecologies: Dialogues in the South on Nature and Knowledge*, edited by Lesley Green, 141–161. Cape Town: HSRC Press.

Whitehead, Alfred N. 1967. *Science and the Modern World*. New York: Free Press.

Whitehead, Alfred N. 1968. *Modes of Thought*. New York: Free Press.

SPECULATIVE FABULATIONS FOR TECHNOCULTURE'S GENERATIONS

FOUR

Taking Care of Unexpected Country

DONNA J. HARAWAY

WHEN I FIRST SAW Patricia Piccinini's work a few years ago, I recognized a sister in technoculture, a coworker committed to taking "naturecultures" seriously without the soporific seductions of a return to Eden or the palpitating frisson of a jeremiad warning of the coming technological apocalypse.[1] I experienced her as a compelling storyteller in the radical experimental lineage of feminist science fiction (SF). In a SF sense, Piccinini's objects are replete with narrative speculative fabulation. Her visual and sculptural art is about worlding, that is, "naturaltechnical" worlds at stake, worlds needy for care and response, worlds full of unsettling but oddly familiar critters who turn out to be simultaneously near kin and alien colonists. Piccinini's worlds require curiosity, emotional engagement, and investigation, and they do not yield to clean judgments or bottom lines—especially not about what is living or nonliving, organic or technological, promising or threatening. Lindsay Kelley, a graduate student in my 2004 seminar in bioart and critical theory, playing brilliantly with *Still Life with Stem Cells* and *The Young Family* (figures 4.1 and 4.2), awakened my passion for Piccinini's corporeal practice of ethically inquisitive fabulating in the heterogeneous media of her collaborative work habits. So I set about learning what these worlds might be like and how they invite the risk of response, of becoming someone one was not before encountering her human and nonhuman critters.

Piccinini's worlds are full of youngsters—including pink and blue truck babies promising to tell where grown-up trucks come from, ambiguously fetal-like transgenics in *Science Story*, eager if blob-ish stem cell playgroups with a girl in a polka-dot smock, Euro-Australian children paired with fabulated introduced species of indeterminate age, anamorphic motorcycle neonates in *Nest*, vividly colored cyclepups, naked pink synthetic pedomorphic "siren moles" in the SO2 series, and gestating wombats in the dorsal pouches of protector Surrogates (see figures 4.3 and 4.4). She invites those willing to inhabit her worlds to dedifferentiate in order to risk bioengineered redifferentiating as part of a queer family whose members require us to rethink what taking care of this country, taking care of these generations, might mean.

From the start, I knew Piccinini lived and worked in Australia; like me, she is the offspring of white settler colonies, their frontier practices, their ongoing immigrations, and their bad memories and troubled discourses of indigeneity, belonging, appropriation, wastelands, progress, and exclusion. Twenty-first-century technoscience and technoculture are nothing if not frontier practices, always announcing new worlds, proposing the novel as the solution to the old, figuring creation as radical invention and replacement, rushing toward a future that wobbles between ultimate salvation and destruction but has little truck with thick pasts or presents (Kenney 2007). But in her sensuous sculptural and graphic stories of terran critters who were not on Earth before now and whose evolutionary and ecological habitats are the installation, the mall, the website, and the lab, Piccinini seems to me to be proposing not another frontier but rather something more akin to a decolonizing ethic indebted to Australian Aboriginal practices of taking care of Country and accounting for generations of entangled human and nonhuman entities.

In this little essay, I want to think about Piccinini's art in conversation with the anthropologist Deborah Bird Rose's *Reports from a Wild Country*

71

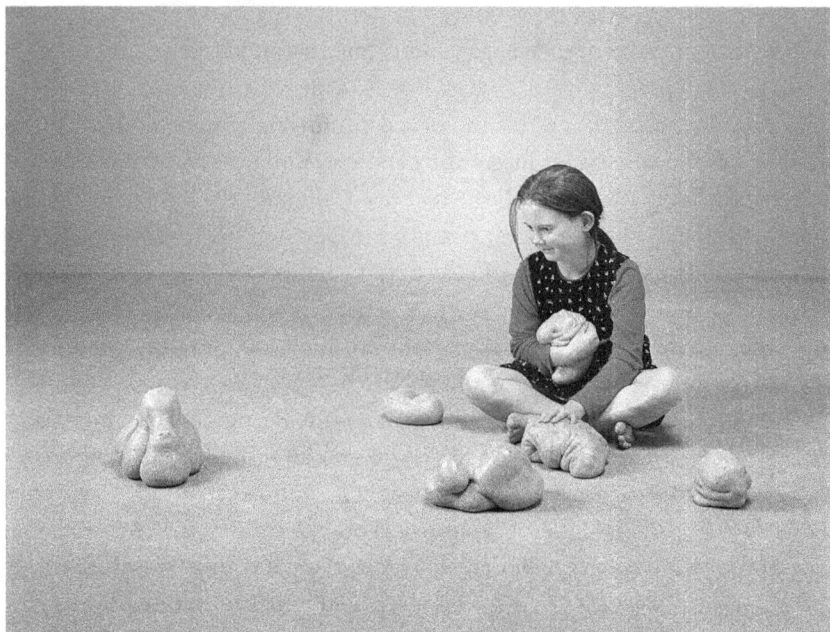

4.1 Patricia Piccinini, *Still Life with Stem Cells*, 2002. Silicone, polyurethane, human hair, clothing, carpet, life-size (dimensions variable). PHOTO BY GRAHAM BARING. COURTESY OF THE ARTIST, TOLARNO GALLERIES, AND ROSLYN OXLEY9 GALLERY.

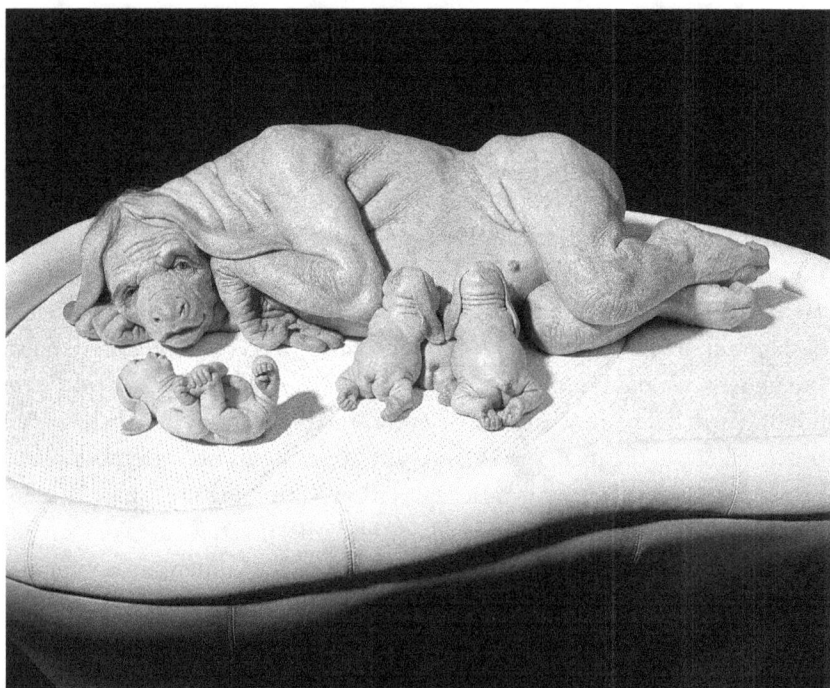

4.2 Patricia Piccinini, *The Young Family*, 2002. Silicone, fiberglass, leather, human hair, plywood, 85 × 150 × 120 cm (approx.). PHOTO BY GRAHAM BARING. COURTESY OF THE ARTIST, TOLARNO GALLERIES, AND ROSLYN OXLEY9 GALLERY.

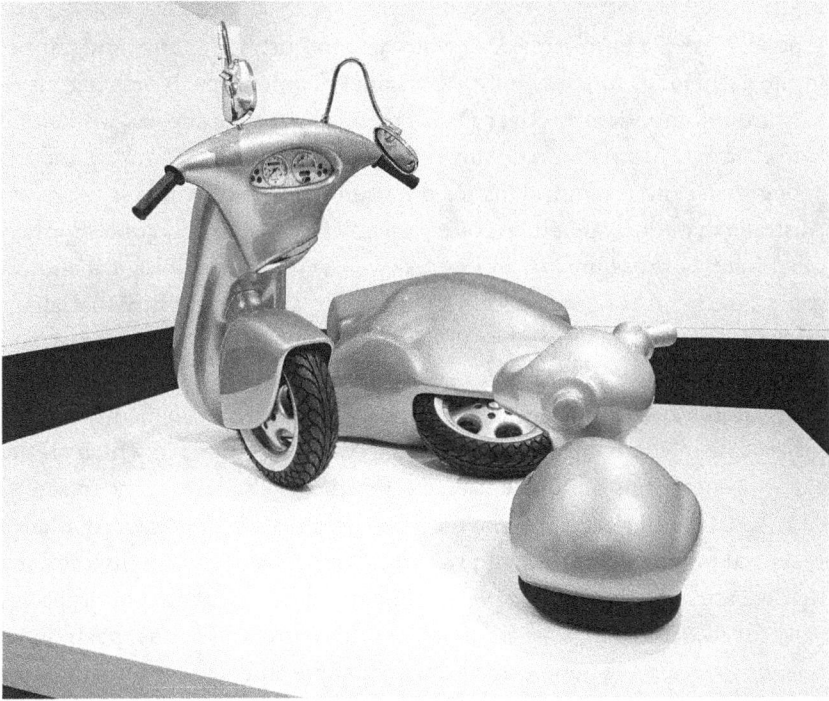

4.3 Patricia Piccinini, *Nest*, 2006. Fiberglass, automotive paint, leather, plastic, metal, rubber, mirror, 104 × 197 × 186 cm (variable). PHOTO BY GRAHAM BARING. COURTESY OF THE ARTIST, TOLARNO GALLERIES, AND ROSLYN OXLEY9 GALLERY.

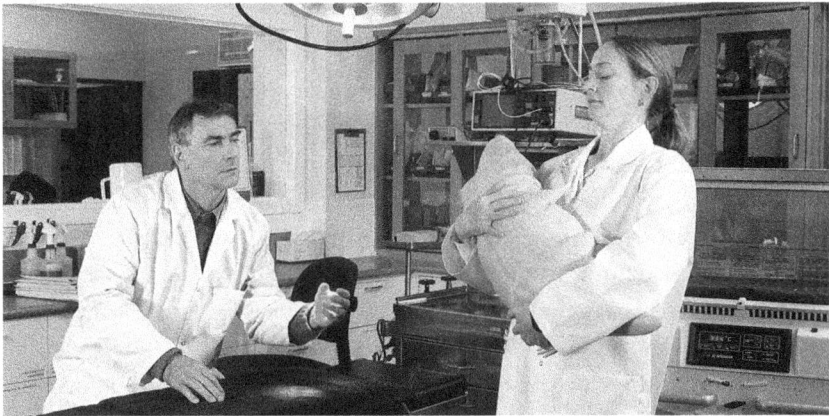

4.4 Patricia Piccinini, *Science Story Part II: Ethical Issues*, 2001. Digital C-type photograph, 100 × 200 cm. COURTESY OF THE ARTIST, TOLARNO GALLERIES, AND ROSLYN OXLEY9 GALLERY.

(2004). Rose is a Euro-American who came to Australia as an ethnographer in the early 1980s to study with Aboriginal people in the Northern Territory around the Victoria River District. Since that time she has worked on land claims, collaboratively documenting sacred sites, and refiguring and enacting social and ecological justice on wounded but still-vital places across Australia that must somehow collect up all of their past and contemporary inhabitants—those human and not, as well as those technological and organic. She, her Aboriginal teachers and friends, and many other Australians work to reground responsibility and accountability to time, generations, and place in a way that might lead to ecological and social restoration and reconciliation. Rose was taught to see the difference between violently blasted places called "the wild" and "quiet country—the country in which all the care of generations of people is evident to those who know how to see it" (4). Across settler societies like the United States and Australia, "violence is central both to conquest and to progress. . . . We cannot help knowing that we are here through dispossession and death. . . . What alternatives exist for us, and what is asked of us? . . . Alternatives arise unexpectedly in relationships among people and between people and place. Alternatives are entangled in the midst of the wild, and may depend on the wild even as they resist it" (4, 6). The crucial question is how to face settler heritage differently, to participate in decolonizing generational practices, in a state of what Rose calls "responsive attentiveness."

To me, and I think to Piccinini, that question is especially pressing in the land I call *technoculture*, where the artist's critters all gestate and proliferate. I experience Piccinini as cultivating a practice of decolonizing responsive attentiveness. Could the worlds of technoculture ever come to be quiet country? It depends, Piccinini's critters suggest, on taking care of generations and doing so in all-too-wild country like the mall, the highway, the lab, and the installation. How might a speculatively fabulated SF art object help morph eroded and disowned no-places into flourishing and cared-for places?

Orientation to time must be the first consideration. Rose emphasizes that, shaped by Christian temporality, European societies "face" the future, while the past is behind and is to be overcome, succeeded, surpassed. In that teleological, goal-directed orientation, the present is nothing but a vanishing point of transition toward what is to come, whether that be destruction or redemption. In contrast, the fundamentally nonteleological time of Aboriginal Country is 180 degrees the other way around; people "face" the past, for which they bear the responsibility of ongoing care in a thick and consequential present that is also responsible to those who come behind, that is, the next generations. Indwelling that sort of time, Country is a multidimensional matrix of relationships: "It consists of people, animals, plants, Dreamings, underground, earth, soils, minerals, waters, surface water, and air. . . . All living things are held to have an interest in the life of the country . . . those who destroy their country destroy themselves" (Rose 2004, 153–154). Furthermore, countries are not equivalent, interchangeable, abstract; Country is materially and semiotically distinctive, each with its own human beings created for that Country and responsible for it through the generations.

Nothing could seem less like modern "Western" science and its future-besotted biotechnological and cyborgian global offspring, who are seemingly innocent of—and so radically destructive of—place. But Piccinini suggests something else is possible in technoculture, not to mention necessary, and I am on her side. Growing up in the presence of Piccinini's plethora of SF elder youngsters is to face the past and care for the generations with verve and ethical imagination. To show why I think that, I need to start again with *Still Life with Stem Cells* and *Young Family*, take a moment with the anatomical niceties of *Leather Landscape* even though its beings are absent from the Artium show, and then embrace my unsafe progenitors and offspring among the critters of the series Piccinini calls *Nature's Little Helpers*. As the artist's exhibition at the Venice Biennale in 2003 proclaimed, "We are family." Happily, this is not the world-famous heterosexual nuclear family of Christian settler imaginations and of all-too-current national policy.

Most of Piccinini's works are premised on bioscientific practices of manipulation and alteration of living beings, of creating "new worlds" if "only" in art. Stem cell research, genetic engineering, cloning, bioelectronics, and technologically mediated ecological restoration and kin formation loom large. Reorienting the arrow of time, both *Still Life* and *Young Family* provoke the onto-ethical question of care for the intra- and inter-acting generations that is not asked often enough in technoculture, especially not about its own progenitors and offspring. The important question is not found in the false opposition of nature and technology. Rather, what matters is who and what lives and dies, where, when, and how? What is wild, and what quiet? What is the heritage for which technocultural beings are both accountable and indebted? What must the practices of love look like in this tangled wild/quiet country? Piccinini's essay "In Another Life" poses the question of care in words: "I am particularly fascinated by the unexpected consequences, the stuff we don't want but must somehow accommodate. There is no question as to whether there will be undesired outcomes; my interest is in whether we will be able to love them" (2006, 13). Replying to a questioner at her 2003 lecture at the

Tokyo University of Fine Art, Piccinini laid out her large, queer, nonhetero-normative view of our technocultural family: "In my work, perhaps I am saying that whether you like them or you don't like them, we actually have a duty to care. We created them, so we've got to look after them." Looking after imperfect, messy, really existing, mortal beings is much more demanding—not to mention playful, intellectually interesting, and emotionally satisfying—than living the futuristic nightmare of techno-immortality.

Piccinini insists in word and object that the people of technoculture have a familial, generational duty to their failures as well as their accomplishments. Natural or not, good or not, safe or not, the critters of technoculture make a body- and soul-changing claim on their "creators" that is rooted in the generational *obligation of* and *capacity for* responsive attentiveness. To care is to know how to nurture quiet country through the often-unexpected generations, not to point toward future utopia or dystopia. To care is wet, emotional, messy, and demanding of the best thinking one has ever done (Puig de la Bellacasa 2017). That is one reason we need speculative fabulation.

The cell-blob/human-girl playgroup in *Still Life with Stem Cells* is neither utopian nor dystopian; it is seriously *playful* and so curious, inquisitive, and risky. Encountering either this romp or the *Young Family* of mop-eared, porcine transgenics (do they exist to provide sick, wealthy humans with organs and tissues?), both the artist and visitors to the exhibit palpably run the risk of coming to care about, even to love, the fabulated blobs and the unlovely chimeric litter with a shrivel-skinned, big-rumped, heavy-lidded, all-too-humanoid mama.

Commenting on those big-headed and ungainly synthetic organisms called *siren moles*, such as the one on the blue car seat in the Artium exhibit's S02 (series) *Waiting for Jennifer* (2000; figure 4.5), the Sydney writer on Australian contemporary art Jacquelyn Millner (2001) concluded, "Unlike Dr Frankenstein who grew to hate his creation and suffered the consequences, Piccinini would urge us to bring an attitude of love to the products of technology, to accept our ethical mantle as creators, to take care of all our progeny, even of the artificial variety. The love she appears to propose is not of the romantic, infatuated ilk—classic technophilia—but of the familial variety, with its overtones of responsibility, ethical guidance and life-long commitment." I would only add that Rose's understanding of Aboriginal material and ethical guidance on taking care of Country insists that we learn to care for ancestors as well as offspring. We face ancestors, and progeny come after; learning how to tell time that way in technoculture would be truly revolutionary. It would mean taking the present seriously, not just passing through it to elsewhere.

76

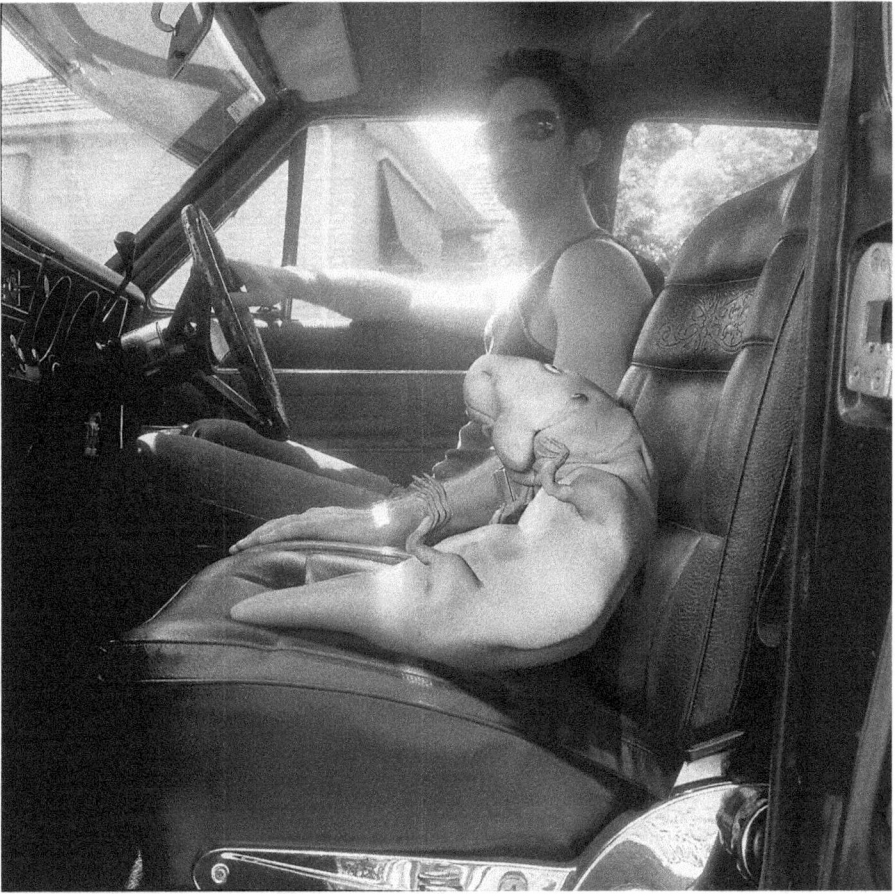

4.5 Patricia Piccinini, *Waiting for Jennifer*, from the series SO2, 2000. Digital C-type photograph, 80 × 80 cm. COURTESY OF THE ARTIST, TOLARNO GALLERIES, AND ROSLYN OXLEY9 GALLERY.

This brings me to my favorite Piccinini critters: *Nature's Little Helpers*. Alerting viewers to both danger and possibility, these drawings, installations, and sculptures palpably argue that the artist has fallen in love with her speculatively fabulated progeny; she has certainly made me do so. To get to *Nature's Little Helpers*, where I will encounter the intriguing dorsal pouches on a protector species fabulated for gestating the young of an endangered species of wombat, I mentally pass by the colony of humanoid, transgenic, African meerkat–like beings in *The Leather Landscape* (2003), exhibited in "We Are Family" at the Venice Biennale but not in the Artium show (figure 4.6).

4.6 Patricia Piccinini, *Leather Landscape*, 2003. Silicone, fiberglass, leather, human hair, clothing, timber, 290 × 175 × 165 cm (irregular). COURTESY OF THE ARTIST, TOLARNO GALLERIES, AND ROSLYN OXLEY9 GALLERY.

What arrests me in this more-than-natural colony is not the pink-suited blond human toddler face-to-face with a fabulated potential playmate living on soft white leather in the museum space. Rather, I am struck by the four-breasted female sitting peaceably on the next level up of the pyramidal habitat, with her milk-lusty babies nestled between her legs ready to attach to her alluring array of ventral teats (figure 4.7).

If I had not seen the critters from *Nature's Little Helpers* first, I might not have noticed the "natural" feature of ventral teats on the transgenic mother in *Leather Landscape* or paused at the number four. But I did see the dorsal pouches first, and now I cannot let go of the image of the fronts and backs of progenitors and guardians all covered with organs to feed and shelter off-category offspring. I cannot let go of the capacious, inventive arrangements Piccinini makes to take care of unexpected, vulnerable, hungry progeny of whatever species, natural or not. Look what the stork brought!

DONNA J. HARAWAY

4.7 Patricia Piccinini, *Leather Landscape* (detail), 2003. Silicone, fiberglass, leather, human hair, clothing, timber, 290 × 175 × 165 cm (irregular). COURTESY OF THE ARTIST, TOLARNO GALLERIES, AND ROSLYN OXLEY9 GALLERY.

With *Nature's Little Helpers*, Piccinini focuses her questions more on ecology and evolution than on genetic engineering or cloning, but the domains are not cleanly separated either. For one thing, the Helpers are all SF humanoids with dubious naturalcultural genealogies. In the stark heritage of destroyed human and nonhuman beings and blasted country, acknowledged or not, the past surges into the present and shapes possible futures just as it does in Rose's reports from a wild country. The pressing question is *how* to inherit, how to face, the living—and killing—past. The urgent need is to learn how to do that in order to be able to take the present seriously, in order to be able to move toward multispecies reconciliation. But in settler societies and their "global" heirs, the category of "endangered species" takes hold of organisms, including people, and subjects them to the ambiguous grace of salvation, specifically being saved through a regulatory and technological apparatus of ecological and reproductive management. Salvation is proposed in the time frame of barely secularized "Western" science. Apocalypse looms; in that story, the past—nature—is the time outside time and must be restored in all its innocence. That kind of time is utterly wild, that is, outside the care of responsible generations. Thick, contingent, and relational, naturalcultural history disappears once again in the dream of natural wilderness, a frontier category of the first rank in the lineage of settler societies. Prodded by Rose, I experience Piccinini's art as proposing another kind of time and place for vulnerable creatures of diverse species and generations. Piccinini's art is tuned to reconciliation and taking care of always-situated place and its denizens.

To do so, Piccinini introduces a bestiary of SF protector species paired with Australian officially endangered species. The speculatively fabulated protectors are not altogether reassuring, nor should they be. The settler habit of introducing species that quickly add problems to those they were supposed to solve is in the forefront of Piccinini's thinking. She remembers Australia's and Aotearoa New Zealand's naturalcultural history of introduced species, human and nonhuman alike, with modern examples such as the cane toad, brought from the neotropics to munch repressively on the cane beetle that eats the sugarcane that gobbles up laboring people, who need the money from sugar to feed their children. She remembers the exterminist consequences of well-intentioned introductions of companion species—in this example, the consequences for the unintended meal, that is, the endemic amphibians gobbled up by voracious, prolific, mobile cane toads. In addition to the fact that they were not fabulated to watch out for people, the protectors are emphatically introduced species. If they have them at all, their home

80

DONNA J. HARAWAY

worlds are elsewhere. How can one not see in Piccinini's narrative art the not always so well-intentioned introductions of the settlers themselves and their exterminist consequences? The Helpers might watch out for officially endangered species, but someone will have to watch out for the protectors too—in every sense of *watch out*.

There will be unexpected consequences. Taking care of unexpected country will be required—again and always. Reconciliation is not guaranteed; it is proffered, suggested, haltingly pictured. Any reconciliation will depend on descendants of settler worlds letting go of salvation history and instead learning to live in technoculture in something more like the time of Aboriginal Country, facing ancestors of many kinds and responsible for those who come after. Technocultural people must study how to live in actual places, cultivate practices of care, and risk ongoing face-to-face encounters with unexpected partners. Well-tuned people have to be *present* in Country for it to flourish; thus, there will be no perfection, but there can be ongoing and effective care that stays alert to many sorts of history. This kind of time and place is utterly contemporary, that is, committed to a flourishing present, not a present that is only a pivot between past and future. Learning how to live in a flourishing present is indebted to Aboriginal practices and ideas but not in the mode of colonial or postcolonial settlers finding salvation in the indigenous to heal the scars of the modern and technological. That way of understanding reconciliation completely misses the point about another conception of time and place, another way to *face* histories, or what feminist theorist Katie King (2010) calls "pastpresents." The unbridgeable dichotomy between the traditional and the modern is as much a frontier myth as the cordon sanitaire between nature and culture, or between the organic and the technological.

What is certain in Piccinini's world is that nature and culture are tightly knotted in bodies, ecologies, technologies, and times. Take tiny, brightly colored birds living in Victoria, golden helmeted honeyeaters, or HeHos, as an example. These birds are multiply dependent on companion-species relations among gum trees, a kind of possum, and their feathered selves in order to get their sugary meals of oozing sap. Their survival is threatened by ignorant or greedy humans encroaching on their places and cutting down their gum trees. Their living arrangements need people who know how to recognize and live with HeHo ecologies. Only fifteen breeding pairs are known to survive. Piccinini invented a protector for HeHos called the Bodyguard. Armored adult Bodyguards look fearsome, with their serious canine teeth and imposing threatening postures. Several photographs in the Artium exhibit picture the Bodyguard and HeHos in their complex naturalcultural ecologies and

81

economies with contemporary people (*Arcadia, Getaway, Roadkill, Thunderdome*). In one graphite drawing at the Artium exhibit, the Bodyguard is sitting beside young Alice. Both the human and off-human critters are using cell phones; their speculatively playful conversation is corporeally a tangle of the organic and technological. In another drawing, the infant Bodyguard is sitting with baby Hector; these youngsters do not find each other strange; they are coeval, in shared time. They are full of the promise of reconciliation if their parents can learn to face the past in the present. Unlike the HeHos and the Aboriginal people historically responsible for taking care of Country, both sets of parents for the youngsters in the drawing—those for the Bodyguards and those for Hector—are introduced settler species in Australia. That fact implies a long and steep learning curve for knowing how to recognize and care for place and time.

The ecological, evolutionary, and assisted-reproduction narratives of *Nature's Little Helpers* all pulsate with pastpresent lives and the ongoing care they demand. Endangered species by legal definition signal the threat of the final loss of "heritage." But that global-speak, settler-nation kind of heritage culture or heritage nature is not what Piccinini's Helpers are concerned with, as I experience these storied drawings, photographs, and installations. The Helpers seem to have a much more relational and mundane task on their hands. Without the supposed comfort of attending to their own "natural" offspring (*natural* in their case would mean transgenic, if not SF, progeny), the introduced protectors' job seems to be *to parent* their unsafe, endemic, and too-few xeno-specific charges. The Helpers' job is to nurture these charges into full contemporary naturalcultural sociality, to locate them in a flourishing present replete with its expected, unexpected, and ontologically heterogeneous beings. To parent is to instruct, guard, carry, nurture, and finally let go. The principal charges of the Helpers whom Piccinini has introduced so far are HeHos, Leadbeater's possums, and northern hairy-nosed wombats, not human beings, a point people would do well to remember in the presence of these protectors.

Just look at *The Embrace* (2005) in the Artium exhibit for clarity on this matter (figure 4.8). Reminiscent of images of the parasitizing monster from the film series *Alien*, the Progenitor for the Leadbeater's Possum glues its whole self alarmingly onto the face of a human woman. Perhaps she looked too closely. Perhaps she had no respect. She certainly did not face in the right direction and may never be able to correct her error.

But in this exhibit, we see, too, the other side of the protectors—their unaccountable interest in and seeming openness to those who come behind

82

4.8 Patricia Piccinini, *The Embrace*, 2005. Silicone, fiberglass, leather, plywood, human hair, clothing (dimensions variable). PHOTO BY GUY ROBINSON. COURTESY OF THE ARTIST, TOLARNO GALLERIES, AND ROSLYN OXLEY9 GALLERY.

the settlers who imposed a frontier naturalcultural ecology and frontier knowledges, including so much of technoscience. The progeny of endangered species—those who will exist in generations past, present, and future because of their SF protectors' effective care—will meet human youngsters descended from the wild settler species who are willing to learn what contemporary quiet country might still be, including a technoscience committed to flourishing pastpresents. Nurtured by their teachers, alien and aboriginal, these youngsters might yet track a path to reconciliation in their reports from a wild country.

Look closely at the blue-sheeted bed with life-size figures made of silicone, hair, and acrylic resin in *Undivided* (2004; figure 4.9). A settler-descended human child sleeps spooning with an adult Surrogate for the northern hairy-nosed wombat. The scene is peaceful; the Surrogate seems

83

4.9 Patricia Piccinini, *Undivided*, 2004. Silicone, fiberglass, human hair, flannelette, mixed media, 101 × 74 × 127 cm. PHOTO BY GRAHAM BARING. COURTESY OF THE ARTIST, TOLARNO GALLERIES, AND ROSLYN OXLEY9 GALLERY.

utterly unthreatening, the human child embraced tenderly. Walk around to the back of the sleeping Surrogate to see the two rows of drawstring dorsal pouches running along the Helper's spine, six in all (see figure 4.13). Each pocket shelters an immature marsupial wombat, with the earliest still-fetal stages, no bigger than a jelly bean, gestating at the anterior end and the ready-to-face-the-world older joey poking out of the posterior pocket. That furry

youngster seems likely to pop out of the pouch by morning to meet the child before the Surrogate even wakes up. That meeting could surprise all the parents and guardians in these off-category species assemblages.

DONNA J. HARAWAY

4.10 Patricia Piccinini, *Laura*, 2006. Graphite on paper, 57 × 77 cm. COURTESY OF THE ARTIST, TOLARNO GALLERIES, AND ROSLYN OXLEY9 GALLERY.

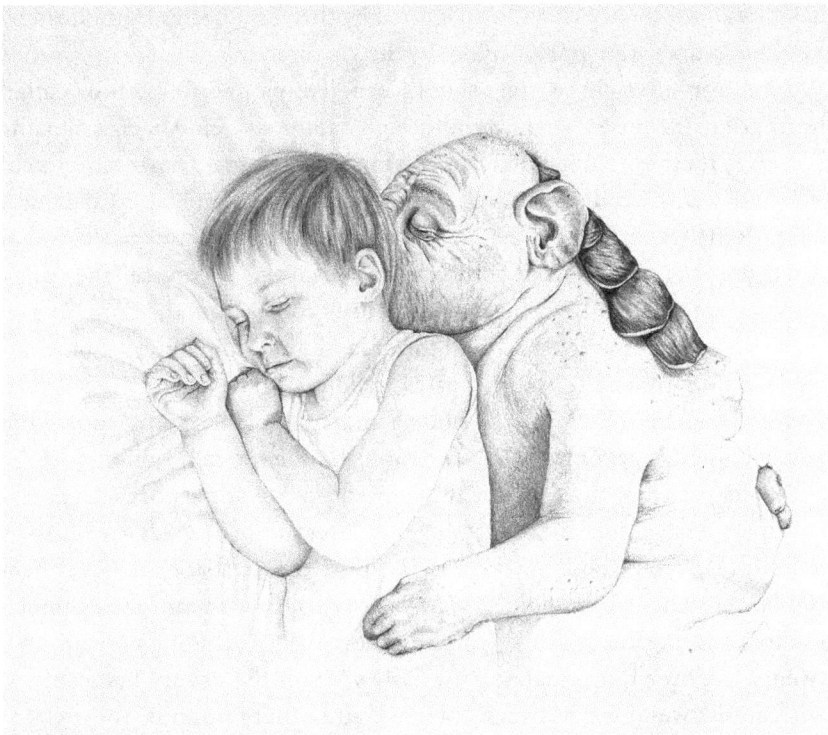

4.11 Patricia Piccinini, *Leo*, 2006. Graphite on paper, 57 × 77 cm. COURTESY OF THE ARTIST, TOLARNO GALLERIES, AND ROSLYN OXLEY9 GALLERY.

The two drawings of human children and Surrogates in the Artium exhibit, *Laura* and *Leo*, also seem to portray benign companions (figures 4.10 and 4.11). Indeed, *Leo* is a portrait of the little guy snoozing with the Surrogate in *Undivided*. Still, I know that human babies often hurt the other critters they play with. I trained with my dogs and children on loan from my graduate students, so that the canids might tolerate such exploratory excesses by badly coordinated, unaccountable, tiny hominids unwisely endowed too early in their development with grasping hands. Are the Surrogates so well instructed? Why should they be? The adult Surrogates and the children are awfully close, maybe too close for a human child and an alien guardian species.

The appealing, full-frontal Surrogate in color on the cover of the Wellington exhibition catalog, *Patricia Piccinini: In Another World*, does not calm my anxiety or Piccinini's (see figure 4.12). The creature's ventral surface *does* sport a proper navel, indicating some kind of mammalian kinship, however reconfigured in SF technochimeras and however foreign to the nonuterine gestational needs of marsupial wombats. The Surrogate was not fabulated to be a protector for *Homo sapiens*, after all, but for *Lasiorhinus kreftii*, whose habitats and associates have been blasted by the very species introduced by Leo and Laura's ancestral kin, if not by the kin directly.

I am not sure what Queensland's Indigenous peoples call or called northern hairy-nosed wombats, although Yaminon is an Aboriginal name (whose?) for these animals that appears in global internet conservation websites today without discussion of the human/nonhuman historical naturecultures that generated that name. I am even less sure what names different Aboriginal peoples might give the dorsally armored Surrogate. The young certainly come behind! The term *wombat* itself comes from the Eora Aboriginal community that lived around the area of modern Sydney.[2] But whatever the proper names, the Surrogates could reasonably decide that Laura, Leo, and the girl in *Undivided* do not fall under their writ of protection if the young hominids get unruly with the wombats, intentionally or not.

Let us consider for a moment a contemporary adult northern hairy-nosed wombat, sometimes called the bulldozer of the bush, as she burrows intently in the dry woodland floor of the Epping Forest National Park in central Queensland. Keeping the dirt out, the female's backward-facing pouch shelters a youngster attached to a teat on her belly. Including perhaps only twenty-five breeding females in the early years of the twenty-first century, with adults weighing between fifty-five and ninety pounds, these roguish but vulnerable marsupials are among the world's rarest large mammals

4.12 Patricia Piccinini, *Surrogate*, 2005. Silicone, fiberglass, leather, plywood, human hair, 103 × 180 × 306 cm. PHOTO BY GUY ROBINSON. COURTESY OF THE ARTIST, TOLARNO GALLERIES, AND ROSLYN OXLEY9 GALLERY.

(Flannery and Kendall 1990). It might seem tragically easy to count these wombats—if only the nocturnal and crepuscular, generally solitary and secretive critters would show themselves to the census takers. Working with the Queensland wombat for over ten years, Dr. Andrea Taylor of Monash University in Melbourne "has developed a low disturbance genetic technique to census the wombat population. Wombat hair is collected on sticky tape strung across wombat burrows and DNA in the follicle is used to identify the sex and the 'owner' of the hair" (Yaminon Defense Fund n.d., image tab 5). In her noninvasive and smart technique, I consider Taylor to be practicing care. Living endangered means living in technoculture; it is a condition of flourishing—or not—on Earth now for most critters. Living well in technoculture is part of the obligation of taking care of unexpected country.

However, all is not well in these wombats' tiny remaining patch of earth. Piccinini knows that the African buffel grass planted for European cattle in the white settler colony outcompetes the native grasses on which the wombats depend and that the threatened wombats contend for food and habitat with cattle, sheep, and rabbits. These marsupials also endure predation by dingoes—mammals dating from much earlier introductions, who have unstably achieved ecological charismatic macrofauna status today after a lamentably unfinished career as vermin to Euro-Australians and a deep—and, with great difficulty, ongoing—history as companion species to Aboriginals. Yet the modern rehabilitated nationalist dingoes, even after the cattle have been evicted and the buffel grass discouraged in the work of ecological restoration, have to be fenced out of the patch of Queensland semiarid grassland and woodland that is the only place left where northern hairy-nosed wombats burrow and dine.

But then, Piccinini knows, living beings in knotted and dynamic ecologies are opportunistic, not idealistic, and it is not surprising to find many native species flourishing in both new and old places because of the resources provided by interlopers from other lands and waters. Think of the kookaburras, displaced from their own former ranges, eating introduced pest snails and slugs alongside European starlings. Piccinini knows, in short, that introducing species (from another watershed, another continent, or another imagination) is often a world-destroying cut, as well as sometimes an opening to healing or even to new kinds of flourishing.[3] Piccinini's fabulated companion species to endangered species may be one more handy newcomer, among many, rather than a destructive invader, among many—or they may be both, the more usual course of things.

88

DONNA J. HARAWAY

The crucial question has to be not "Are they original and pure (natural in that sense)?" but rather "What do they contribute to the flourishing and health of the land and its critters (naturalcultural in that sense)?" That question does not invite a disengaged "liberal" ethics or politics but requires examined lives that take risks to nurture some ways of getting on together and *not* others. With their generally positive attitudes toward animals Europeans have disparagingly called *feral*, Australian Aboriginal peoples have tended to evaluate what Westerners call *species assemblages*, new and old, in terms of what sustains the human/nonhuman, storied, changing, and lived world that in English is called *Country*. As feminist science studies scholar Karen Barad put it for ears tuned to Western philosophy and science: "Embodiment is a matter not of being specifically situated in the world, but rather of being in the world in its dynamic specificity. . . . Ethics is therefore not about right response to a radically exterior/ized other, but about responsibility and accountability for the lively relationalities of becoming of which we are a part" (2007, 377, 393).

That brings us back to the Surrogates. Look again at the three pairs of gestational pouches running down the spine of the protector companion species, nurturing three stages of wombat development (figure 4.13).

Aligned with that of other marsupials like the red kangaroo, Surrogate wombat reproduction seems to be run on just-in-time principles for stocking embryos on the gestating body. Just out of the birth canal and plucked from the hairs of its wombat mama's belly while struggling up to crawl into a pouch to finish making a wombat, a barely formed embryo surely inhabits the Surrogate's top pouch. Attached to a teat? Does the Surrogate have teats in those odd sphincter-ringed, drawstring pouches? How not? Normal northern hairy-nosed wombats have only two teats in their single, backward-facing pouch, so they can't handle three young out of the body at once, much less six, and they give birth to only one young at a time, once a year. Joeys stay in the pouch eight to nine months. But if they are like kangaroos, these wombats could have arrested embryos ready to speed up their life course if the senior joey dies—or is disappeared by aliens. Northern hairy-nosed wombats like to have their babies in the rainy season, and getting a replacement joey into the pouch too late, when the succulent grasses are drying out, would not bode well for that reproductive cycle anyway. Maybe the Surrogates pluck just-emerged and still-fetal joeys from wombat females and put them in their own pouches, thus forcing the wombats to get another embryo out of their body sooner and multiplying the numbers of young who can

89

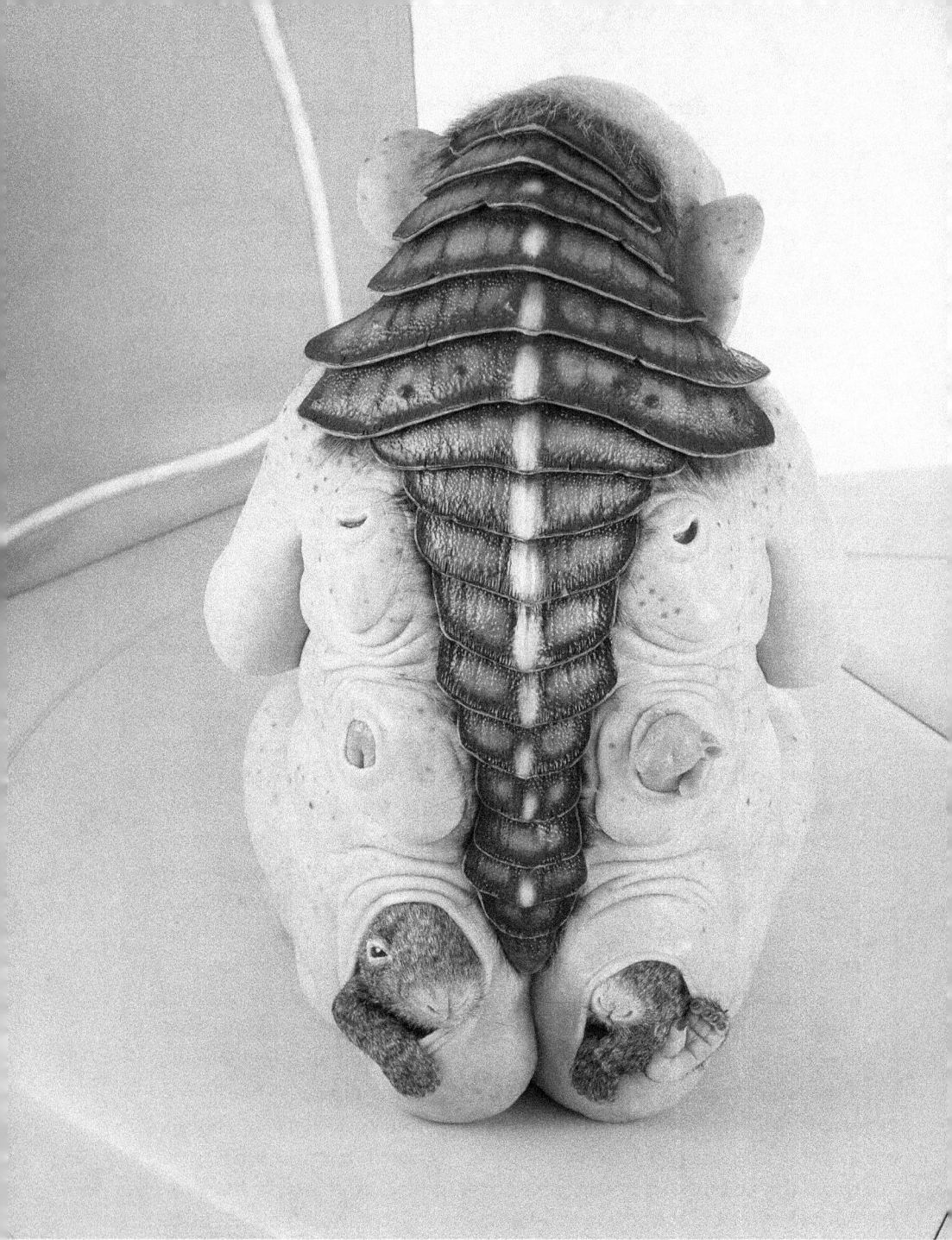

4.13 Patricia Piccinini, *Surrogate* (alternate view), 2005. Silicone, fiberglass, leather, plywood, human hair, 103 × 180 × 306 cm. Photo by Guy Robinson. COURTESY OF THE ARTIST, TOLARNO GALLERIES, AND ROSLYN OXLEY9 GALLERY.

be raised in a season? This would not be the first time that forced reproduction was employed as an evolutionary and ecological rescue technology. Ask any tiger in a Species Survival Plan® database. I am reminded that only about twenty-five breeding female northern hairy-nosed wombats live on planet Earth to gestate the young of their species. Being female in such a world never comes without paying the price of value. No wonder Piccinini is suspicious, as well as open to another world. Unexpected country will be full of surprises, good and bad, even as it is fully webbed in pastpresents.

The middle rung of Surrogate pouches houses more developed but still-hairless baby wombats; they are far from ready to explore the outside world. A teat, a pouch, and a vigilant Surrogate's armored spine are all that is required for now. The third rung of pouches holds mature furry baby wombats, and we see in *Undivided* that one is ready to crawl out of the pocket to begin its risky encounters in a wider world. For a few months, this joey can leap back into the pouch when things get too scary and supplement grass with milk, but even the best wombs or pouches, alien or native, give time-limited protection.

I'd love to call the Surrogate "queer" and let it go with a celebratory frisson that comes so cost-free to those not made to inhabit the category, but I am sure Piccinini would wince if I tried to get away with that. The Surrogate remains a creature that nourishes indigestion, that is, a kind of dyspepsia with regard to proper place and function that queer theory is really all about. The Surrogate is nothing if not the *Mutter*/matter of gestation out of place, a necessary if not sufficient cut into the female-defining function called *reproduction*. To be out of place is often to be in danger and sometimes also to be free, in the open, not yet nailed by value and purpose, but full of pastpresents. The point for me in Piccinini's *Nature's Little Helpers* is *parenting*, not *reproducing*. Parenting is about caring for generations, one's own or not; reproducing is about making more of oneself to populate the future, quite a different matter.

There is no fourth rung of guarded gestation. The human and wombat youngsters will find each other soon. Then, what the world of companion species might become is open. The past has not laid enough ground for optimism concerning relations between white settler humans and wombats. Yet the past is far from absent or without rich offerings for reconciliation. The past, present, and future are all very much knotted into each other, full of what we need for the work and play of naturalcultural restoration: less deadly curiosity, materially entangled ethics and politics, and technical and organic well-being. Experienced together, Rose's writing and Piccinini's art tell about attention to alien and native beings linked in learning how to take care of unexpected country, in alliance with those called traditional owners of the land who see better the difference between wild and quiet because they face those who came before and care also for those who come behind, in all their demanding and unfinished kinds.

NOTES

This chapter was previously published in the Artium exhibit catalog, Vitoria, Spain, October 2007.

1. For more on naturecultures and Piccinini's *Surrogate (for the Northern Hairy-Nosed Wombat)* (2004), see Haraway (2008).

2. Wikipedia, s.v. "Wombat," last modified March 20, 2021, 2:51 (UTC), http://en.wikipedia.org/wiki/Wombat.

3. For the shaping of "new natures" composed of the mixed native/introduced species assemblages of every place on Earth by the twenty-first century, see the controversial work of the Australian Tim Low (*The New Nature*, 2002). For integration of Low's approaches with science studies, sociology, colonial and postcolonial cultural studies, and considerations of animal well-being from both ecological and rights perspectives, see Franklin (2006); the kookaburra example is on p. 230.

REFERENCES

Barad, Karen. 2007. *Meeting the Universe Halfway: Quantum Physics and the Entanglement of Matter and Meaning.* Durham, NC: Duke University Press.

Flannery, Tim, and Paula Kendall. 1990. *Australia's Vanishing Mammals.* Sydney: R. D. Press.

Franklin, Adrian. 2006. *Animal Nation: The True Story of Animals and Australia.* Sydney: University of New South Wales Press.

Haraway, Donna J. 2008. *When Species Meet.* Minneapolis: University of Minnesota Press.

Kenney, Martha. 2007. "Frontier Epistemologies." Paper presented to GeoFeminisms II: Phylogeographies, History of Consciousness and Anthropology Departments, University of California, Santa Cruz, June 2007.

King, Katie. 2010. "Pastpresents: Playing Cats Cradle with Donna Haraway." Accessed June 28, 2021. http://partywriting.blogspot.com/. Also at http://playingcatscradle.blogspot.com/2010/10/katie-king-womens-studies-university-of.html.

Low, Tim. 2002. *The New Nature: Winners and Losers in Wild Australia.* Sydney: Penguin.

Millner, Jacquelyn. 2001. "Patricia Piccinini: Ethical Aesthetics." Patricia Piccinini's website. http://www.patriciapiccinini.net/writing/4/497/96.

Piccinini, Patricia. 2006. "In Another Life." In *Patricia Piccinini: In Another Life,* 12–13. Wellington: City Gallery. Published in conjunction with an exhibition

of the same title at City Gallery, Wellington, New Zealand, February 19–
June 11, 2006.

Puig de la Bellacasa, Maria. 2017. *Matters of Care: Speculative Ethics in More Than Human Worlds*. Minneapolis: University of Minnesota Press.

Rose, Deborah Bird. 2004. *Reports from a Wild Country: Ethics for Decolonisation*. Sydney: University of New South Wales Press.

Yaminon Defense Fund. n.d. "Gallery." Accessed December 9, 2010. http://www.yaminon.org.

THE DISAPPEARING SNAILS OF HAWAI'I

FIVE

Storytelling for a Time of Extinctions

THOM VAN DOOREN

THE DIRT TRACK WE WERE WALKING ON wove its way along a rocky ridge-line of the Wai'anae mountain range on the island of O'ahu. Each side of the track was lined by an assortment of scraggly and windswept plants, foremost among them the 'ōhi'a with their hardy branches and bright red blossoms. These branches, once upon a time, would likely also have been laden with another colorful presence, that of the kāhuli, the tree snails. In decades past, upland forests like this one were thick with snails; hundreds of their brightly colored forms might have been found clinging to the leaves of a single tree. Unlike the predominantly white and gray leaf-eating garden snails more familiar to most of us, these brightly colored and intricately patterned kāhuli would not have harmed their botanical hosts. Rather, their diet consisted exclusively of the thin layer of fungi and other microbes that line the surface of leaves. As they moved across a leaf, they cleaned as they went. Around the trunks of these plants, in the decomposing leaf matter, other, less conspicuous snails would once also have roamed. Consumers of dead leaf matter, detritivores, these snails would have contributed to the health of Hawai'i's forests by breaking down organic materials and releasing nutrients back into the soil. But as we walked through this place, we encountered none of these snails, not in the branches or among the decaying leaves. We walked through a landscape now missing most of the diverse species of gastropods that once called this place home. But we walked *toward* snails, nonetheless.

My guides were two conservationists, Dave Sischo and Kupaʻa Hee. More accurately, I was tagging along on one of their routine trips to one of the few places where snails can still be found reliably in this mountain range—indeed, one of the few places where they are now to be found in abundance anywhere in the Hawaiian Islands. After about an hour of walking up and down, through the undulating and often-muddy terrain, we arrived at our destination. The forest opened into a small clearing, and in front of us stood a shoulder-height green metal fence: the Palikea exclosure.

Encircling roughly 1,600 square meters of vegetated land, the exclosure is a place of refuge for rare snails who have been rescued from surrounding forests or released from the growing captive-breeding program. It is called an *exclosure* rather than an *enclosure* because its function is not primarily to keep these snails in (although it probably does this) but rather to keep others out, specifically, to exclude the many predators of snails that have arrived in these islands with their human inhabitants, predators like rats, Jackson's chameleons, and, most important of all, the rosy wolfsnail (*Euglandina rosea*), a species of carnivorous snail that tracks and consumes the local species with incredible and insidious efficiency.

Keeping all of these animals out is no small feat. A complex series of barriers line the exclosure walls, from a curved lip that stops rats from getting up and over, through to a set of solar-powered wires that deliver an electric shock to any predatory wolfsnails that might be trying to make their way up the walls. These exclosures are a key component of the work of the Snail Extinction Prevention Program, a partnership program of the Hawai'i state government and the US Fish and Wildlife Service, headed up by Dave. In partnership with the US Army, they run nine exclosures across the island of Oʻahu, with two more under construction. But these facilities can protect only a fraction of Hawai'i's threatened snails.

The Hawaiian Islands were once home to an incredible diversity of land snails. In all, over 750 species have been recognized by taxonomists, but the real number is likely considerably higher. Even at 750 species, however, Hawai'i had one of the most diverse assemblages of snails anywhere on Earth. To put this in some sort of context, Hawai'i had two-thirds the number of snail species that are found in the whole of North America, a landmass roughly 1,700 times the size. Sadly, however, most of these snail species are now extinct: an estimated 65 to 90 percent of Hawai'i's land snails are thought to be gone, depending on the taxonomic family in question. In addition, the majority of those species that still remain are thought to be headed swiftly towards extinction.

While current conservation efforts are significant, they are at best a stopgap measure. As Dave explained to me, restoration of these species is just not possible at the moment: extinction prevention is the best we can hope for. And even that isn't always possible. All over the island of O'ahu, and beyond when resources allow, Dave and the Snail Extinction Prevention Program team are engaged in what he thinks of as an evacuation: trying desperately to locate the last remnants of snail species. Just a few years ago, they would try to take only a small number of snails from these populations as a backup, leaving the rest in the forest. In the intervening years, however, they have seen about fifteen formerly robust populations, each comprising hundreds of snails, completely disappear. Some, like that of *Achatinella lila*, were the last known free-living populations of their species. As a result, they are now often pulling out every snail they can find, carefully packing them into containers and bringing them into the captive-breeding population in the lab or an exclosure—if there is a suitable space available for them.

At a time that is increasingly being thought about as the sixth mass extinction event in Earth's history, we need multiple stories, diverse efforts to experiment and explore, to thicken and enliven, the many forms of life that are slipping away. Deborah Bird Rose was a passionate advocate for the many roles of storytelling in the face of "the great unmaking of ecological, social and intellectual systems" (2013, 2). She told extinction stories that explored the entangled significance of these processes of loss, the way in which the disappearance of forms of plant and animal life ripples out into the world to impact on diverse human and nonhuman lives and possibilities, the way in which extinction arises out of and takes form in lands already shaped by historical and ongoing processes of colonization, globalization, and their many violences. Through the slow, careful work of paying attention to the world—in our own and others' stories—Debbie argued that we come to understand, to be connected, to be redone, in ways that just might enable better possibilities for life. But even when this is no longer possible, she insisted that storytelling in the mode of bearing witness was a vital responsibility. To refuse to turn away, she argued, was "to remain true to the lives within which ours are entangled, whether or not we can accomplish great change" (9).

This chapter offers a series of snail stories, woven together around questions of knowing and relating, of wonder and mystery. Inspired by Debbie's extinction stories and our decade of collaboration on this theme, it is an effort to weave together some of the many strands of this loss: to mourn and bear witness but also to celebrate what has been and might still be, and so to turn toward the living earth: "to cherish birth and growth, and to love that which is perilous" (Rose 2011, 118). At its core, this chapter is a response to a single question that I found myself more and more preoccupied by during my time conducting research on Hawaiʻi's snails: How did a global center of terrestrial snail diversity end up out in the middle of the Pacific Ocean? Snails, after all, are not commonly known for their propensity to undertake long journeys—not by land, and certainly not by sea, where their low tolerance for salt water must surely cause significant problems. So how did they all get here? And equally as important at our present time, how might the ongoing extinctions of snails be understood differently if we pay attention to these deep-time processes? What might this context help us to see, appreciate, and perhaps hold on to?

As I stood in the Palikea exclosure on the day of my visit, these questions of extinction and loss preoccupied me. But I had another interest, too. Standing among one particularly nice cluster of about seven critically endangered *Achatinella mustelina*, their vibrant white shells in the leaves around me, I took the opportunity to listen. Listening is not something that one ordinarily does with snails, but in this case I did so because it is said that the kāhuli sing in the forest. In fact, another Hawaiian name for these snails is *pūpū-kani-oe*, literally translating as "shell sounding long" (Sato, Price, and Vaughan 2018, 324). This singing is one of the strongest and most consistent themes associated with snails in Kanaka Maoli (Native Hawaiian) mele and moʻolelo (chants and stories). It isn't clear what form this singing might take: it is described by some as beautiful; others told me it was a single high-pitched note. In the texts where it is mentioned, the singing of kāhuli is deeply meaningful, often occurring as a sign that after a series of adventures, changes, or turbulence, all is pono again—all is righteous, correct, and good (Sato, Price, and Vaughan 2018, 326). But while I listened for singing that day, I heard no song. Perhaps this was because snails cannot sing, as many biologists I asked about this phenomenon told me. Perhaps it was because it was daytime and snails only sing at night, when they are active. Or perhaps they did not sing that day and do not sing much, if ever, anymore because everything is a long, long, way from being right in the world.

⚓

EACH NEW DRAWER WE OPENED REVEALED another set of wonders, another surprising color or variation in shape or size. In one drawer we encountered the cone shells of *Carelia turricula*, a now-extinct ground-dwelling snail that is thought to have once been the largest in the Hawaiian Islands. In another drawer we saw the delicate, translucent forms of *Succinea lumbalis*. In many others we found the glossy, colorful forms of *Achatinella* tree snails, some with bands and stripes, others patterned in ways reminiscent of tweed or tortoiseshell. Drawer after drawer, cabinet after cabinet, row after row, we moved through the Malacology Collection of the Bernice Pauahi Bishop Museum in Honolulu, ultimately seeing only a tiny fraction of the shells held there. My guide was Nori Yeung, curator of this collection of roughly six million Pacific Island snail shells, the largest of its kind in the world. While much of this collecting was done by museum staff, many of these shells were donated to the museum by private collectors or their families.

In fact, it seems that almost as soon as Europeans and Americans started arriving in these islands, they began collecting snails' shells—in some cases on a staggering scale (Hadfield 1986): from the scientific collectors of early European expeditions through to the hobbyists and picnicking families who made a game of collecting in the late nineteenth and twentieth centuries engaged in what some locals of the period referred to as "land shell fever" (Baldwin 1887). In this way, shell collecting became part of the larger domesticating processes that "settled" these people in this new land during a period in which the Hawaiian monarchy and government were overthrown and the islands became a settler-colonial dominion of the United States.[1] Numerous reports exist from this period of people traveling into the mountains for a few hours of snail-centered fun, returning with saddlebags full of shells. Today there are likely fewer individual snails of a whole range of species left on the entire island of Oʻahu than were collected by some of these groups in a few hours.

There is no doubt that these collecting practices had a significant impact on Hawaiʻi's snails, perhaps even causing the extinction of some species.[2] As has so often happened, in at least some cases, it seems that collection was explicitly motivated by a desire to catalog this diversity before it was lost. But snail shell collecting has had its day in Hawaiʻi. It is now a minor, even negligible, consideration in the decline of these species. Rather, as I saw firsthand

THOM VAN DOOREN

at the Palikea exclosure, a host of introduced predators are now thought to be the key drivers of snail extinctions.

In addition, however, Hawai'i's snails are struggling with the long legacies and steadily escalating realities of a transforming environment. To a certain extent, this decline really began with the arrival of Polynesian peoples about 1,000 years ago, as they cleared lowland forests to make room for kalo (taro) and the other agricultural plants that would allow these islands to sustain human life. But these processes were drastically ramped up from the early nineteenth century as vast areas of land, including many forested lands, were taken over by plantations and ranching, and later by tourism, urban, and military developments. These are complex and charged stories of environmental decline, bound up with the ongoing processes through which Kānaka Maoli were themselves dispossessed of their ancestral lands to become, as J. Kēhaulani Kauanui has succinctly put it, "largely a landless people" (2008, 75).[3]

As Nori and I moved through the Bishop Museum collection that day, she told me about the diverse threats faced by Hawai'i's snails. She also explained some of what is known about the species whose shells we encountered: their environments, their conservation statuses, their life histories. With each drawer it became apparent both what a remarkable collection this is and at the same time how utterly it fails to capture and contain the incredible diversity of the islands' snails. Even something as seemingly straightforward as color cannot really be retained in the collection in any full way: the color in a snail's shell, it turns out, resides only in the outer layer, the periostracum, which decays after death to eventually leave behind only a white calcium carbonate core. Depending on the conditions, this process can take a few years or be delayed for centuries in a climate-controlled collection in a museum. Even the uncolored, translucent shells do not readily reveal the living forms of their former occupants: for example, as they moved through the misty rain forests of the island of Kaua'i, *Succinea lumbalis* would actually have been red to the human observer, in this case because their shell reveals the colorful flesh that lies below and even some of the internal organs.

In other words, a shell collection is not a substitute for living snails in the world. While it is a vitally important resource for the crafting of all sorts of knowledges—not least the kind of information that might aid in snail conservation—there is so much that it cannot tell us about how these snails once lived and mattered in their environments. Even more important, this collection cannot hold on to and sustain those diverse, living relationships themselves; it cannot enable the ongoing interactions among

99

snails, people, trees, and soils that have in their own ways, small or large, shaped life for everyone in these islands.

Λ

THE FIRST SNAILS I ENCOUNTERED in the Hawaiian forest were of a far less showy variety than those of the genus *Achatinella*. In fact, they were actually pretty hard to see. A few weeks before my visit to the Palikea exclosure, I was hiking with Brenden Holland, a snail biologist with a passion for biogeography, on Puʻu ʻŌhiʻa (Mount Tantalus) on the edge of Honolulu. We had come to see a few of the smaller endemic tree snail species that persist in this forest just outside the city. As we walked, Brenden pointed out snails of a few different species, each of them not more than a millimeter or two in length. I quizzed him about snail biogeography as we went. In particular, I wanted to know how the diverse land snails of Hawaiʻi made their way to these remote oceanic islands. The short answer, I discovered, is that we really don't know for certain.

Terrestrial snails are generally a pretty sedentary bunch, spending their lives close to the spot they happened to be born or hatched on. When we add to this situation their very low tolerance for sea water—as they have no control over their salt absorption and thus dehydrate readily—the diverse range of snail species found in this remote archipelago becomes even more confounding. The Hawaiian island chain formed over a volcanic hot spot, out in the middle of the Pacific Ocean. This means that all of the diverse species of plants and animals that have made their homes in this place arrived across vast expanses of water or evolved from an ancestor who did. This situation has left a lasting impact on the islands' animal biota. In simple terms, they tend to have wings. In fact, when it comes to vertebrate animals, Hawaiʻi was for the longest time a land of birds. Until people introduced them, there were no terrestrial mammals or reptiles, with the sole exception of a winged mammal, the hoary bat. When one looks around the Hawaiian forest, this all seems quite logical: that is, until the intricate form of a large, brightly colored tree snail comes into view.

This situation is in no way unique to Hawaiʻi. Terrestrial snails are found on pretty much every tropical and subtropical island around the world. We are faced, then, with a kind of snail paradox, as Brenden put it: How do organisms that are so sedentary end up being so incredibly widely dispersed? Biologists have long puzzled over this question. Charles Darwin, in a letter to Alfred Russel Wallace in 1857, summed the situation up succinctly: "One of the subjects on which I have been experimentising and which cost me much trouble, is the means of distribution of all organic beings found on oceanic islands and any facts on this subject would be most gratefully received: Land-Molluscs are a great perplexity to me" (quoted in Holland 2009, 538).

Today it is thought that snails likely use—or get caught up in—a variety of modes of long-distance movement. Not all of those methods are immediately obvious, though, if we only look at these snails in their current forms. This was one of the reasons that Brenden had suggested we make this trip. The tiny *Auriculella diaphana* and the even smaller members of the subfamily Tornatellidinae that we encountered on Puʻu ʻŌhiʻa, he explained to me, are close relatives of the much larger tree snails of the genus *Achatinella*. While *Achatinella* snails grow to about two centimeters in length, these relatives can be as small as two millimeters when fully grown, about the size of a grain of rice. If the ancestors of the larger *Achatinella* snails were tiny creatures like this—only becoming "gigantic," relatively speaking, after generations of life on Oʻahu—then they might have had other modes of transportation open to them. Most important, Brenden thinks, the tiny ancestral forms might have traveled here by bird. The basic idea is that these snails climbed on board as a migratory bird perched or nested overnight—snails, after all, are nocturnal. These snails then hunkered down deep in the bird's feathers, only climbing off once they had safely arrived at their destination.

This is a proposal that, I must admit, I was quite dubious about—that is, until I saw the tiny forms of *Auriculella diaphana* and the Tornatellidinae snails. While it still seems horribly unlikely that this sequence of events would ever take place, in the fullness of evolutionary time those are actually pretty reasonable odds. Other biologists I spoke to agreed. The almost universal view I encountered among the community of snail biologists in Hawaiʻi is that this kind of avian dispersal, especially of smaller ancestral species, is the most likely avenue for their arrival.

There are, however, several other possibilities for snail movement across oceans, especially for the shorter trips between islands in the chain that genetics research indicates have taken place at various points in the history of some species. Some of these snails may have traveled *inside* birds: recent studies have shown that a variety of species of snails around the world survive passage through avian digestive tracts at a relatively high frequency (Wada, Kawakami, and Chiba 2012). Others might have flown on leaves or other debris, high in the airstream. Yet others likely rafted over on logs or bark. While snails don't do well with salt water, it seems that they do have a few tricks for survival. Most land snails can form an epiphragm, which is essentially a temporary cover of mucus used to seal their aperture to prevent them from drying out. Studies going back at least as far as Darwin have found that dormant (estivating) snails submerged in salt water can survive for weeks at a time (Ożgo et al. 2016). There haven't been significant experiments of this kind on Hawai'i's snails, with the exception of a small trial conducted by Brenden and Robert Cowie that showed that individuals of one nonendangered species, *Succinea caduca*, might survive in salt water at least long enough to make short interisland trips via raft (Holland and Cowie 2007).

These are undoubtedly all rather unreliable ways to travel. For every snail that successfully arrived in a strange new land on a bird or a floating branch or log, countless millions must have been washed, blown, or flown out to sea without such luck. The odds must be slightly better traveling by bird than log: at least in theory, if you hop onto or into a migratory bird in a forest, you are quite likely to be taken to another forest. Of course, for those snails unfortunate enough to be traveling *inside* the bird, they would have to survive the journey through the digestive system, too.

Snails are largely at the whim of external forces in these movements, subject to what biologists call *passive dispersal*. As Brenden helpfully summed it up for me, "biogeographically, snails are plants"—both groups share many of the same vectors for movement, the latter usually traveling by seed or spore. This is clearly a "system" of island dispersal that can hope to achieve results only with immense periods of time at its disposal. Over millions of years, a few lucky snails made these journeys successfully. We really can't know for certain how many times this happened in the Hawaiian Islands. At an absolute minimum, however, in order to have ended up with the diverse range of known terrestrial snails, things must have worked out for around twenty intrepid travelers over roughly the past five million years.[4] This means that the vast majority of Hawai'i's snail species evolved in the islands from a relatively small number of common ancestors.

While snails undoubtedly have many things working against them in these travels, the simple fact that they are found on islands almost everywhere tells us that—despite appearances—they are actually very good at dispersing and establishing themselves in new places. While they might not fly or enjoy salt water, they are small and robust enough to take advantage of other modes of movement. But these snails have another dispersal advantage over many other animals that only really becomes apparent after arrival—a *reproductive* advantage. Hawai'i's land snails, like most others around the world, are hermaphrodites. This means that for successful establishment to take place, any two individuals will do. In fact, in some cases one might be enough: some snails seem to be capable of "selfing" (i.e., self-fertilization), and others seem to be able to store sperm from copulation for long periods of time to utilize at a later date.

There is clearly something very passive about this dispersal of snails around the world: always at the whim of others, be they birds, storms, or tides, traveling under their steam and direction. But this also isn't the whole of the story. Deep, multigenerational evolutionary histories have produced the kinds of living beings that can move around the world in these ways. These modes of passive movement work only because snails have evolved some pretty remarkable traits that enable dispersal, survival, and reproduction across and into isolated new lands: from epiphragms to hermaphroditism, sperm storage, and self-fertilization. Millions of years and countless generations of more or less successful journeying have selected for those individuals that survived and established themselves best.

A profound kind of evolutionary agency is at work here, a creative, experimental, adaptive working out of living forms with particular capacities and propensities.[5] For the most part, individual snails are indeed relatively passive in all this. They are not, however, irrelevant. The particular actions of those little beings that crawled onto a bird, that opted to seal up their apertures, that safely stored away sperm for future use, mattered profoundly. But snails are also not involved in the more active, sometimes even deliberate, dispersal undertaken by many other animals. Instead, if we pay attention, they must amaze us with their capacity to move so far, to spread so widely, while doing so little.

This, it seems to me, is one of the real marvels of snail biogeography. Individual snails do not need to exert great effort because those incredible processes of natural selection have acted for them, acted on them, acted with them, to produce these beings that are so unexpectedly but uniquely suited to this particular from of travel, drifting. From such a perspective, rather than being any kind of deficiency, the highly successful passivity of snails might be seen as a remarkable evolutionary *achievement*.

There is so much more to learn here. So much to learn about the processes that have given rise to these gastropod forms of life that are so oddly suited to islands. So much to learn about not just the vectors but the patterns in which dispersal takes place: Are they perhaps laid down by atmospheric and oceanic currents or by the paths of avian migration? And yet to some extent this must remain a space of uncertainty and even mystery. How can one really study processes of biogeography that take place across such vast periods of time and space? As Brenden reminded me, it's likely that in the history of these islands, on average one species of snail has arrived and successfully

103

THE DISAPPEARING SNAILS OF HAWAI'I

established itself roughly every 300,000 years. Put simply, it's not something that any of us are likely to ever see, let alone study, firsthand.

In all, over 750 species of Hawaiian land snails have been recognized to date. This is an incredible diversity of snails for these tiny landmasses to have once supported. It is likely that far fewer than half of these species remain in the islands today, in various states of precariousness. This is perhaps a particular tragedy because over 99 percent of these species are not found anywhere else. In fact, almost all of the larger snail species were what biologists call *single-island endemics*, found only on one island and in many cases only in a single mountain range or, within that range, a single volcano or valley. The cause of this very high level of endemism, of course, is the fact that most species evolved in the islands: single-arrival events giving rise to one new species, and then another, and then another, as populations separated and diverged.

But why did so many different species evolve in these tiny areas of land? In no small way, the Hawaiian Islands themselves produced the conditions for this incredible diversity. They did so through the relatively ideal environment they provided: plenty of moist forests that were entirely or largely predator-free. These environments provided gastropods with a variety of adaptive possibilities, niches they might occupy and explore. But perhaps more important, the Hawaiian Islands also offered remarkable opportunities for the kind of separation and isolation that allow snail populations to simply drift apart into different species.

The main Hawaiian Islands, the high islands, are lands of incredible ecological diversity and patchiness, with rainfall and vegetation often varying dramatically across relatively short distances. Many of these landscape features form impassable barriers for snails, at least most of the time. Unlike birds and other highly mobile animals that can spread across an island into all areas of similar suitable habitat, snails rely on occasional dispersal across barriers by intermittent forces such as hurricanes, floods, and slope failures. This means that snail populations, once separated, are less likely to reconnect over intervals of hundreds of thousands, perhaps even millions, of years (Holland and Hadfield 2007). This kind of isolation creates ideal conditions for populations to simply drift off in different evolutionary directions, giving rise to one or more new species in each locale.

In other cases, movement of the land itself might open up new barriers. This could happen through a landslide that carries some snails out to sea and over to another island, or it may happen over immense periods of time as a deep valley is eroded out of a volcanic mountain chain, creating a warmer and drier barrier zone that is less hospitable for snails between the two peaks.[6] There are numerous paths to this kind of separation of one or a few snails from a larger population. While the landscape of the Hawaiian Islands offered an ideal environment for this kind of speciation, snails, too, played their part. Snails are themselves ideally suited to this kind of speciation as a result of their largely sedentary form of life that is punctuated by occasional moments of long-distance dispersal.

$$\text{\^{A}}$$

THE CURATOR REMOVED A SMALL BOX, about the size of a dinner plate, from the cabinet; walked over to the bench; and set it down. Inside, two delicately interwoven strands of kāhuli shells, all of the genus *Achatinella*, combined to form a stunning lei. I was in another part of the Bishop Museum, the ethological collection, this time to see the one and only lei that they hold that is composed entirely of terrestrial Hawaiian snail shells. This lei is also distinguished by its former owner: Queen Liliʻuokalani, the last monarch of the sovereign nation of Hawaiʻi, whose government was overthrown in 1893 by a group of mostly American citizens and Hawaiian subjects of American descent, with the assistance of US Marines. Little is known for certain about this lei: how, why, or when Liliʻuokalani acquired it. In fact, while leis made from marine shells are very common in Hawaiʻi, the shells of *forest* snails seem to have been used far less frequently in this way.

This lei reminds us that the lives of the Hawaiian people, the Kānaka Maoli, have long been tangled up with snails. Their shells were used to adorn the bodies of hula dancers and their kuahu (altars). According to occasional references in the literature, some larger snails may have been eaten by people—both raw and cooked inside the leaves of the ti plant (Stewart 1912). But more important than any of these kinds of uses, snails are potent symbols and omens in people's lives and stories, often indicating positive and righteous action and circumstance. This is, as I have already mentioned, something that the stories tell us snails do most powerfully through their singing.

People whom I spoke to in Hawaiʻi had a range of ideas about this snail singing. Referencing a lack of vocal cords, most people I asked told me that snails do not sing and offered one of two explanations for these stories. In the first case, it was said that this notion of singing was metaphorical, referring to the whistling sound that might be made as the wind rushed over the opening of a snail shell as it hung from a leaf or branch. In centuries past, when the forest was thick with snails, this sound might have combined to produce

105

a melody of sorts. Others felt that this was unlikely. The biologist Michael Hadfield told me that these shells were just too small. What's more, snails tend to assiduously keep their apertures covered. As Michael put it, "no self-respecting snail would give up its moisture by sitting their gaping into the wind" (pers. com., April 30, 2018).

A second possible explanation for these stories of singing that I heard from several people was expressed most eloquently by Sam 'Ohu Gon, a biologist and distinguished kumu oli, a singer and teacher of chants. Sam pointed out to me that Hawaiians were, and are, extremely observant people, but in this case he thinks that perhaps the chirping of crickets might have been associated with the much more readily visible kāhuli. He asked me to imagine visiting a dark forest at night with only the light of a sputtering torch to guide the way. "You'd be surrounded by the sound of high-pitched singing, because in Hawai'i there are hundreds of species of crickets." But, he pointed out, as you approached the crickets, they would become quiet and even move away. "You come over with your torch and you want to see what is making that sound. You turn over the leaves, and the crickets have long since jumped away, but there are snails sitting there under the leaves, beautiful snails no less. It would be very easy to associate that singing, whistling sound with those snails. And you've disturbed them, so of course if you put your ear to them, you're not going to hear a thing. It's only when you put the leaf back and sit quietly for a minute that the singing begins again" (pers. com., May 3, 2018).

※

STANDING WITHIN THE PALIKEA exclosure on the day of my visit—encircled by a fence fitted with layers of barriers, itself surrounded by a moat of cleared land—I could not fail to appreciate how profoundly fractured and isolated the lives and possibilities of Hawai'i's snails have become. This situation is perhaps exemplified in the story of one specific occupant of the exclosure: *Amastra spirizona*. This striking species, with a brown, conical shell about 1.5 centimeters in length, is now thought to be found nowhere else. The last thirty or so individuals were brought into the exclosure and placed within a large wooden box with wire mesh on one side. The box keeps them together to ensure that a core breeding population can find each other to reproduce, while also allowing smaller juveniles to disperse through the mesh into the exclosure beyond. Happily, this is exactly what has been happening: the current population is over 150 snails.

While *Amastra spirizona* is no doubt an extreme case, the sad reality is that most of Hawai'i's remaining snails can only survive in tiny, isolated pockets of space: from the captive populations in the lab through to the various spaces of the exclosure. In short, they can only survive cut off from the environments, processes, and relationships that birthed them. Environments that once provided the conditions not only for survival but for an incredible radiation of diversity have become lethal. In this way, to borrow James Hatley's apt term from his chapter in this volume, snails are being "deanimated" as the "creaturely ties" that bind them to humans and countless others are broken down.

As I stood in the presence of these snails in the Palikea exclosure, I remembered a conversation earlier that week with Puakea Nogelmeier, an expert in Hawaiian language and culture. When I asked Puakea about the traditional stories and ideas about snails singing, he replied with a story of his own. Many years earlier, Auntie Edith Kanaka'ole, the renowned composer and kumu hula (teacher of hula), told him and a group of her chant students that scientists had taken her to their lab to explain how impossible it was, biologically, for a snail to sing. He continued, "Auntie Edith's take on that was: 'Isn't that sad, they won't sing for the scientists'" (pers. com., May 4, 2018).

Auntie Edith's understanding draws us into another space of uncertainty, or mystery, in the unfolding story of these snails. Uncertainty and mystery are not the same thing. While the former describes a lack of knowledge that might at some stage be acquired, mystery—at least in the strong sense of the term—is an acknowledgment that the world is not, even in principle, fully *knowable* (Cooper 2007). Auntie Edith reminds us that the world and the other living beings that constitute it are not objects transparent to our gaze, readily revealed. Each of us—scientist, kumu hula, philosopher, snail—knows one another, knows the world, from the *inside*. Which is to say that each of us only ever knows the world in a partial way; much will always remain, must always remain, unknowable, or simply knowable in other ways.

Debbie argued that this kind of mystery is an inherent and unavoidable feature of life. As she put it, "One cannot remove one's self from the system under examination, and because one is a part of the system the whole remains outside the possibility of one's comprehension" (Rose 2005, n.p.). But, Debbie insisted, this mystery is a cause for celebration; it is something to be respected, cherished, even guarded. Mystery signals the complexity and integrity of our world. A system that is entirely knowable is a dead or dying one: "Total predictability would signal crisis—loss of connection" (Rose

2005, n.p.). From this perspective, mystery is inseparable from the vitality of the living world. This is by no means a celebration of ignorance but rather a humble acknowledgment of the many layers and possibilities of our shared world. It might perhaps be seen as an acknowledgment of what is called *kaona* in Hawaiian, a term that is often used to refer to the many meanings— some of them hidden—carried within a text but that, as Kanaka historian Noelani Arista notes, might also describe the more general "tolerance and preference" in Hawaiian thought "for multiplicity in the relation between not only words but also *worlds*" (2010, 666).[7]

For as long as they or we endure, Hawai'i's snails will continue to draw us into worlds of uncertainty and indeed mystery. These spaces of not-knowing might reside in the one or many vectors by which these snails arrived in the islands, or in relation to the ways in which they might sing and make meaning in the world with and for the peoples of Hawai'i. As these snails disappear, the vitality of these mysteries is threatened too. While these diverse spaces of not-knowing cannot really be lost in any absolute sense, the possibility of our *living well* with them can be: the possibility of inhabiting the world in a spirit of respectful curiosity, humility, and wonder.

As Hawai'i's many incredible snail species slip away, one by one, and as the worlds of those that manage to survive become increasingly fractured and simplified, we undermine our ability to find ways to relate to and value a world that is much bigger and more complex than we can know. We undermine the possibility of looking at a snail shell and seeing a mystery that can never be uncoiled but that must rather, simply, be lived with. Questioned, explored, wondered about, chanted, danced, and sung with but ultimately always to remain at least partly unknown.

Snails are just one way, or rather one constellation of ways, into a sense of a world that exceeds us. None of the snails I encountered in Hawai'i sang in my presence, or if they did, I was not able to hear them. But thinking carefully with and about snails nonetheless drew me into new understandings, new modes of appreciation and respect. For me at least, the immense biogeographical and evolutionary stories coiled into their tiny shells provided a potent portal into a world of incredible scope and complexity, of exciting understanding alongside ongoing and profound mystery. It is hard to really make sense of this vast assemblage of Hawaiian snail life. I imagine it as something like a giant network with strands stretching out across the Pacific Ocean and beyond, stretching back over evolutionary and geological time frames. Each strand represents one of hundreds of unique species. Millions of years of unlikely journeys—nestled into a bird's feathers, or perhaps stuck to a floating branch—heading to destinations unknown. Millions of years of evolutionary agency that produced these intrepid, even if somewhat unlikely, island dispersers with the reproductive and other adaptations that made these movements possible. And then, after that most fortuitous of arrivals, countless generations more of chance movements giving rise to isolation and speciation: drifting snails, drifting valleys and hills, drifting genes. Each strand is a unique line of movement, of relationships, of branching transformations. These are at least some of the processes that have produced the intricate webs of lives and possibilities that are, that *were*, the worlds of Hawaiian snails, a remarkable, breathtakingly diverse, utterly unrepeatable assemblage of life.

To labor to hold this network in mind, however imperfectly, however impossibly, might offer us a glimpse into at least one of the many ways in which these snails matter, and so the significance of what is being lost in their extinction. Doing so might remind us that each of the fragile, fleshy, little individuals of *Achatinella mustelina* or *Amastra spirizona* surviving in the Palikea exclosure is not so much a member of a species as it is a participant in a lineage, one link in a vast, improbable intergenerational project.

As Hawai'i's snails remind us so well, each of these specific projects is a shifting and emergent one. Through processes of adaptation, of isolation, of drift, a species is always becoming other than itself: changing, diversifying, multiplying. As such, what is lost with each species is not "just" its current form—not just the particular mode of life and physical manifestation of these snails we see around us today—but all of what they have been, and all of what in the fullness of evolutionary time they might have become. The world is dispossessed of a diversity of potentialities, left hovering just beyond the edge of the real; of all of those other incredible snail species that don't yet quite exist, not to mention the other plants and animals that might have emerged in relationship with them.[8] As Debbie insisted, to kill species, to kill generations, is in an important sense to kill time itself (Rose 2012).[9]

In Hawai'i today, the lives, histories, and possibilities of diverse snail species are being radically truncated, or simply shorn off, all within the space of a few generations of human life. With them are disappearing countless unique ways of life and the vast evolutionary heritage that they together represent. But with them is also disappearing the possibility of our learning to be at home in the world in a way that is responsible for other modes of life: not in isolation, not as barely surviving populations and organisms, but as ongoing processes of entangled life and death stretching across oceans of time and space that we cannot comprehend.

THE DISAPPEARING SNAILS OF HAWAI'I

NOTES

1. For a fuller discussion of this topic, see Osorio (2002); Goodyear-Kaʻōpua, Hussey, and Kahunawaikaʻala (2014); Silva (2004); and Banner (2007).

2. Brenden Holland drew to my attention the collecting efforts of d'Alté Welch, who, with the aid of assistants, collected 15,176 *Achatinella mustelina* in a five-year period throughout a wide variety of sites in the Waiʻanae Range (see Holland and Hadfield 2007, 54).

3. See also Silva (2004). For contemporary politics related to ʻaina (land) in Hawaiʻi, see Goodyear-Kaʻōpua, Hussey, and Kahunawaikaʻala (2014); and Yamashiro and Goodyear-Kaʻōpua (2014).

4. That is, since the formation of Kauaʻi, the oldest of the current high islands with suitable snail habitat.

5. On this topic, also see Plumwood (2009, 125).

6. These are, respectively, examples of processes that biogeographers refer to as *dispersal* and *vicariance*.

7. For a discussion of the difficulties and importance of exploring the spaces of overlap and divergence between worlds, see Anna Lowenhaupt Tsing's discussion of "edge effects" in her chapter in this volume.

8. This is a topic that I have explored in greater detail in van Dooren (2014, 21–44).

9. Also see Kate Wright's chapter in this volume.

REFERENCES

Arista, Noelani. 2010. "Navigating Uncharted Oceans of Meaning: Kaona as Historical and Interpretive Method." *PMLA* 125 (3): 663–669.

Baldwin, David D. 1887. "The Land Shells of the Hawaiian Islands." *Hawaiian Almanac and Annual*: 55–63.

Banner, Stuart. 2007. *Possessing the Pacific: Land, Settlers, and Indigenous People from Australia to Alaska*. Cambridge, MA: Harvard University Press.

Cooper, David E. 2007. *The Measure of Things: Humanism, Humility, and Mystery*. Oxford: Oxford University Press.

Goodyear-Kaʻōpua, Noelani, Ikaika Hussey, and Erin Kahunawaikaʻala, eds. 2014. *A Nation Rising: Hawaiian Movements for Life, Land, and Sovereignty*. Durham, NC: Duke University Press.

Hadfield, Michael G. 1986. "Extinction in Hawaiian *Achatinelline* Snails." *Malacologia* 27 (1): 67–81.

Holland, Brenden S. 2009. "Land Snails." In *Encyclopedia of Islands*, edited by Rosemary Gillespie and David Clague, 537–542. Los Angeles: University of California Press.

Holland, Brenden S., and Rob H. Cowie. 2007. "A Geographic Mosaic of Passive Dispersal: Population Structure in the Endemic Hawaiian Amber Snail *Succinea caduca* (Mighels, 1845)." *Molecular Ecology* 16 (12): 2422–2435.

THOM VAN DOOREN

Holland, Brenden S., and Michael G. Hadfield. 2007. "Molecular Systematics of
   the Endangered Oʻahu Tree Snail *Achatinella mustelina*: Synonymization of
   Subspecies and Estimation of Gene Flow between Chiral Morphs." *Pacific
   Science* 61 (1): 53–66.
Kauanui, J. Kēhaulani. 2008. *Hawaiian Blood: Colonialism and the Politics of Sover-
   eignty and Indigeneity*. Durham, NC: Duke University Press.
Osorio, Jonathan Kay Kamakawiwoʻole. 2002. *Dismembering Lahui: A History of the
   Hawaiian Nation to 1887*. Honolulu: University of Hawaiʻi Press.
Ożgo, Małgorzata, Aydin Örstan, Małgorzata Kirschenstein, and Robert Cameron.
   2016. "Dispersal of Land Snails by Sea Storms." *Journal of Molluscan Studies* 82
   (2): 341–343.
Plumwood, Val. 2009. "Nature in the Active Voice." *Australian Humanities Review*,
   no. 46, 113–129.
Rose, Deborah Bird. 2005. "Pattern, Connection, Desire: In Honour of Gregory
   Bateson." *Australian Humanities Review*, no. 35: n.p.
Rose, Deborah Bird. 2011. *Wild Dog Dreaming: Love and Extinction*. Charlottesville:
   University of Virginia Press.
Rose, Deborah Bird. 2012. "Multispecies Knots of Ethical Time." *Environmental
   Philosophy* 9 (1): 127–140.
Rose, Deborah Bird. 2013. "Slowly ~ Writing into the Anthropocene." In "Writing
   Creates Ecology and Ecology Creates Writing." Special issue, TEXT, no. 20,
   1–14. http://www.textjournal.com.au/speciss/issue20/Rose.pdf.
Sato, Aimee You, Melissa Renae Price, and Mehana Blaich Vaughan. 2018. "Kāhuli:
   Uncovering Indigenous Ecological Knowledge to Conserve Endangered
   Hawaiian Land Snails." *Society and Natural Resources* 31 (3): 320–334.
Silva, Noenoe K. 2004. *Aloha Betrayed: Native Hawaiian Resistance to American
   Colonialism*. Durham, NC: Duke University Press.
Stewart, Charles Samuel. 1912. "Addenda: Achatina stewartii and A. oahuensis
   [1823]." *Manual of Conchology* 22:404–407.
van Dooren, Thom. 2014. *Flight Ways: Life and Loss at the Edge of Extinction*. New
   York: Columbia University Press.
Wada, Shinichiro, Kazuto Kawakami, and Satoshi Chiba. 2012. "Snails Can Survive
   Passage through a Bird's Digestive System." *Journal of Biogeography* 39 (1):
   69–73.
Yamashiro, Aiko, and Noelani Goodyear-Kaʻōpua, eds. 2014. *The Value of Hawaii 2:
   Ancestral Roots, Oceanic Visions*. Honolulu: University of Hawaiʻi Press.

ROADKILL SIX

Multispecies Mobility and Everyday Ecocide

KATE RIGBY AND OWAIN JONES

ENTERING THE DEATHZONE

BODIES OF DEAD OTHERS LITTER our everyday life of commute and travel. The corpses of road-killed animals are often left in view—sometimes repeatedly run over until they are no more than stains on the tarmac. In this chapter we take the seemingly unremarkable—and mostly unremarked-upon—routine sight of animal corpses on modern roadways to open up a set of narratives that speak of the continuing gulf in political and ethical status between animals and humans within modern industrialized society. While we acknowledge how some animals are able to take advantage of roadways, we highlight the ways in which the phenomenon of roadkill discloses the violent and asymmetrical intersection of human and nonhuman everyday motilities.

Our chapter is, in part, simply a lament, not only for the dead animals encountered, but also for the wider era of ecocide unfolding around us, of which roads are, in many ways, harbingers and facilitators. What is the salience of roadkill, we wonder, in an era of escalating extinction? We also explore the question of what one should do on encountering the corpse of another—and in some instances the young of a deceased parent—and consider strategies for rendering other-than-human road fatalities both more meaningful and less common. Attending responsively to our encounters with road-killed kindred creatures, we contend, affords an "awakening to the call of others," which, as Isabelle Stengers discusses in this volume, lies at the heart of Deborah Bird Rose's "ecological existentialism."

"In the shadow of all this death": this phrase, the title of Rose's contribution to a 2013 volume entitled *Animal Death* (edited by Jay Johnston and Fiona Probyn-Rapsey), haunts us, now especially, in the wake of Rose's own untimely demise. Those of us who find ourselves living on in the shadow of her death feel called to redouble our endeavors to stay true to her lifelong project of taking "a stand for life," whereby this means also "taking a stand for faith in life's meaningfulness" (Rose 2017, G61). Life, of course, encompasses death, in the time frame both of individual beings and, on an evolutionary scale, of entire kinds of being, those defined as species in the language of the modern biological sciences. As Rose writes in *Wild Dog Dreaming*, "Living things are bound into ecological communities of life and death, and within these communities life is always making and unmaking itself in time and place" (2011, 82). What counts in this context—one in which pain and sorrow and loss do not, ultimately, overwhelm the potential for pleasure and joy and replenishment—is that death is forever folded back into life.

But in the intimate and intricate dance of multispecies lifedeath, if death is allowed to take the lead, life is liable to stumble. If this happens, we enter the zone of what Rose identified as "double death": the zone of human-caused mass death, whether genocidal or ecocidal, in which the dead are "left with no living descendants" (2004, 176). "In the shadow of all this death": the *all* here, in the essay of that name, refers specifically to the mass death of escalating anthropogenic extinctions, which is cutting off the regenerative potential of entire kinds of living beings at a rate and on a scale that far exceeds the background rate of extinction inherent to evolutionary processes, unraveling ecologies, deanimating entire multispecies worlds, and causing untold suffering along the way, as individual lives are traumatized and truncated, and breeding attempts, such as those of the grief-stricken albatross pair whose story Rose relates in *Animal Death*, fail, and fail again.

The deathzone with which we are concerned in this chapter is situated somewhere between the everyday dance of lifedeath and the endgame of

113

double death, yet it touches on both. "In the shadow of all *this* death": this phrase comes back to haunt us, almost daily, as we make our way, generally by car, and not always slowly and mindfully enough, along the narrow rural lanes and busy roads of England's superficially "green and pleasant" southwest. For in the midst of the mad dash of our twenty-first-century academic lives, we are all too often brought up short by yet another corpse, the mortal remains of yet another animal victim of our motorized transportation system.

"Roadkill": for many urban people, this is now the main way in which they are likely to encounter free-living other-than-human mammals. Yet this pervasive modality of animal death within contemporary industrialized and industrializing countries has, until very recently, received surprisingly little sustained consideration in human-animal studies or the environmental humanities. Indeed, we are struck by the absence of the term *roadkill* in the index of *Animal Death*, although several of the contributions to that volume, including Rose's, are germane to our concerns in this chapter.

In keeping with the practice of "passionate immersion" in the lives (and in this case, especially, the deaths) of others that has become a hallmark of multispecies studies (see van Dooren, Kirksey, and Münster 2016; van Dooren and Rose 2016), this chapter alternates between two different types of writing. The first is expository, entailing coauthored reflections on historical, geographical, ecological, and philosophical aspects of roadkill. The second is performative and poetic, arising from some of the many personal encounters that each author has experienced with the bodies of road-killed animals. By attending to the phenomenality of such encounters, together with the questions to which they have given rise, we hope to both bear witness to the dead and advance a more bio-inclusive ethos of multispecies coexistence in a world of proliferating tarmac and diminishing biodiversity.

KR: DISREGARDED DEATHS, DEVALUED LIVES

Throughout the month of November 2008, as I made my daily trek from the historical research center of the National Museum of Australia, where I was spending my weekday mornings, to the Canberra Hospital, where I spent most afternoons with my mother at my father's bedside, I passed the disintegrating carcass of a kangaroo, left to molder on the sun-scorched grass of the median strip dividing the four-lane roadway where she or he had been struck.[1] By chance, the dead roo lay close to a cross that had been placed in a prominent position on a low rise on one side of the road.

KATE RIGBY AND OWAIN JONES

The research that I was conducting at the time concerned the environmental history of the Canberra area, and I had become fascinated by the ways in which the planners of Australia's federal capital (my old hometown, as it happens) had succeeded, as least in part, in realizing Walter Burley Griffin's vision of a city that was not only in but of the landscape (Taylor 2006). Canberra's geometrically designed formal center is aligned with the surrounding mountains and the river that once traversed the Limestone Plains (now dammed to create the lake that bears Griffin's name), its ceremonial boulevards forever leading the gaze beyond the built environment, while the radiating suburbs are traversed by messy remnant bushland, perpetually interrupting the expansion of its tidy city streets. There is a downside, though, to Canberra's "open space" plan: while the incorporation of ribbons of grassy woodland and unbuilt hillsides into the urban environment affords Canberrans the opportunity for regular encounters with native flora, fauna, and granite outcrops, it also increases the risk that any bushfires sweeping down from those picturesque mountains will be ferried to, and through, the doors of their homes (a risk much amplified in some areas by the commercial pine plantations that contributed to the devastation of several suburbs in the catastrophic firestorm of February 2003). The riskiness of this ecotopian town planning, though, is even greater for other-than-human Canberrans: the segmentation of their territory by roads spells deadly danger for the city's wildlife, with kangaroos being the most commonly encountered casualties. What struck me about this one, though, was its proximity to a cross memorializing another kind of road fatality: evidently, a human one.

The practice of honoring the dead, while perhaps not exclusively human, is an anthropic constant, with mortuary sites constituting one of the most important markers of early human presence for archaeology.[2] Overseeing the passage of deceased kin into whatever afterlife they were believed to be entering has been a crucial task for religion throughout human history. Among those who today erect crosses to mark the site where loved ones have been involved in fatal traffic accidents, many might no longer subscribe to a specifically Christian view of the afterlife; but in deploying this culturally resonant symbol, they are effectively turning their private loss into a public memorial. Juxtaposed with the disregarded roo carcass, then, this particular cross offers every passerby a potent lesson in human exceptionalism, proclaiming that while the death of any human being, even a complete stranger, should concern us all as fellow humans, the accidental killing of a fellow living being categorized as an animal is a matter of complete indifference. This indifference, bespeaking a disavowal of cross-species kinship, communion, and care, potentially places other nonhuman lives in peril as well, as scavenging birds and mammals, drawn to the moldering roo corpse, are at risk of being struck in turn while endeavoring to feed.[3] Roadkill can become a death trap: this, too, might be considered a form of double death.

VIOLENCE

This incident from Canberra is sobering, not least because it shows how a modern city with some environmental, even ecotopian, ambitions embedded in its design—the bringing of nature into the city (Rigby 2005)—ends up creating greater risk to both human and nonhuman safety through the juxtaposition of habitat and roads. In essence, roadkill arises from the collision of two forms of mobility: human and nonhuman animal; as environmental historian Gary Kroll observes, both are situated within contingent natural-cultural histories. From this perspective, roadkill also represents a collision of cultural history and natural history, and an examination of that collision has much to reveal about the relationship between humans and (other) animals within modernity (Kroll 2015).

Motorized road vehicles are extraordinarily violent things when in use. Stand by any road with fast-moving traffic—the noise, the pulse of air, the swirling eddies in their wake are testaments to the violent forces at play. Motorized mobility is so everyday and commonplace that the fact of its violence has become just background noise to everyday modern life. Motor vehicles are hostile to all bodies not inside them (and often also to the ones inside). Whether or not animals are able to sense this, it is apparent that most generally find it hard to negotiate the weird spatio-temporal-material alien that is a fast-moving vehicle in *their* everyday mobilities. We might not be able to get inside the minds of other critters (or, thankfully, even those of others of our own kind: not yet, anyway). But a growing body of research in ethology, comparative psychology, and zoosemiotics is beginning to give us some fascinating glimpses into how other animals perceive their environment, think, feel, and communicate (see, for example, Bekoff 2007; Bekoff and Pierce 2009; Uexküll 2010). As discussed further later on, moreover, the arts have long had ways of engaging our empathic imagination, opening a path to the recognition of a shared creatureliness, whether found in the experience of enjoyment, the discernment of meaning, or the susceptibility to injury, illness, suffering, and death.

Something of the potential trauma of animal encounters with human roadways can be sensed in a video entitled "Transience 1. Oh—Bird" from

KATE RIGBY AND OWAIN JONES

2008 by the English multimedia performance artist Sue Palmer. The frame is filled with a human hand gently enclosing a small bird, a young great tit, which the artist had found by the side of a road in a woodland. The bird is moving slightly, and his or her beak is just poking out above the cup of the hand. Slowly, from nothing and afar, a rushing noise grows. An unseen lorry is approaching. As the noise grows to a roar, the slightly fluffed-out feathers on the bird's head close and flatten, and at the same time he or she hunkers down into the shelter of the cupped hand in fear—in way more fear than from being held by some huge unknown alien. Palmer's comments take the form of what we read as a prose poem:

> may 22 2008 driving through Culmstock tiny bird standing facing white line at edge of road stopped looked small bird standing still stunned picked it up you know that amazing feeling when you hold a small bird i filmed it sorry small bird but we had to collaborate somehow fast heart beat fluttering body held light in my rapt warm hand i sensed the power of my strength in the lightness of its eye i saw its head flatten at the passing of the truck that could have been its end breath thinnest legs placed on grass bird still bird looking around then flew up into the tree and gone turn back to the car. (S. Palmer 2008)

The conflict between modern terrestrial transport systems and animal becoming nonetheless precedes the advent of the motorcar. The shockingly violent character of modern machine-powered human mobility was made palpable by the painter Joseph Mallord William Turner in his ambivalent tribute to the Great Western Railway, *Rain, Steam, and Speed* (1844).[4] While technophiliacs might take pleasure in the phallic upsurge of the train bearing down on them, few have remarked the small animal, a hare, barely visible in the misting rain. The famously fast-moving hare is itself an exemplar of speed. Here, though, it is rendered as a victim of speed: that embodied in the powerful new machine surging towards it. The hare is not crossing but running before the train in confused panic, as animals often do, and it is highly likely to be crushed.

Alongside this nonhuman member of the multispecies community that had long co-constituted the preindustrial countryside of Britain, Turner recalls some of its human members, too, in the ghostly group of rural workers, similarly veiled by mist, as if on the verge of disappearing. While they wave jauntily, the immanent, if forever suspended, death of the hare becomes presciently metonymic of the erasure of a whole multispecies way of life. Elsewhere the steam locomotive was also instrumental in the dispossession and displacement of colonized peoples, together with those culturally as well as ecologically keystone species with whom their lives were enmeshed. Among those were the buffalo of Montana, the genocide of which is recalled in a mural discussed by James Hatley in this volume, in which a train is shown charging "into a herd of a more-than-human living kind, crushing them into the earth, even as they struggle with the locomotive in their plight" (Hatley, this volume).

To an even greater extent than railways, roads expose the fact that modern industrial society has produced chronically striated space that radically transforms the co-becoming of terrestrial life, creating certain novel affordances for nonhumans as well as humans, to be sure, but also engendering new regimes of risk.[5] In her research into the ecology of roads in the field of transport studies, Alisa Coffin points out that in motorized societies, "the nature of road systems as network structures renders vast areas of the landscape as road-affected, with small patches of isolated habitat remaining beyond the ecological influence of roads" (2007, 396). Roads cut up the territories and the routeways of animal becoming and the becoming of the land in more vertical exchanges. As Tim Ingold notes:

> Under the rubric of the "built environment", human industry has created an infrastructure of hard surfaces, fitted out with objects of all sorts, upon which the play of life is supposed to be enacted. Thus the rigid separation of substances from the medium that [James J.] Gibson took to be a natural state of affairs has in fact been engineered in an attempt to get the world to conform to our expectations of it, and to provide it with the coherent surface we always thought it had. Yet while designed to ease the transport of occupants across it, the hard surfacing of the earth actually blocks the very intermingling of substances with the medium that is essential to life, growth and habitation. (2011, 124)

Many things might be hailed as the epitome of what Kate Wright (in this volume) refers to as the "Earth-shattering violence" of expansionist industrial-capitalist society. But cars, roads, and their consequences and casualties could claim to be high on the list. Roads are one of the ubiquitous and essential parts of modern "civilization." They allow the everyday mobility through which the processual fabric of modern society functions. Throughout the world, "development" goes hand in hand with road building. As Graham Lawton (2018) has observed, "The world is experiencing an unprecedented highway building boom—with untold consequences for the planet's wildlife," with an estimated 12 million kilometers of new roads built since 2000 and a further "25 million [kilometers] of roads estimated to be built by 2050." These new roads, paving the way for all manner of other developments, including large infrastructure projects, damage and fragment habitat, and they can also provide a vector for the spread of invasive species. Inevitably, this will expand the experience of roadkill to new species, cultures, and places. The roadways that from one perspective signal the advancement of civilization produce spaces that Rose's Aboriginal teachers would categorize as wild: spaces, that is, where the "care of generations" devoted to the cultivation of "quiet" places of collective flourishing is disrupted or undone, leading to a proliferation of heedless violence and unheeded death.[6]

ECOCIDE

The longer we have been dwelling in the deathzone of roadkill, the more we have become convinced that roads are a harbinger of ecocide and one of the primary means through which ecocide is enacted.

In *Reports from a Wild Country*, Rose introduces the dire term *ecocide* in the sense in which it was deployed by Donald Grinde and Bruce Johansen in their 1995 history of the "environmental destruction of Indian lands and peoples" in North America.[7] In Australia, too, as Rose demonstrates, genocide and ecocide have gone hand in hand, leading to the "loss of around 90 per cent of the original Aboriginal population, the loss of all but a small number of Aboriginal languages," and the "loss of large numbers of plant and animal species, including the highest rate of mammalian extinction in the contemporary world" (Rose 2004, 34–35). Here we want to extend this notion of ecocide to encompass also the psychological degradation highlighted by Félix Guattari in *The Three Ecologies*, first published in French in 1989. As Ian Pindar and Paul Sutton explain in their translators' introduction, "Guattari's contention is that IWC [Integrated World Capitalism] is not only destroying the natural environment and eroding social relations, but is also engaged in a far more insidious and invisible 'penetration of people's attitudes, sensibility and minds.' . . . Human subjectivity, in all its uniqueness—what Guattari calls its 'singularity'—is as endangered as those rare species that are disappearing from the planet every day" (2000, 6).

With respect to the erosion of the oikos of other-than-human kinds, awareness of the collateral damage inflicted on animals was evident in the United States, the pioneering heartland of car culture, by the 1930s, leading to the publication in 1938 of the first book-length study of "automobile-killed animals," James R. Simmons's *Feathers and Fur on the Turnpike*. While Simmons's taxonomy of "roadside casualties" tends toward a normalization of this disconcerting phenomenon, namely, as something to be accepted as an inevitable consequence of advances in transportation, the shocking statistic made public by the Humane Society in 1960, of some one million road-killed animals per day, was intended to raise concern and goad efforts to redress the carnage (Monahan 2016, 152). The escalation of animal road fatalities during this decade suggests that roadkill should be added to the many existing hockey-stick graphs charting the "Great Acceleration" of industrial modernity's grievous impacts on the planet.

Roadkill is just one negative eco-impact of roads, and while there are some eco-benefits stemming from road networks, such as road-verge biodiversity (as discussed further later in this chapter), they are also a source of damaging pollution: of waterways through runoff, along with noise pollution, light pollution, and, of course, airborne pollution from exhaust emissions. Where motorized vehicles are fueled by the combustion of the fossilized remains of ancient marine animal life, as most are, they contribute significantly to those anthropogenic climatic changes that not only are set to escalate an already high extinction rate but are already bringing death and suffering to numberless animals, human and otherwise, through the increasing frequency and intensity of extreme weather events.

For many endangered species, moreover, the risk of getting killed on the road constitutes one more threat to the species' survival. In the United States, a 2008 report to Congress identified twenty-one federally listed threatened or endangered animal species, including the Hawaiian goose, the desert tortoise, and the San Joaquin kit fox, "for which road mortality is among the major threats to the survival of the species" (Huijser et al. 2008, 9).[8] Similarly, in Australia, koalas, whose numbers have been declining precipitously largely owing to habitat loss, malnutrition, and disease and who are also suffering from the increasing frequency and intensity of droughts and bushfires, are highly susceptible to being struck by motorized vehicles (International Union for Conservation of Nature, n.d.; Taylor-Brown et al. 2019). In the United Kingdom, endangered species that are at risk on the roads include barn owls, who hunt at night, flying low over grassland, quartering fields, and skimming over the hedgerows bounding rural laneways. In a typical year, Britain's 4,000 pairs of barn owls produce roughly 12,000 young, and it is estimated that a shocking 3,000–5,000 of these are killed by motorized vehicles (Barn Owl Trust, n.d.). In the horizon of anthropogenic mass extinction, then, roadkill acquires a new and dreadful salience.

With regard to the second of Guattari's three ecologies, cars and roads also create spatially dispersed social relations, eroding place-based forms of employment, consumption, and conviviality. Historically, road building was integral to the inauguration of what Anna Lowenhaupt Tsing and Donna

J. Haraway have termed the *Plantationocene* (Haraway 2015). Beginning in the sixteenth century with "the devastating transformation of diverse kinds of human-tended farms, pastures, and forests into extractive and enclosed plantations, relying on slave labor and other forms of exploited, alienated, and usually spatially transported labor," the Plantationocene "continues with ever-greater ferocity in globalized factory meat production, monocrop agribusiness, and immense substitutions of crops like palm oil for multispecies forests and their products that sustain human and nonhuman critters alike" (Haraway 2015, 162). As ever more corners of the globe get caught up in the transnational web of turbocharged capitalist industrialization, roads open frontiers for resource extraction that undermines ecocultural diversity. As is widely recognized, this is currently the case for the forest-dwelling peoples of Amazonia, whose oikos is coming under increased pressure as a consequence of the policies of Brazilian president Jair Bolsonaro and those whose economic interests (notably, in agricultural production and oil excavation) they are serving. Less well known is the plight of the Orang Rimba, an Indigenous people of the rain forests of Sumatra, whose richly biodiverse dwelling places have been almost entirely converted into palm oil plantations, creating a silent wasteland crisscrossed with death-dealing roads, rendering it impossible for most of the survivors to maintain their traditional way of life (Knudson 2009).

As harbingers of ecocide, then, roads and the vehicles that traverse them bring a form of quadruple death—directly, by causing road fatalities, by destroying and fragmenting habitat, by contributing to climate change, and by eroding local cultures: not the mythical four horsemen of the apocalypse, perhaps, but a material network wreaking Earth system changes of apocalyptic proportions.

Moreover, in our analysis, the daily spectacle of disregarded roadkill also has a psychospiritual impact pertaining to the third of Guattari's three ecologies: namely, to the extent that we become inured to animal death and suffering in a way that reinforces human exceptionalism and self-enclosure, eroding or impeding more bio-inclusive social relations entailing the recognition of cross-species kinship and the cultivation of care. This degradation of the ecology of affect is made manifest, for example, in the popularity of a game known as roadkill bingo, in which players score by spotting dead animals on the road and ticking them off on a bingo card, the winner being the first to mark five different animals in one row or column (Burnside 2012).[9] Less brutally but more insidiously, we might consider the popular Road Runner cartoons, first screened in 1949, in which Wile E. Coyote's repeated flattening is a source of humor, while his repeated recovery, as Linda Monahan notes, effectively releases viewers from "any trace of guilt over the consequences of American car culture as they fixated on the [amusingly] mutable moment of death and its undoing" (2016, 152).

KR: DEER

One morning, early, as we round the corner from a rural laneway onto a busier two-way road, we are pulled up short by a deer. A trail of blood shows where the corpse has been dragged to the edge of the tarmac to lie alongside a hedged embankment, where it still partially blocks our passage. Nor do we try to heave it up and over: too heavy, too bloody, too time-consuming. The deer is entirely headless, the bone, muscle, and sinews of the neck clearly visible to our gaze. Had the antlers become snared in the undercarriage? Or had somebody snaffled the head as a trophy? And how? The head appeared to have been severed rather than ripped, but the cut was not clean. Beyond our immediate recoil from the abject grisliness of this spectacle, what is most striking is how the facelessness of this poor creature alters our affective response. On reflection, I realize that it is precisely in this that the decapitated deer discloses the bitter truth of roadkill: to the extent that their death and suffering are considered inconsequential, their everyday journeys and objectives disregarded, none of these animals has a "face," in the Levinasian sense: that is, in none do we encounter an other who has an ethical call upon us: "The Other becomes my neighbour precisely through the way the face summons me, calls for me, begs for me, and in so doing recalls my responsibility, and calls me into question" (Levinas 1989, 83).[10]

While Emmanuel Levinas insisted that only humans could be thus encountered, Rose, drawing on what she had learned from her Aboriginal teachers about multispecies kinship, and in conversation with James Hatley, opened this ethic up to include other others, especially animals. From this perspective, practices that police the impermeable boundary between human and animal life make it "possible to ignore animal deaths" (Rose 2011, 22). If, for Levinas, "the justification of the neighbor's pain is certainly the source of all immorality" (Levinas 1988, 163), and if, as Rose insists, countering ecocide requires that we consider animals, too, as neighbors, fellow members of multispecies collectives, then the blithe acceptance of other-than-human road fatalities as the inevitable price for the development and expansion of motorized transportation systems surely counts as deeply unethical. Indeed, the very term *roadkill* contributes to this systematic discounting of other-than-human road fatalities. As labor studies scholar Dennis Soron observes, "'Road kill' is just as de-animalized as 'beef' and just as open to cultural meanings that are bracketed off from the embodied experience of the suffering animal" (2011, 63). To this, Monahan adds that it presupposes that the road is an exclusively human space, implying that animals trespass at their peril and transforming individual victims into an "anonymous aggregate" (2016, 155).

The psychic violence entailed in the suppression of fellow feeling for a nonhuman creature can also have horrendous implications for the treatment of fellow humans who have been relegated to the subordinate side of the human-animal binary, as Theodor Adorno observed in the wake of the Shoah: "The possibility of pogroms is decided in the moment when the gaze of a fatally-wounded animal falls on a human being. The defiance with which he repels this gaze—'after all, it's only an animal'—reappears irresistibly in cruelties done to human beings, the perpetrators having again and again to reassure themselves that it is 'only an animal,' because they could never fully believe this even of animals" (1978, 105). And yet, despite the continued, although possibly weakening, prevalence of human exceptionalism, many do care, and their stories, too, need to be told.

OJ: RABBIT

6.1 Rabbit, local lanes, Somerset, 2015. © OWAIN JONES.

Again in the lanes, driving alone, away from home. A bright summer's day. Just at the top of a steep little dip down to where the road crosses a stream, I see a car is stopped, door open, and a woman is running up the road in front of her car. I can just see past the stationary vehicle. She is running with her hands half to her head. Obviously in distress. My windows are shut. I see her running forward but hear nothing. It looks, from behind, as if she is crying. "My God," I think," someone, a child maybe, has been run over." But then she stops and bends and picks up a rabbit, dead, limp in her hands. Its head flops backward, no doubt still as warm as it was alive a few seconds previously. Road-killed rabbits are among the most common animal corpses to be seen in the lanes around our village (figure 6.1) I guess that a car preceding hers had struck this one and sped on. Perhaps she witnessed the tumbling body. Perhaps she had run it over herself.

She carries the rabbit tenderly back to near her car, still with silent movements of distress. Then she lays it in the long grass on the verge. At that point she notices me waiting behind. I recognize her as a fellow villager. She gives a sort of tearful, apologetic half smile and wave. Then she gets underway. I was moved and, in a sense, heartened, by her grief and tender placing of the rabbit in the grass. We see each other at the occasional village function but never broach this incident. She might not even realize it was me in the other car.

This incident recalls Barry Lopez's moving essay "Apologia," where the author describes doing just this for a whole series of road-killed animals encountered on a single journey:

> A few miles east of home in the Cascades I slow down and pull over for two raccoons, sprawled still as stones in the road. I carry them to the side and lay them in sunshot, windblown grass in the barrow pit. In eastern Oregon, along U.S. 20, black-tailed jackrabbits lie like welts of sod—three, four, then a fifth. By the bridge over Jordan Creek, just shy of the Idaho border in the drainage of the Owyhee River, a crumpled adolescent porcupine leers up almost maniacally over its blood-flecked teeth. I carry each one away from the pavement into a cover of grass or brush out of decency, I think. And worry. Who are these animals, their lights gone out? What journeys have fallen apart here? (Lopez 1998, 133)

Commenting on this passage, Scottish poet John Burnside (2012) observes that to "handle another animal in this way is to reassert one's own, usually concealed bond with the creaturely. Because such handling demands tact and real tenderness, it becomes a highly charged event, an assumption of responsibility and a declaration not of guilt, which is something else, but penitence."

"Wild" spaces, as Rose acknowledges, can themselves become sites for the emergence of alternatives to the regimes of violence, dispossession, and death that produce them: "Alternatives arise unexpectedly in relationships among people and between people and place. Alternatives are entangled in the midst of the wild, and may depend on the wild even as they resist it" (2004, 6).[11] Yet what is particularly striking about Owain's encounter with the woman and the road-killed rabbit is that her tender concern was evidently a source of embarrassment, a quasi-covert act—one that implicitly challenges the systems of domination that structure so many everyday dimensions of human-nonhuman relations.

MITIGATION AND MOURNING

There are, of course, several ways in which the incidence of roadkill can be mitigated: individuals might choose to drive more slowly, especially at night, and this can be encouraged by appropriate signage. Culverts, underpasses, and overpasses, in combination with appropriate fencing, are being added to enable animals to more safely negotiate human roadways, as proposed by advocates of the "permeable highway" since the 1970s (Kroll 2015). Meanwhile, communities of carers have been called into being to tend injured animals and, in Australia, to hand-rear the young of female marsupials who have survived their mother's death on the road.

Yet the precondition for the normalization of such mitigation strategies, conceived as part of a wider movement to reduce adverse human impacts on our Earth others, is a fundamental ethico-political shift that, as one marsupial foster mother, ecofeminist philosopher Val Plumwood, put it, would resituate nonhumans in ethical terms, as the necessary counterpart to resituating humans ecologically (2002, 8–9). In Levinasian language (as read, with Rose, through Judith Butler), this would entail restoring to animals the privilege of the face, which "'awakens us to the precariousness of the lives of others, and thereby to the precariousness of all life'" (Rose 2017, 11). With respect to roadkill, this might begin with cultivating practices of honoring the dead, in pointed opposition to the current status of road-killed animals (and, with the exception of domestic companions, animals in general) as "ungrievable" (Butler 2004).

There is a memorial in Bath (United Kingdom) "to lives lost and broken on our roads in the South West" (figure 6.2). There is no indication of who erected it. The emblem on the plaque is an abstract representation of a dove drawn out of the curl of a road. It has road markings as part of the design. On reflection, it looks like a dove that has been run over, yet that is clearly not the point, for its meaning is purely symbolic. Instead of appropriating the image

125

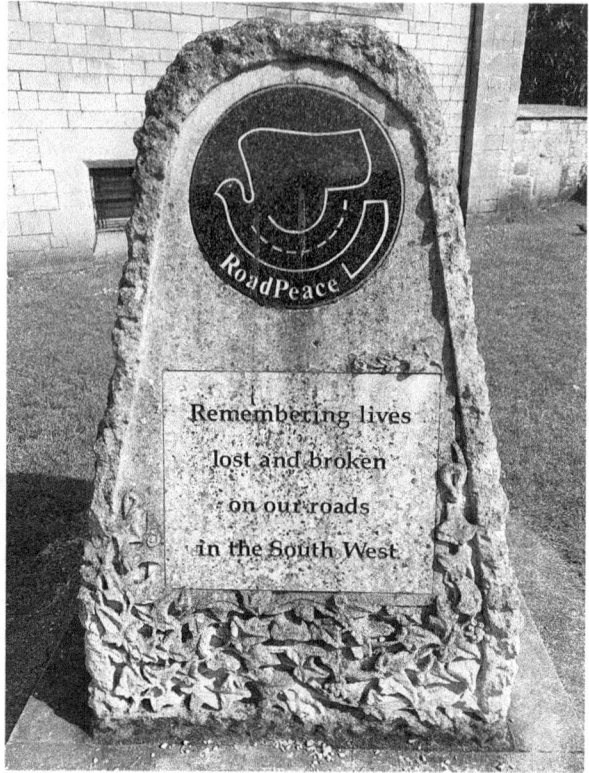

6.2 Road fatality memorial, Bath, 2016. © OWAIN JONES.

of the animal for the purpose of exclusively human remembrance, veiling the other-than-human "lives lost and broken," we propose multispecies modes of memorialization, in which the quest for "RoadPeace" is extended to all creatures, as suggested in our image of the cruciform pigeon (figure 6.3), which we have elsewhere superimposed on the purely symbolic dove in our photo of the road fatality memorial (image not available). Such memorials could be considered acts of "penitential witness" (Hatley 2011) and might be accompanied by public forms of the private rituals that are possibly more common than we know.

But they might also take the form of confronting artworks, such as Australian artist John Reid's startling *Performance for 25 Passing Vehicles* (figure 6.4), in which he posed naked at the opposite end of a road sign from a dead kangaroo—at the end pointing to a posher destination but with his human body echoing the shape of the animal other—on the Newell Highway while

126

KATE RIGBY AND OWAIN JONES

6.3 Cruciform pigeon, 2015. © OWAIN JONES.

6.4 John Reid, *Performance for 25 Passing Vehicles, Newell Highway, NSW*, 1989. Gelatin silver print, 48 × 143 cm. © JOHN REID.

twenty-five vehicles, most of them trucks, sailed right on by without so much as varying their speed—a testament, Reid speculates, "to the ease at which we can differentiate between art and life" (2014, n.p.). And yet the photographic record remains as a powerful statement of solidarity with the animal dead, comprising a kind of interspecies "liturgy," in Hatley's terms: a "mode of expression . . . in which one would speak 'for another,' not in the sense of speaking in place of the other but rather in the sense of speaking as a mode of service to the other" (this volume).

For Reid (2014), "the work addresses our high-energy, high-speed careless life style and reasserts the proposition that our fate is bound to the fate of other life around us. . . . Subject to the messages of my own work, each time I see a reproduction of this image I renew my commitment to a nighttime curfew for driving in wildlife territory. Despite this I am guilty of killing animals in the course of my personal transportation. I need a new ethical testament on this important matter."[12]

ANIMAL AGENCY

Yet it is also important to avoid perpetuating a colonizing gesture by construing animals purely as victims of motorized transportation.

Roads provide affordances of various kinds for some animals. Birds are often standing and pecking about in the lanes where we live. We think they

128

are gathering grit for their gizzards. On occasion in the laneways one can be lucky enough to end up driving behind a hunting sparrow hawk. They fly low and fast, just above the tarmac, and then, expressing a stunning hunting technique, suddenly flip over the hedge or through a gateway to surprise a blackbird or some other smaller bird that is their preferred prey. Road verges, especially if left unmown, can become wildlife corridors, with wildflowers providing nectar for pollinators and grasses that are food for grazing animals.[13] Meanwhile, scavengers can derive benefit from those who have died, so long as their corpses are removed from the road to reduce the risk to those seeking to make a meal of the dead. This might be especially valuable where animals are stocked indoors, reducing the amount of carrion in the countryside, which is part of the food chain for buzzards, crows, foxes, and others. As Jonathan Clark (2017) has observed in articulating "an ethical approach to roadkill," "Adopting an ecological perspective helps us think about death and decomposition in a more positive way. Instead of fixating on the sight or smell of the rotting carcass, or on the violent death that produced it, a wider, ecological vision enables us to appreciate that a carcass is also a source of life."

While liturgical acts of penitential witness draw us into community with (other) animals as mourners (recalling that we cannot assume that we are the only ones who grieve for lost loved ones), so, too, might the respectful consumption of roadkill affirm our kinship with fellow scavengers. Indeed, for meat eaters, this is probably the most ethical way to come by animal flesh and certainly is preferable to the barbarity of factory farming.

DEFAMILIARIZING THE DEATHZONE, REFUSING COLDHEARTEDNESS

While our emphasis throughout this essay has been on human responseability and animal grievability in the matter of roadkill, it is only by affirming animals' independent agency, together with their ethical considerability, that we might move toward creating more life-sustaining modes of multispecies mobility across shared spaces.

As we have been writing this chapter, we have become much more aware of and uncomfortable with the whole notion and practice of motorized transport—especially sole car journeys. The cities where we live are badly clogged with cars, and roadways form a dense, dominating network on the landscape. Where the roads are not clogged, the speed and violence are unnerving. We are fleshy bipedal creatures who routinely propel ourselves in relatively huge, complicated, powerful, violent, and costly machines, at the expense of the environment and other species (and frequently ourselves). The car and its speed and violence are becoming strange to us.

Clearly, wide-ranging structural changes (political, economic, social, and technological, as well as cultural) are needed to redress the destructive impacts of those motorized transportation systems that are now proliferating around the world. In the meantime, we want to end by affirming the pertinence of what Rose has written regarding other deathzones with respect to the deathzone that is made manifest in the mangled bodies of road-killed animals: "The expression of our ethical lives will be visible in how we inhabit the deathzone: how we call out, how we refuse to abandon others, how we refuse hard-heartedness, and thus how we embrace the precious beauty of the home of life" (2017, 4).

NOTES

1. This segment is adapted from KR's editorial profile, as posted on the old *Environmental Humanities* journal website (Rigby 2014).

2. There is evidence, not only of grief, but also of something akin to funeral rites for the dead among some animals, including African elephants, dolphins, and other primates. See Bekoff (2009); Harrod (2014); and Ritter (2007).

3. On the common disavowal of cross-species kinship, see also Colin Dayan (this volume).

4. A high-resolution photographic reproduction of the original, which is held in the National Gallery in London, can be viewed online. Accessed October 8, 2019. https://www.nationalgallery.org.uk/paintings/joseph-mallord-william-turner-rain -steam-and-speed-the-great-western-railway.

5. On animal affordances in urban environments, see, e.g., Wolch (2002); C. Palmer (2003); and Thomson (2007).

6. On the distinction between "quiet" and "wild" country, see Rose (2004, 3–4). See also Haraway, this volume.

7. On this nexus, see also James Hatley, this volume, who shows that "what begins, then, as Buffalo genocide culminates in prairie ecocide, as the entire world in which Buffalo functioned as an ecological kind is in turn unraveled."

8. This report is also cited by Kroll (2015, 6).

9. John Burnside (2012) notes that this game became a news item when US troops were described playing a modified version of it during the Desert Storm campaign. According to the Roadkill Bingo website, "The Sergeant explained the Roadkill Bingo rules: 'If your vehicle hits an animal, the games [sic] is over' and announced some critical substitutions required to play the game on the Main Supply Route, (MSR Dodge) to Daharan. 'Abandoned cars, camels and empty water bottles were substituted for the "*deer*", "*rabbit*" and "*skunk*" on the West Coast version'" (Roadkill Bingo Co., n.d.).

10. In our commitment to documenting such encounters as a step toward a practice of bearing witness, we snapped a photo of what remained of this hapless creature. Fearing that reproducing it here would perpetuate or deepen the disrespect the deer had already suffered, however, we have decided to withhold this image, and we include the others with a sense of ethical unease.

11. In her contribution to this volume, Haraway discusses such alternatives in the work of the artist Patricia Piccinini.

12. Among a growing number of other artists whose work raises salient questions about the phenomenon of roadkill are Kimberley Witham, Sophie Raynor, and Steve Baker. See, e.g., Little (2016); ABC Radio Darwin (2017); and Baker (n.d.).

13. In the United Kingdom, there are plans to incorporate road verges into conservation strategy. See Barkham (2019).

REFERENCES

ABC Radio Darwin. 2017. "Apologies to Roadkill: Contemporary Art Exhibition Highlights Beauty of Dead Animals." ABC News, January 29, 2017. https://www.abc.net.au/news/2017-01-30/roadkill-inspires-contemporary-art-exhibition-katherine/8222898.

Adorno, Theodor. 1978. *Minima Moralia: Reflections from Damaged Life*. Translated by E. F. N. Jephcott. London: Verso.

Baker, Steve. n.d. "Roadside." Steve Baker's website. Accessed October 31, 2017. http://steve-baker.com/artwork/roadside/.

Barkham, Patrick. 2019. "UK Roadsides on Verge of Becoming Wildlife Corridors, Say Experts." *Guardian*, September 27, 2019. https://www.theguardian.com/environment/2019/sep/27/uk-roadsides-verge-wildlife-corridors-guidelines-wildflowers.

Barn Owl Trust. n.d. "Barn Owl Hazards: Major Roads." Accessed January 25, 2019. https://www.barnowltrust.org.uk/hazards-solutions/barn-owls-major-roads.

Bekoff, Marc. 2007. *The Emotional Lives of Animals*. Novato, CA: New World Library.

Bekoff, Marc. 2009. "Grief in Animals: It's Arrogant to Think We're the Only Animals Who Mourn." *Psychology Today*, Animal Emotions blog October 29, 2009. https://www.psychologytoday.com/gb/blog/animal-emotions/200910/grief-in-animals-its-arrogant-think-were-the-only-animals-who-mourn.

Bekoff, Marc, and Jessica Pierce. 2009. *Wild Justice: The Moral Lives of Animals*. Chicago: University of Chicago Press.

Burnside, John. 2012. "The Beauty of Roadkill." *New Statesman*, June 6, 2012. http://www.newstatesman.com/culture/culture/2012/06/beauty-roadkill.

Butler, Judith. 2004. *Precarious Life: The Powers of Mourning and Violence*. London: Verso.

Clark, Jonathan L. 2017. "Consider the Vulture: An Ethical Approach to Roadkill." *Discard Studies: Social Studies of Waste, Pollution and Externalities,*

December 4, 2017. https://discardstudies.com/2017/12/04/consider-the-vulture-an-ethical-approach-to-roadkill/.

Coffin, Alisa W. 2007. "From Roadkill to Road Ecology: A Review of the Ecological Effects of Roads." *Journal of Transport Ecology* 15 (5): 396–406.

Grinde, Donald A., and Bruce E. Johansen. 1995. *Ecocide of Native America: Environmental Destruction of Indian Lands and Peoples.* Santa Fe, NM: Clear Light.

Haraway, Donna. 2015. "Anthropocene, Capitalocene, Plantationocene, Chthulucene: Making Kin." *Environmental Humanities* 6 (1): 159–165.

Harrod, James B. 2014. "The Case for Chimpanzee Religion." *Journal for the Study of Religion, Nature and Culture* 8 (1): 16–25.

Hatley, James. 2011. "Blaspheming Humans: Levinasian Politics and *The Cove.*" *Environmental Philosophy* 8 (2): 1–21.

Huijser, Marcel P., P. McGowen, J. Fuller, A. Hardy, A. Kociolek, A. P. Clevenger, D. Smith, and R. Ament. 2008. "Wildlife-Vehicle Collision Reduction Study: Report to Congress." FHWAHRT-08-034. US Department of Transportation, Federal Highway Administration. Washington, DC: US Government Printing Office.

Ingold, Tim. 2011. *Being Alive: Essays on Movement, Knowledge and Description.* London: Routledge.

International Union for Conservation of Nature (IUCN). n.d. "Koalas and Climate Change: Hungry for CO_2 Cuts." IUCN Red List Fact Sheet. Accessed June 18, 2021. https://www.iucn.org/sites/dev/files/import/downloads/fact_sheet_red_list_koala_v2.pdf

Johnston, Jay, and Fiona Probyn-Rapsey, eds. 2013. *Animal Death.* Sydney: Sydney University Press.

Knudson, Tom. 2009. "The Cost of the Biofuel Boom: Destroying Indonesia's Forests." *Yale Environment 360,* January 19, 2009. https://e360.yale.edu/features/the_cost_of_the_biofuel_boom_destroying_indonesias_forests.

Kroll, Gary. 2015. "An Environmental History of Roadkill: Road Ecology and the Making of the Permeable Highway." *Environmental History* 20 (1): 4–28.

Lawton, Graham. 2018. "Road Kill." *New Scientist,* September 1, 2018, 36–41.

Levinas, Emmanuel. 1988. "Useless Suffering." In *The Provocation of Levinas: Rethinking the Other,* edited by Robert Bernasconi and David Wood, 156–167. London: Routledge.

Levinas, Emmanuel. 1989. "Ethics as First Philosophy." In *The Levinas Reader,* edited by Sean Hand, 75–87. Oxford: Blackwell.

Little, Becky. 2016. "Making Ethical Art from Dead Animals." *National Geographic,* February 17, 2016. https://www.nationalgeographic.com/adventure/article/160217-video-taxidermy-art-animals-death-ethics.

Lopez, Barry. 1998. "Apologia." In *About This Life: Journeys on the Threshold of Memory,* 113–118. New York: Vintage.

Monahan, Linda. 2016. "Mourning the Mundane: Memorializing Road-Killed Animals in North America." In *Mourning Animals: Rituals and Practices Surrounding*

Animal Death, edited by Margo Demello, 151–158. East Lansing: Michigan
State University Press.

Palmer, Clare. 2003. "Colonization, Urbanization, and Animals." *Philosophy and Geography* 6 (1): 47–58.

Palmer, Sue. 2008. "Transience 1. Oh—Bird." May 22, 2008. YouTube video, 0:45.
https://www.youtube.com/watch?v=gtMaOooknbo.

Pindar, Ian, and Paul Sutton. 2000. "Translators' Introduction." In *The Three Ecologies*, by Félix Guattari, 1–20. translated by Ian Pindar and Paul Sutton.
London: Athlone.

Plumwood, Val. 2002. *Environmental Culture: The Ecological Crisis of Reason.* London: Routledge.

Reid, John. 2014. "Spotlight: Road Kill." *Plumwood Mountain: An Australian Journal of Ecopoetry and Ecopoetics* 5 (2): n.p.

Rigby, Kate. 2005. "(Not) by Design: Utopian Moments in the Creation of Canberra." In "Imagining the Future: Utopia and Dystopia," edited by Andrew Milner, Matthew Ryan, and Robert Savage. Special issue, *Arena Journal*, n.s., nos. 25-26 (Fall): 155–177.

Rigby, Kate. 2014. Editorial profile. *Environmental Humanities* journal website, January 18, 2014. Accessed September 1, 2017. http://environmentalhumanities.
org/2014/01/18/editorial-profile-kate-rigby/ (no longer available online).

Ritter, Fabian. 2007. "Behavioural Responses of Rough-Toothed Dolphins to a Dead Newborn Calf." *Marine Mammal Science* 23 (2): 429–433.

Roadkill Bingo Co. n.d. "Roadkill Bingo Played during Operation Desert Storm."
Accessed October 8, 2019. http://www.netads.com/tccc/ds.html.

Rose, Deborah Bird. 2004. *Reports from a Wild Country: Ethics for Decolonisation.*
Sydney: University of New South Wales Press.

Rose, Deborah Bird. 2011. *Wild Dog Dreaming: Love and Extinction.* Charlottesville:
University of Virginia Press.

Rose, Deborah Bird. 2013. "In the Shadow of All This Death." In *Animal Death*,
edited by Jay Johnston and Fiona Probyn-Rapsey, 1–20. Sydney: Sydney
University Press.

Rose, Deborah Bird. 2017. "Shimmer: When All You Love Is Being Trashed." In *Arts of Living on a Damaged Planet*, edited by Anna Tsing, Heather Swanson, Elaine Gan, and Nils Bubandt, G51–63. Minneapolis: University of Minnesota Press.

Simmons, James R. 1938. *Feathers and Fur on the Turnpike.* Boston: Christopher Publishing House.

Soron, Dennis. 2011. "Road Kill: Commodity Fetishism and Structural Violence."
In *Critical Theory and Animal Liberation*, edited by John Sanbonmatsu, 55–70.
New York: Rowman and Littlefield.

Taylor, Ken. 2006. *Canberra: City in the Landscape.* Broadway, NSW: Halstead.

Taylor-Brown, Alyce, Rosie Booth, Amber Gillett, Erica Mealy, Steven M. Ogbourne, Adam Polkinghorne, and Gabriel C. Conroy. 2019. "The Impact of Human Activities on Australian Wildlife." *PLoS ONE* 14 (1): n.p. https://
journals.plos.org/plosone/article?id=10.1371/journal.pone.0206958

Thomson, Melanie S. 2007. "Placing the Wild in the City: 'Thinking with' Melbourne's Bats." *Society and Animals* 15 (1): 79–95.

Uexküll, Jacob von. 2010. *A Foray into the Worlds of Animals and Humans, with a Theory of Meaning*. Translated by Joseph D. O'Neill. Minneapolis: University of Minnesota Press.

van Dooren, Thom, Eben Kirksey, and Ursula Münster. 2016. "Multispecies Studies: Cultivating Arts of Attentiveness." *Environmental Humanities* 8 (1): 1–23.

van Dooren, Thom, and Deborah Bird Rose. 2016. "Lively Ethography: Storying Animist Worlds." *Environmental Humanities* 8 (1): 77–94.

Wolch, Jennifer. 2002. "Anima Urbis." *Progress in Human Geography* 26 (6): 721–742.

KATE RIGBY AND OWAIN JONES

AFTER NATURE

SEVEN

Totemism Revisited

STEPHEN MUECKE

Astonishing, isn't it, that the one big in-your-face fact—that "totems" are your kin in a world of sentient beings—just never hit the horizon!
—DEBORAH BIRD ROSE, September 2, 2018

TOTEMISM HAS HAD AN EXTENSIVE career in anthropology, ever since the Ojibwe (Canada and the northern midwestern United States) word *ototeman* first entered English in the late eighteenth century (Descola 2013, 167). Totems caught the popular imagination after many of the founding fathers of anthropology wrote books on the subject (Sir James Frazer, Émile Durkheim, Alfred Radcliffe-Brown, Claude Lévi-Strauss . . . not to mention Sigmund Freud as well), and totemism has been seen as a basis for primitive religion, joining the fetish as an object of modernist iconoclasm (Latour 2010). Yes, the Moderns (as Bruno Latour calls them) can't take seriously

Indigenous peoples' totemic *practices* but take really seriously *their own belief* that these totems are symbolic (of something else, something more "profound" that fits the Moderns' analytic and conceptual frameworks) or that they are "functioning" to organize society. Deborah Bird Rose thought quite differently about totemism, as she came to describe it as "a common property institution for long-term ecological management" (2013, 127). But she had already been thinking before 1992, in her pioneering fashion, about "a more thorough analysis of Dreaming ecology and Aboriginal and European constructs of 'nature' and productivity'" (Rose 1992, 237).

When Debbie came to Australia in 1980 to do the doctoral work that became *Dingo Makes Us Human* (1992), she would have been well aware that she was landing on a continent whose cultures had long been characterized as totemic, initially via what Durkheim derived from his reading of Walter Baldwin Spencer and Francis James Gillen (Watts Miller 2012). The word *totem* is not indexed in *Dingo Makes Us Human*, but the term for "matrimoieties" among the people at Yarralin is *ngurlu*: "*Ngurlu* is a relationship between people and one or more plant or animal species. People of the same *ngurlu* share the same flesh with each other and with their *ngurlu* species" (Rose 1992, 82). This is a fairly standard definition of a totemic relationship: beings of different appearance but with the same life force. They have a literal and intimate relationship rather than a figurative or representative one; an inalienable life force flows through all members of a totemic network. We learn from Deborah that her ngurlu is flying fox in a matrilineal line: "My skin is Namija. I was also assigned flying fox *ngurlu* on the basis of my close relationship with my 'sister,' Mirmir. She is flying fox because her mother and her mother's mother are flying fox" (1992, 82). But "the particular species with which one's *ngurlu* is identified is called one's *warpiri*" (83), and there are especially intense relationships associated with them. Wisely, Deborah resisted conflating ngurlu and warpiri under the heading of "totem" because these concepts that inalienably link humans and nonhumans are plural and complicated.

The European system that was trying to come to terms with these exotic "beliefs" had, post-Enlightenment, settled into what Philippe Descola calls *naturalism*, "the coexistence of a single unifying nature and a multiplicity of cultures" (2013, 146). It establishes a material continuity "out there" in nature, where everything is composed of basically the same stuff, while only the human has the privilege of interiority or a soul. Anthropology itself was founded on this naturalist ontology based on the separation of nature and culture, and to this day many of its practitioners can't think without it. After

136

STEPHEN MUECKE

all, anthropology is the study of *human* society, by definition, and in its traditional form, it is predicated on the nature-culture division, as Deborah understood well before her important article "Common Property Regimes in Aboriginal Australia: Totemism Revisited" was published in 2013: "I believe that we must consider that this project, of distinguishing civilisation from savagery, and culture from nature, was given special urgency by the pressure placed on key concepts of western thought under the intellectual revolution taking place in conjunction with secularisation and Darwinian theory. A *key feature of western thought since the Enlightenment, the disjunction between nature and culture,* was powerfully threatened by evolutionary theory, for if humans are descended from animals, where is the boundary between them?" (2013, 132, my emphasis).[1] Only recently have we seen the advent of multispecies ethnography, a reconfiguration with which anthropology can recognize that we live with nonhumans as viable actors; its attribution of *agency* to animals and plants is restorative of what has been erased by naturalism, for it insists that nonhuman lives relate (to each other and to humans) in specific, meaningful ways (Mitchell 2002). I say "erased" because Christianity suppressed paganism (see Tsing, this volume), the modern sciences suppressed ancient know-how, and today only children's stories and fantastic genres retain the vestiges of animal agency and interiority.

It is very clear why Lévi-Strauss, for example, could not see beyond the naturalist ontology. He saw the discontinuities of "the natural world" (different types of birds, trees, etc.) as being used by people as symbols to index social classifications, so that people, who would otherwise resemble each other, can "create differences among themselves" (Descola 2013, 108). So, he didn't think totemism was anything real but rather an intellectual construction, whereby primitive peoples chose natural species (as totems) "not because they are 'good to eat' but because they are 'good to think'" (Descola 2013, 89).

The nature-culture opposition was so firmly embedded as axiomatic in Lévi-Strauss's structuralist system and so firmly absent in so-called totemic systems that Lévi-Strauss had to reject totemism (and the way it expresses nature-culture continuities) as a mere intellectual plaything, as a "mystification" (Descola 2013, 144). In their critique of structuralism, Gilles Deleuze and Félix Guattari say, "It is no longer a question of instituting a serial organisation of the imaginary, but instead a structural order of understanding. It is no longer a question of graduating resemblances, ultimately arriving at an identification of Man and Animal at the heart of a mystical participation" (1988, 236). Then they put the structuralist homology more explicitly: "A

137

man can never say: 'I am a bull, a wolf . . .' But he can say: 'I am to a woman what a bull is to a cow, I am to another man what the wolf is to a sheep.' Structuralism represents a great revolution; the whole world becomes more relational" (237).

We know from the work of Eduardo Viveiros de Castro (2014) that many, perhaps most, Indigenous societies did not, and do not, operate with a nature-culture opposition. There is typically no word for nature as a whole, as something distant, or as a backdrop to our human-centric dramas. In the modern European version of nature, humans' links to nonhumans were broken and relegated to myth: animals or plants were no longer ancestors, sacred or part of the extended kinship system, living beings with whom one has rights and obligations. Nature was constructed as composed of nonactive materials, either dead or about to be dead, sitting passively out there as resources for humans to profit from.

UNIVERSES AND MULTIVERSES

This vision of human societies opposed to a singular material nature leaves us with only one reality to deal with. European naturalism constructs what ethnopsychiatrist Tobie Nathan calls a "single universe society" (Nathan 2018; de la Cadena and Blaser 2018), a *uni-verse*, if you like, as opposed to William James's *pluriverse*. So-called totemic or animist societies are what Nathan would call "multiple universe societies," and what pagan European life was more like before the recent dominance of naturalism. In such a world made up of multiple realities, you would have to ask what it is like to live, for instance, with gods or the spirits of ancestors. It is not as if you and they are part of *one society*, as if you can walk to the train in the morning and wave to your great-great-grandmother working in the fields. Or that you are astounded to find that the spirit of Julius Caesar is a competitor for the job you are applying for. No, it is rather that there would be, in any multiple universe society—animist or totemic—elaborate rituals and techniques for making contact with ancestor spirits. If one has to enter another "world" (a church, for instance, in contemporary contexts) to interact with the world of spirits and ancestors, single universe societies tend to treat this as the realm of (mere) belief, without the kinds of ecological connections that a totemic system makes explicit. So, to accept religion as a mode of existence with its own rules, as *another* part of a more complex real world, is to go some way toward restoring the pluriverse. And societies with so-called totemism have many gods, so to speak, rather than one: the elevation of a singular god in the

138

Abrahamic religions facilitated a dislocation from place(s) and the mobilization of proselytizing religions of the book. It is not important that Moses handed the tablets down from a particular mountain, Mount Sinai, but that the law was written and could be distributed.[2] Totems always belong to their territories, but they are not necessarily rigid. The famous anthropologist Marshall Sahlins, in his discussion of the Manambu of New Guinea, encourages us to embrace a great fluidity in the definitions of various "totems," and even in their politics, that extends the idea of totem to the present:

> The roster of totems is characteristically expanded by political moves that appropriate beings from more powerful cultural realms beyond it. . . . So when a certain Manambu subclan claimed the clothing of colonial officials as one of its totems—on the ground that its honorific address form was homonymous with the term for the European-introduced laplap—it was trumped by a rival subclan who claimed the Queen herself for their totem— on the ground that the Australian government crest on school exercise books depicted one of its own traditional totems, the cassowary. (Actually, it was an emu, the Australian colonials' own native totem.). (2014, 285)

Sahlins's analysis gives us permission, in a way, to see totemic relations in their contemporary political fluidity and not just as vestiges of primitive superstition. There is a real totemic logic, as I shall argue in conclusion, and it could be deployed more fully once again, "revisited" more seriously, as Debbie says. Sahlins mentions the emu—perhaps half jesting, as his references jump from the exercise book to the queen to the cassowary to the emu—as the totem of settler society. The emu and the kangaroo stand opposed to each other on the Australian coat of arms, the very symbol of state power. As these images of unique Australian fauna are brought into society, they, too, are totemic relations to the extent that they *are made into the essence of Australian nationhood* by being installed at the very top of its power hierarchy, which is actually an inversion of the animals' disposable power, which at the moment is virtually nil.[3] It thus tells a story of their particular subjugation in this set of colonies, which unified under their symbol to become a nation in 1901. And it speaks more generally of the subjugation of nature by Man's dominion, as ordained in Eden by the singular God. The "magic of the state," as anthropologist Michael Taussig (1997) would say, is condensed into these animal symbols that we don't notice anymore, that we treat as merely symbolic, because we "know" the operations of power to be really happening elsewhere. I can imagine, though, that Aboriginal people have sometimes looked at these totemic figures high on the wall of the High Court or Parliament House, or on a police badge, in a slightly different way, possibly as *their* totems, which would distribute the operations of their *law* differently: to the partial authority of people belonging to an emu or kangaroo clan, not to a "whole society" from the top down. They might wonder how the emu and kangaroo totemic clans got to dominate the whole country.

BEING, BECOMING, AND BELONGING

There are three verbs I have to experiment with before I can get to my practical example: *being, becoming,* and *belonging.* They are also concepts, and as concepts I want to see what kind of work they do in relating us language users to our worlds. As concepts they can be generative; they help make our worlds the way they are. Being, of course, is at the heart of Western existentialist philosophies, discussed by Isabelle Stengers in this volume, and of course I won't be delving into Martin Heidegger and Jean-Paul Sartre, with their habits of thinking alone and thinking that truth is "the child of protracted solitude" (Foucault 1984, 72), gloomily pondering existence and nothingness.

It is enormously enlightening to take the concept of existence to Indigenous Australia and watch it sink out of sight. Australian Aboriginal philosophies are not existentialist. In an obvious way, this is marked by the common absence of the verb "to be." "To be or not to be" is *not* the question, making Hamlet's famous speech very difficult to translate. Belonging is far more important, and this is often marked by a comitative suffix, like *-tjara*, meaning "having" or "with"—as in, Pitjantjatjara speakers are those who have *pitjantja* as their word for "going."

I can, with my three verbs, roughly sketch a genealogy of the uptake of totemism. We saw, with the structuralist appropriation, hinging around the all-important nature-culture divide operating in a naturalist ontological frame, that human *beings* used other minor beings to structure their thought, thus enriching that internal life that it was their destiny to fulfill. There is no doubt that human culture was central in this configuration, and nonhuman nature was there as a support act.

Then, taking Deleuze and Guattari as poststructuralists, it could be argued that their concept of *becomings* might stand as a critique, or replacement, for structuralist relations of *beings* as "internal homologies." They say that "Levi-Strauss is always encountering these rapid acts by which a human becomes an animal at the same time as the animal becomes . . . (Becomes what? Human, or something else?). It is always possible to try to explain these blocks of becoming by a correspondence between two relations, but to do so most

140

STEPHEN MUECKE

certainly impoverishes the phenomenon under study" (1988, 237). They elaborate on the value of becomings: "Becomings-animal are neither dreams nor phantasies. They are perfectly real. But which reality is at issue here? For if becoming animal does not consist in playing animal or imitating an animal, it is clear that the human being does not 'really' become an animal any more than the animal 'really' becomes something else. Becoming produces nothing other than itself. We fall into a false alternative if we say that you either imitate or you are. What is real is the becoming itself, the block of becoming, not the supposedly fixed terms through which that which becomes passes" (238). Becomings are thus a useful poststructuralist correction. They eschew fixed identities; they are real, and they embrace metamorphic imaginaries; they are attractively emancipatory because becomings can only emerge from minoritarian positions; they allow for symbiosis (as opposed to Darwinism): "There is a block of becoming that snaps up the wasp and the orchid, but from which no wasp-orchid can ever descend" (238). The wasp-orchid relationship is not classically totemic, but there is a mutual becoming. Neither is dominant in their symbiotic life. Likewise, the men of the pelican totem look after that animal, and there are mutual becomings in more than one way: when the men dress up with pelican headdresses for the pelican ceremony and sing the songs, when the men follow the seasonal life cycle of pelicans and care for them, then the life cycle of the pelicans starts to govern the life of the clansmen in turn. Perhaps this is what Barbara Glowczewski means by *totemic becomings*, as she picks up on the Deleuzo-Guattarian concept.

Glowczewski's 2015 book, *Totemic Becomings*, refuses any essentialist definition of totem, recognizing that an Indigenous Australian subject is "always a constellation of totems" (136), that these totems "reticulate" as nonhierarchical networks. She goes on to say, very importantly, "There is no such thing as 'the environment' but simply an elongation in the form of metamorphoses" (145) so that the Indigenous subject constantly flashes between being, say, a woman, a landform, an animal, and a constellation in the sky. A cosmopolitical understanding is thus something many Indigenous peoples already had as a massive intellectual achievement, something that Europeans unwisely undid when they invented the concept of nature as a way to classify nonhuman life, the better to treat it as exploitable dead matter.

Because human beings are not doing everything on their own, becomings have done the enormously useful work of restoring certain nature-culture continuities, even though, as I said, they embraced a generalist emancipatory program, which is essentially modernist. To be modern is to be free to roam, without attachments to place. As long as Deleuze and Guattari don't make

141

explicit where they are coming from in their own text (someone has to write a critical ethnography that describes how their discourse emerged among Parisian intellectual elites post-1968, and so on), they remain complicit in a modernist will-to-expand.[4] The aspiration to universalize has nothing inherently wrong with it, to the extent that it can mean finding new relevance in different contexts. Indigenous knowledges, often kept local by the overarching operations of universalizing (social) sciences, have also, in recent years, found relevant nonlocal connections.

But I suspect that the intellectual exhilaration about becomings has been short-lived, perhaps because there is nothing very pragmatic about a becoming—Isabelle Stengers (2005), who was influenced by Deleuze and Guattari, nonetheless preferred to talk of "ecologies of practices." And Debbie and I, conscious of the significance of Aboriginal ontologies of place, might prefer to ask where this wasp-orchid becoming is located. Is it in Europe? It can't happen everywhere; it must have a territory or territories that it *belongs* to, so that we can recognize that place as the place of the wasp-orchid becomings. You can see where I am heading using language like this: it sounds like Australian literature, or rather what that literature is in the process of becoming when it listens to the great traditions of the continent (Muecke 2013).

WHAT'S IT GOT GOING FOR IT?

To be properly descriptive we should ask about the attributes of a being or thing that keep it alive as it is, ask what it *has* rather than what it *is*, pay attention to prepositions like *with* and to comitative suffixes. This takes me to my third verb, *belonging*, a concept that is central to the much-elaborated ontologies of place in Australian Aboriginal thought and its commentaries. Totemic *belongings* or attachments are what Indigenous Australian societies "have got going for them" as pretty robust and long-lived systems. The totemic principle of sharing one's life with a nonhuman (plant, animal, etc.) is not only magical (as it is constantly performed as Dreaming metamorphoses) but pragmatic and ecological. Deborah Bird Rose has revisited totemism precisely in this way. We saw how she defines totemism as "a common property institution for long-term ecological management." *Common property* means here what is held in common by a society of humans and nonhumans, and *management* a form of governance that distributes rights and responsibilities. At a certain time of year, a clan, identified totemically, will look after an animal resource (say, red kangaroo) that is coming into season. At that time there may be a ceremonial performance where they are responsible for singing the red kangaroo increase song, and so on and so forth for different clans and different species within the territory. It is distributed rather than hierarchical authority. The red kangaroo men and the red kangaroo belong to each other and belong to a part of the country, and there is a red kangaroo ancestor (the *krantji* myth famously explored by A. E. Newsome [1980] in Central Australia) traveling through Arrernte country. It is a multiple set of mutual belongings held in a beautiful tension. The "common property" lies in the ways these entities belong to each other, with the practical outcome that kangaroo-humans and kangaroos look after each other on the basis of what each is capable of doing. The same logic applies to honey ant or bush onion clans, whose responsibility and activity arise at different times of the year and in different parts of the country.

Daisy Bates wrote a lot about totems in Broome at the turn of the twentieth century; she could have been influenced in her language by Sir James Frazer's *Golden Bough*, which was published in 1890. She makes explicit the notion of inalienable shared life, using a Frazer-like concept of sympathetic magic, under the heading of *ngargulala*, a now-unused word for "totem" in the West Kimberley:

> A special circumstance attaching to the cave, rock, spring and other non-edible totems, gives them a certain significance, and still more completely identifies them with their owners. If a cave in some district which is the Ngargulala totem of a man, falls in, or a portion becomes loosened, the cave totem man will die. If the spring which is his totem dries up, the spring totem man follows it, if a rock splits or breaks, the rock totem man dies soon afterwards. If the totem is any kind of seed, and the seed fails to come in its season, the seed totem person will die (Bates n.d., 169).

Are these Goolarabooloo people deluded? Surely they don't believe in this kind of sympathetic magic, that if a seed dies, the seed man dies with it? It is easy to ridicule isolated statements as mere belief, without explaining the whole ecology of practices that goes with the statement. Such ridicule always presumes that a more enlightened, modernist view is about to replace the superstitious belief. But one can't pull one such relationship—call it totemic—out of this world because it is supported, and has been for millennia, by a whole system of similar, self-sustaining ideas, concepts, feelings, and relationships. And it is not just in this territory, because the mob down the road will have a quite similar system.

You can counterargue, "Surely these Moderns don't believe that nature is on one side of a divide and humans have their cultures exclusively on

143

the other?" What madness! Precisely this mad scheme has accelerated the destruction of those things called natural, deprived, as they were, of their capacity to answer back—that answering back, by the way, was what the seed threatened to do to the seed man if he neglected his care for Country. Looking after the seeds might be not only common sense but a kind of rationality. When asked a fundamental question, "On what basis do human and nonhuman life coexist?," the Western "naturalist" solution is to put humans firmly in cultures, and nonhumans in nature. But the solution in so-called totemic societies, which refuse the singular concept of nature, is an extraordinary invention: totemism, which I would now define as an *expert Indigenous scientific construction pertaining to the crucial importance of the continuity of nature and culture.* While the Western system has radically divided nature from culture, the better to exploit the former, Indigenous "sciences" may have invented totemism as an extended multispecies kinship system that makes rights and responsibilities in relation to nonhumans explicit in their Law.[5]

This is what Bruno Latour, talking of being "earthbound," identifies as a challenge to "rationality" and "objectivity":

> It is hardly astonishing that the word rationality has become somewhat frightening. Before accusing ordinary people of attaching no value to the facts of which so-called rational people want to convince them, let us recall that, if they have lost all common sense, it is because they have been masterfully betrayed.
>
> To restore positive meaning to the words "realistic," "objective," "efficient," or "rational," we have to turn them away from the Global, where they have so clearly failed, and toward the Terrestrial.
>
> How can this difference in orientation be defined? The two poles are almost the same, except that the Globe grasps all things from *far away*, as if they were *external* to the social world and completely *indifferent* to human concerns. The Terrestrial grasps the same structures from *up close*, as *internal* to the collectivities and *sensitive* to human action, to which they *react* swiftly. (2018, 66–67)

To "land" on Earth once again, we shall have to be refitted, realistically, to the scale of what each territory is capable of sustaining, no longer believing the fantasies of the Moderns about endless global expansion. It seems that with totemism, Aboriginal people have a territorially sensitive and self-regulating system that worked, with all its differences from one territory to the next, over fifty thousand years.

STEPHEN MUECKE

7.1 Bernadette Trench-Thiedeman as a protesting bilby. PHOTOGRAPH BY
STEPHEN MUECKE.

THE BILBY BELONGS...

Earlier, I claimed Marshall Sahlins gave us permission to think of totemism
leaping across cultures to make a political point, as when a Manambu subclan
appropriated the queen of England as their totem. I would like to experiment with the performance activism of installation/theater artist Bernadette
Trench-Thiedeman (see figure 7.1), who learned from Goolarabooloo traditional owners, along with other antimining activists, that bilbies did indeed
belong to the country that Woodside Energy was threatening to destroy by
building a gas plant at James Price Point north of Broome, Western Australia.

How many allies were in the network continuing the process of invasion
in the West Kimberley that we now call *extraction colonialism*, carried out on
behalf of the Global Moderns (who, as you know, have no territory)? We
can count Woodside Energy, the state, the Murdoch press, the police, the
Kimberley Land Council, the Shire Council, the banks, privatized scientists
and anthropologists ... To stop them, those seeing themselves as protectors
of country had to get creative, and I want to claim Trench-Thiedeman's bilby
as being in a kind of relationship of totemic belonging, in the fluid and political sense that Sahlins suggested. No one is fooled into thinking she *is* a bilby.
She may be bilby-*becoming*, but there's no point to that becoming unless
there are bilbies around, in country, backing her up, doubling her up: "the

145

power to both double yet double endlessly, to become Other and engage the image with the reality thus energized," says Michael Taussig (1993, 255) in *Mimesis and Alterity*.[6] She gives the bilbies agency in this intense political atmosphere, not just because they *are* there, not because they can *become* other, but because they inalienably *belong* there, and the Bernie-bilby assemblage expresses human-animal entanglements as a necessary attribute of this place and a part of its ancient heritage. I am arguing that her performance is similar to that of the Goolarabooloo dancers who paint up and wear the pelican headdress when they dance the mayiarda (pelican) nurlu. The bilbies themselves were too skittish to come forward, but how eloquently they spoke through Bernie, bravely mounting the Woodside bulldozer. Her boyfriend, Malcolm Lindsay, citizen scientist, had found the bilbies with the help of the traditional owners (Lindsay 2011). Others found the hawksbill turtles; others counted the numbers of humpback whales for months, found spinner dolphins for the first time . . .

This, then, is how the antimining, green-Indigenous alliance was composed to express, and sometimes express in new ways, the nature-culture continuities that mattered to them—that "one big in-your-face fact—that 'totems' are your kin in a world of sentient beings," as Debbie wrote to me. They were up against the mining consortium, and though they may not have theorized it in this way, they were opposed to the radical nature-culture divide that was the intellectual device that enabled the mining company to be disconnected from nature, the better to extract one of its materials, methane gas.

I have argued, with Debbie, that totemism was no arbitrary or symbolic set of beliefs but was a real system in place in multiple-universe societies. It is very hard to understand within the conceptual architecture of European naturalism, which has the effect of destroying continuities across species, continuities that are not just between humans and nonhumans but also, Debbie notices, among birds: "There is also a vast range of information concerning animal behavior about which men are most vocal. Knowledge of animals, like that of plants, is tied into Dreaming Law and Dreaming identities. Associated with the emu, for example, is a set of small birds, (finches) whose presence signals waterholes and springs; they tell the emu when it is safe to put its head down to drink. Coded both as law and *ngurlu* (matrilineal identity), this knowledge also assists the hunter" (Rose 1992, 100). "Continuity is a key value," asserts Debbie, quoting W. E. H. Stanner. Aboriginal people are not (as many earlier anthropologists tended to assume) parasitical on nature, just extracting things from it; there are "regimes of rights and regimes of responsibilities" that are inseparable, Debbie says, and "they include not only the right to take resources, but also the responsibility to ensure that resources will be there in the future. Totemism appears to constitute just such a jurisprudence of responsibility and right" (Rose 2013, 131).

NOTES

1. While Debbie's article was published in 2013, it begins, "In the closing years of the twentieth century, debates in Australia about Indigenous institutions of common property ownership and management are inseparable from the highly political issues of Native Title" (127).

2. See my discussion of David Mowaljarlai in Muecke (2016, 31).

3. See Rigby and Jones, this volume.

4. The ethnography of Deleuze and Guattari's discourse could be done in the descriptive style of Ian Hunter (2016).

5. These remarks relate only to my understanding of Australian totemism, but see Descola (2013) for an extensive treatment of the topic.

6. "This excessiveness was once in the hands of seers and magicians who worked images to effect other images, who worked spirits to affect other spirits which in turn acted on the real they were the appearance of" (Taussig 1997, 255).

REFERENCES

Bates, Daisy. n.d. Daisy Bates' papers, Box 10 (totems), folio 20. National Library of Australia, Canberra.

de la Cadena, Marisol, and Mario Blaser, eds. 2018. *A World of Many Worlds*. Durham, NC: Duke University Press.

Deleuze, Gilles, and Félix Guattari. 1988. *A Thousand Plateaus: Capitalism and Schizophrenia*. London: Athlone.

Descola, Philippe. 2013. *Beyond Nature and Culture*. Translated by Janet Lloyd. Chicago: University of Chicago Press.

Foucault, Michel. 1984. "Truth and Power." In *The Foucault Reader*, edited by Paul Rabinow, 51–75. New York: Pantheon Books.

Frazer, James George. 2012. *The Golden Bough: A Study in Comparative Religion*. Cambridge: Cambridge University Press.

Glowczewski, Barbara. 2015. *Totemic Becomings: Cosmopolitics of the Dreaming/Devires totêmicos: Cosmopolítica do Sonho*. Sao Paulo: n-1.

Hunter, Ian. 2016. "Heideggerian Mathematics: Badiou's *Being and Event* as Spiritual Pedagogy." *Representations* 134 (1): 116–156.

Latour, Bruno. 2010. *On the Modern Cult of the Factish Gods*. Durham, NC: Duke University Press.

Latour, Bruno. 2018. *Down to Earth: Politics in the New Climatic Regime*. Translated by Cathy Porter. London: Polity.

Lindsay, Malcolm. 2011. "Evidence of the Greater Bilby, *Macrotis lagotis*, at the Site of the Proposed James Price Point Browse LNG Precinct." Report prepared for the Goolarabooloo and Broome No Gas Community, October 2011. https://cdn.wilderness.org.au/archive/pdf/james-price-point-bilby-report.

Mitchell, Timothy. 2002. *Rule of Experts: Egypt, Techno-Politics, Modernity.* Berkeley: University of California Press.

Muecke, Stephen. 2013. "The Great Tradition: Translating Durrudiya's Songs." In *Decolonizing the Landscape: Indigenous Cultures in Australia*, edited by Beate Neumeier and Kay Schaffer, 23–36. Cross-Culture Studies series. Amsterdam: Rodopi.

Muecke, Stephen. 2016. *The Mother's Day Protest and Other Fictocritical Essays.* London: Rowman and Littlefield International.

Nathan, Tobie. 2018. "Towards a Scientific Psychopathology." In *Doctors and Healers*, edited by Tobie Nathan and Isabelle Stengers, 2–29. Translated by Stephen Muecke. London: Polity.

Nathan, Tobie, and Isabelle Stengers. 2018. *Doctors and Healers.* Translated by Stephen Muecke. London: Polity.

Newsome, A. E. 1980. "The Eco-Mythology of the Red Kangaroo in Central Australia." *Mankind* 12 (4): 327–333.

Rose, Deborah Bird. 1992. *Dingo Makes Us Human: Life and Land in an Australian Aboriginal Culture.* Melbourne: Cambridge University Press.

Rose, Deborah Bird. 2013. "Common Property Regimes in Aboriginal Australia: Totemism Revisited." In *The Governance of Common Property in the Pacific*, edited by Peter Larmour, 127–143. Canberra: ANU Press.

Sahlins, Marshall. 2014. "On the Ontological Scheme of Beyond Nature and Culture." *Hau: Journal of Ethnographic Theory* 4 (1): 281–290.

Stengers, Isabelle. 2005. "Introductory Notes on an Ecology of Practices." *Cultural Studies Review* 11 (1): 183–196.

Taussig, Michael. 1993. *Mimesis and Alterity: A Particular History of the Senses.* New York: Routledge.

Taussig, Michael. 1997. *The Magic of the State.* New York: Routledge.

Viveiros de Castro, Eduardo. 2014. *Cannibal Metaphysics.* Edited and translated by Peter Skafish. Chicago: Univocal.

Watts Miller, William. 2012. "Durkheim's Re-imagination of Australia: A Case Study of the Relation between Theory and 'Facts.'" *L'Année sociologique* 62 (2): 329–349.

TELLING ONE'S STORY IN
THE HEARING OF BUFFALO

EIGHT

Liturgical Interventions from Beyond the Year Zero

JAMES HATLEY

AN INVITATION TO COUNTRY

THE FIRST PEOPLES BUFFALO JUMP STATE PARK is located on terrain encompassing one of the largest sites of its kind to be found on the North American continent. Consisting of an elongated sandstone cliff, shaped roughly like a horseshoe, the jump itself runs for several miles along the southern, eastern, and then northern edges of a low-lying butte. That butte in turn emerges, just barely, between two broad, flat-bottomed valleys carved out on either side by seasonal flooding of the Missouri and Sun Rivers. The country here is big sky and arid earth—a mostly treeless, windswept landscape of fenced-in grazing lands and wheat fields rising westward to meet the blue-gray reefs of limestone making up the front range of the Rockies some sixty miles distant. As one looks toward that convergence, the land begins to bunch up, as if a great hand had stuck the butt of its palm into the ground and then pushed until the earth itself buckled and broke into a maze of low-lying ridges and ravines interspersed with chunky, flat-topped buttes rimmed by basalt. To the east, the Great Plains stretch more or less unimpeded for a thousand miles. And to the west, at the very edge of this scene, always, lurking on the horizon, are those limestone teeth capped with snow, ridges and peaks jutting up and then jittering along the blue margins of the earth before all falls away into dreams and unknowing, or at least into designated wilderness and grizzly bears. The Niitsitapi, I am reminded, locate the very place of creation on those distant heights.

Montanans are fond of saying that this is God's country, as if in at least this particular place on the planet, the immensity and power, not to say the righteousness, of what is involved in its creation were still undeniably in evidence. This is arguably the case, particularly if one squints one's eyes ever so slightly so that the grandiose features of an extravagant topography take precedence. But if one focuses one's gaze more narrowly and discerningly on the intimate sites of multispecies habitation and flourishing that are characteristic of what might be termed *land* in the thought of ecologist Aldo Leopold or *Country* by the Australian Aboriginal informants of anthropologist Deborah Bird Rose, then what one encounters quickly turns out to be disconcerting and shameful. One discovers, if one looks on this place with an eye that is ecologically oriented and historically attuned, that the gloriousness of it writ large festers with wounds in its every nook and cranny.

Among the greatest of these involves the gaping hole left by the widespread extirpation and near extinction of Buffalo, the once dominant mammal of this region, whose eradication, Wade Davis has written, "resulted from a campaign of biological terrorism unparalleled in the history of the Americas" (2018, 23). This troubling act was carried out as the explicit expression of an implicit, ongoing policy of Lebensraum that quickly came to govern European settlement of this continent. On the Great Plains, the first wave of that campaign involved Buffalo genocide, as this animal was remorselessly slaughtered wherever it might be found, so that its population dropped within a few decades from some fifty million individuals to barely a thousand by 1890. In a second wave, the diverse presettlement ecosystems characterizing North America's grassland biome, a dynamic patchwork of habitats by which Buffalo, among many other living kinds, was sustained, were undone. On a given stretch of land that once provided a haven for up to 250 species of plants, only 40 would have remained after being submitted to grazing by cattle

JAMES HATLEY

and only one (namely, a monoculture crop) when regularly overturned by the plow (Manning 1995, 19). What begins, then, as Buffalo genocide culminates in prairie ecocide, as the entire world in which Buffalo functioned as an ecological kind is in turn unraveled. Indeed, in this sense, grizzly bears, cougars, wolves, and elk, now to be found living wild in mountainous habitats to the west, shared the same fate as the Buffalo. Like it, these living kinds were wiped off the face of the grasslands in which they were heretofore ecologically at home. As an entire biome was ripped out by its roots, less than 1 percent of the original tall-grass prairie grasslands, once embracing the midsection of an entire continent, was left intact.

Disconcertingly, this result is celebrated as a triumph of ingenuity and enterprise, the very mark by which America is to be understood iconically as America, graced as it is in the minds of its citizens with its amber fields of grain and purple mountain majesty. In this view of the matter, the very soil that once fed Buffalo has now been rightfully claimed and harnessed by settlement culture to feed the world. Richard Hopkins, a grass range specialist who served as the first director for the First Peoples Buffalo Jump State Park, discusses how the earth here, laid down by the retreating ice cap some ten thousand years ago, grows wheat that is unusually high in protein, just as was the case for the diverse host of native grasses on which Buffalo also previously had thrived.[1] Yet, regardless of the transformative activities of the cow and the plow, of grazing and farming, in rendering the Great Plains fruitful in a particular sense of that term, that legacy is permeated by currents of ecological diminishment and cultural displacement that continue to haunt all those who would call themselves at home in this place. Further, as the entire project of agrarian monoculture becomes increasingly tenuous economically in this area, the question of where the future might lead opens up anew possibilities for rethinking the significance of settlement itself.[2]

The establishment of the First Peoples Buffalo Jump State Park, which occurred around twenty-five years ago, functions in its own right as a moment of public critical reevaluation of settlement, even as it has been set up in turn to nurture in those who now visit it the possibilities for further investigation, reflection, and critical discernment.[3] In doing so, it provides a site in which one might not only learn about the history of the relationship of Buffalo with First Peoples but also engage in an ongoing meditation on its implications for the present and future, as one walks the paths set out on the grounds. As time spent on them quickly makes clear, even if the discrete, living bodies of Buffalo are no longer being offered physical access to this landscape, the continued presence of this living kind here is nonetheless undeniable.

151

The management plan for the park, drawn up in collaboration with representatives from more than a dozen tribal nations, "welcomes Native American use for worship and celebration and for reconnection with ancestors" (Aderhold, Monger, and Hagener 2005, 4). Richard Hopkins notes that these activities in this location have been ongoing, however surreptitiously, during the entire time in which settlement has been occurring.[4] Thus, even as Buffalo was being for the most part eradicated by settlement peoples, its palpable, spiritual presence continued to be intimately interwoven with the ceremonial life engaged in here by First Peoples. This occurred in spite of a spate of police actions and legal prohibitions carried out by federal and state governments with a view to suppressing, if not altogether eradicating, the religious practices and lifeways of First Peoples. That this site's legacy, then, is not only historical in its remembrance of how Buffalo were once present here but also ceremonial in its assertion of the continuing relevance of Buffalo to those who now visit here makes it a powerful point of inflection in rethinking anew how this living kind might surmount its near extinction, how it might regain a newfound foothold in a world that had been constructed on the very premise of Buffalo's widespread extirpation, if not its ultimate disappearance as a living kind.

For those who are identified with settlement culture, to visit these environs inevitably leads to questions about the stories one tells about oneself, particularly those in which the very shape of one's humanity is held up for others to recognize and hopefully to celebrate along with oneself. Inevitably, in my own life such stories were deeply interwoven with this landscape and the ways in which it affirmed my own standing within it. Indeed, settlement culture in general has been fixated on telling its story in this manner, as if the land had been waiting from time immemorial to receive and then affirm one's presence in it. Yet, as Jill Stauffer points out, the stories one tells of oneself come not only from one's own experience of the world but also "from what other people say to us, from the values and truths produced by whatever cultures surround us, and from unspoken affective interactions between persons living aside one another" (2015, 10). Indeed in a story well told, as Thom van Dooren and Deborah Bird Rose have argued, a plurality of voices interact with one another in such a manner that no single perspective predominates, even as each is reanimated by its entanglement in the other perspectives through which the story emerges in its telling (van Dooren 2014, 78–79; van Dooren and Rose 2016, 85). Telling a story in this sense is profoundly democratic, as an opportunity is proffered for voices to emerge in the hearing of one another that are not inevitably reducible to one another.

In a similar vein, what Stauffer would have us know is that the very capacity to tell one's story, to celebrate one's very place under the sun, was never ours alone to claim. We are always already indebted to others for the very possibility of holding forth the story of our own emergence into this earthly realm. Yet all too often settlement culture has proceeded as if it is sui generis, as if no other story told by another might inform one concerning the circumstances of one's own birth and ongoing development. Indeed, the very manner of telling settlement's story, as the following discussion makes clear, is to interrupt not only the stories of others but also the manner in which the voices who tell those stories have always been intimately intertwined from the very first word (and even before that word!) with the telling of one's own story.

This neglect of others does not apply only to other humans and their diverse cultures. As the very inauguration of the First Peoples Buffalo Jump State Park makes clear, the drawing near of more-than-human living kinds to the telling of one's story has also been disregarded. What follows is offered not so much in the spirit of a philosophical argument, although at times these do occur, as in that of an ongoing personal meditation on the circumstances of this latter neglect and what it might mean for how one goes forward in the settlement practices of telling one's story.[5] In particular, how might one come to be mindful of and so practice discernment concerning the telling of the story of one's shame in regard to Buffalo genocide? In taking up this task, the remarks that follow should be understood as beginning and ending on the cliffs of the First Peoples Buffalo Jump State Park. One should also prepare oneself to be mindful of how, as this occurs, Buffalo, both among the living and among the dead, even now, has been listening.[6]

A COUNTRY HARROWED AND HARROWING

All too often, public discussions responding to the threat of a living kind's extinction or extirpation remain narrowly focused on the thought of the possible disappearance of that living kind, along with an examination of the measures that might be necessary to avoid this outcome. In this way, the emphasis is put on the survival of a species' genotype or perhaps, if one is a bit more expansive in how one thinks of these things, its lineage. The hidden assumption in this approach is that extinction is to be understood as if it were an antiseptic or clinical event. A living kind is excised from the world in which it once existed, and while that world in the main continues, the living kind does not. As a result, even as empathy for the plight of a living kind is encouraged, the full measure of this empathy is kept tethered, so that the most troubling aspects of the violence involved remain concealed. This approach all too often defers or, worse, simply neglects precisely how the threatened anthropogenic extinction or extirpation of a particular living kind involves not only the question of its prospective dematerialization but also the ongoing deanimation of the very world in which that living kind has heretofore found itself at home. As Thom van Dooren has pointed out, anthropogenic extinction of a living kind is not to be characterized as a scalpel excising one creature from among the many but as a dull knife tearing at and shredding the multiple threads of entanglement by which a living kind has previously both sustained its world and been sustained by it.[7] A living kind, then, is not so much excised from as shredded up and hacked out of its country, and the effect of this on its former habitat and those other living kinds—both human and more than human—with whom that habitat was shared is often as catastrophic as it was for the living kind itself.

As a result, any manner of thinking about anthropogenic species extinction in which one defers or overlooks how the deanimation of country attends upon the loss of a living kind is already hardly innocent. But intensifying this situation, particularly in the settlement context, is how the very language in which this discussion takes place is itself rife with deanimation of another sort, one to be characterized and understood not merely through the dynamics of ecosystem processes but also as a repercussion of a moral or spiritual crisis, as the human beings involved, whether actively or passively, in the conscious and willful carrying out of anthropogenic extinction come to disregard or even repudiate their very kinship with the more-than-human kinds who are involved. Here deanimation not only proves to be a diminishment of biological life, as this is expressed in the collapse and loss of ecosystem processes and the living kinds with which they are intertwined but also works in perverse ways on human beings themselves and the creaturely ties they share not only with one another but also with the other living kinds. As a result, the process of anthropogenic extinction not only wounds humans' capacity to survive biologically but also leaves them in perilous straits in regard to their very readiness to affirm life itself.

In regard to Buffalo genocide, an early account of its deanimation of country is found in the testimony of Pretty Shield, a Crow Medicine Woman, as she walks in the Judith Basin among innumerable carcasses of Buffalo, recently slaughtered for their skins by white hunters and then left rotting in the sun: "My heart fell down when I began to see dead buffalo scattered all over our beautiful country. . . . The whole country there smelled of rotting meat. Even the flowers could not put down the bad smell. Our hearts were like stones" (quoted in Linderman 1974, 144).[8] These words, inscribed on a wall greeting visitors upon their entrance into the interpretive exhibit maintained at the First Peoples Buffalo Jump State Park, chasten all who read them. Here the call for one's empathy in regard to those living kinds suffering in the wake of Buffalo genocide, both human and more than human, is not kept tethered. Instead, one is summoned to become mindful of something approaching the full measure of the violence involved, as one confronts through its palpable details its effect on a human witness to it. In these circumstances, one is called to meditate on what Pretty Shield has said, to let her words turn about in one's thought, even as they settle into one's mind. Indeed, having read them, one feels summoned to a lifetime of contemplation by what is entailed in them, as if there could never have been enough time for their full meaning to have hit home. Having stood before them, one feels one will never have been given leave to leave them behind ever again.

In the moments I have spent with these words, I have been struck by how Pretty Shield characterizes her heart as falling down, even as the reality before her, of the many animals that have fallen indiscriminately before the hunters' bullets, strikes home. What might it be to find one's very heart incapable of standing upright on the face of the earth? Indeed, what might it be to live in a time in which no leave is given to stand anywhere at all for a living kind with whom one has lived in kinship through the generations? I remind myself that the words leading me to these thoughts are not mine to parrot, to take as if they were my own. And yet I cannot help but be accompanied by the words of Pretty Shield wherever I walk on the face of this country. And even as I entertain the questions to which they have led me and wrestle with what they are asking of me, I must also consider how the work of Buffalo skinners, who take only the hide of each animal, treating all else as waste, leave in turn Pretty Shield's fallen heart, as she puts it, hardening like a stone, becoming deadened to its very life. One is invited to imagine being sickened, repulsed, by the smell of the abandoned, rotting flesh of Buffalo, a smell so strong that not even the flowers burgeoning across the prairie can undo its insult to the senses. And as I reflect on this, I find myself connecting the incapacity to stand, to be upright on the face of the earth, with the upwelling of the stench of putrefaction.

Bringing into consideration the matter of Buffalo genocide, then, leaves those who come after not only confronting a landscape shorn of its charismatic, keystone species but also, as a result of the very manner in which this has occurred, debilitated in their very capacity to be consoled by the living world itself in regard to this loss. In these circumstances, one's willingness to affirm creation itself is pushed into crisis. Here Rose's invitation to a posture of "ecological existentialism," discussed in this collection by Isabelle Stengers, finds that the stakes involved are not merely those of witnessing and so mourning the extinction of a particular living kind who has now forever more been rendered silent, now mired in a past lost to our time and so without the means to communicate in its own way the unique senses of its having existed. The silence also registers loss redoubling upon loss, as the very ability of the world that remains to make sense of what has been lost to it is in turn lost. Loss cascading upon loss threatens to engulf the world in senselessness beyond any reprieve. In this vein, an infectious rendering meaningless altogether of things is fomented by Pretty Shield's witnessing of the very willfulness and, so, heartlessness with which Buffalo genocide has been pursued by human others. In anthropogenic extinction, especially when it is being executed as willfully and remorselessly as that of Buffalo, grief for the loss of another living kind is interrupted by the very shamefulness of how one's own kind has comported itself in regard to a more-than-human creation. In the wake of that event, wherever one turns, one finds that the very sense of turning toward any meaning that might have been proffered as consolation has itself been rendered disheartening. One learns that the negation of a world is rendered senseless insofar as one loses increasingly in that negation the very sense of what would have been affirmed had that world not been negated. Or, put otherwise, species genocide is not a species of logical negation, in which meaning is restored through the very axis by which that negation pivots in its dance with affirmation. Rather, species genocide is privative in its effect. It extinguishes meaning and leaves all that exists debilitated in its wake.

Contrasting this debilitation to one sometimes reported by inmates of the death camps of the Nazi genocide is instructive. Sculptor and Holocaust survivor Shelomo Selinger, for example, speaks of his horror before the beauty of nature "so offensively irrelevant to his dereliction" (Chalier 2017) as spring arrives outside the fences of a camp in Nazi Poland, even as within its bounds human beings are being turned into living corpses. In a similar vein, Etty Hillesum meditates on "violet lupins . . . spread out with a princely calm," sun inundating one's face as a massacre takes its course, women gossiping nearby on a crate, and "everything is so incomprehensible" (1996, 274). The implication in these moments is that the very indifference of nature to human suffering, that it would continue to thrive resplendently even as humans themselves were submitted to the very undoing of their humanity, not only fails to console those who are being dehumanized but also cruelly deepens their despair over their plight. In these moments the presence of nature thriving does not counter the extremity of violence, the deanimation of world that is occurring in what has come to be termed, as if any word might name it, a genocidal act, but only serves to punctuate it, to make it even more unbearable that such a thing takes place under the sun.

The flowering spires of two species of lupine, both silvery and silky, *Lupinus argenteus* and *Lupinus siriceus*, were surely among the prairie plants of the Judith Basin witnessed by Pretty Shield that terrible spring day, when the flowers themselves could not put down the rotting smell of Buffalo genocide. Here, then, are flowers of living kinds related to the one that is singled out by Hillesum. Yet the dereliction of Pretty Shield, unlike that of Hillesum, is not in regard to a nature indifferent to the fate of humans but to a Regime of humanity not only indifferent but also hostile to the dwelling of more-than-human creatures in its all-too-human company. Here policies of genocide and ecocide reinforce one another in a manner that is unique to settlement cultures (Rose 2004, 34–36). In their carrying out, Pretty Shield is struck down not only by the inhumanity of settlement culture in regard to other humans, including herself, but also by its inanimity, if one can, however awkwardly, coin this word here, in regard to living things generally. This disregard of the living world leaves that world in turn not only wounded, sickened in its capacity to thrive, but also rendered repugnant and shameful to those who now behold it and must continue to find a way to live in it.

And in the midst of the crisis provoked in acknowledging both the inhumanity and inanimity of Buffalo genocide comes, for me, this especially distressing passage of Pretty Shield's testament: "And yet even then, nobody believed that the white man could kill *all* the buffalo" (quoted in Linderman 1974, 144). This simple statement communicates the shattering realization that the trajectory of a living kind through time can be willfully stopped cold in its tracks, that it is indeed possible to kill every last one of something so that country might be emptied of its presence and inalterably diminished because of it.

The very capacity to work an evil this large had been unimaginable for Pretty Shield and indeed would have been so for most of humankind for most of its residency on the face of the earth. One's ignorance in this regard would have occurred in at least two registers. In the first, one fails to imagine that sufficient destructive force is available to humans to succeed in carrying out this project. In the second, one fails to imagine how the work of extinction might be accomplished not simply as a by-product of greed or as the outcome of indifference but as an actively sought-after result. The very far-heartedness

157

of its project—one that, as Linda Hogan describes it, "sees life, sees other lives as containers for our own uses and not as containers in a greater, holier sense" (2007, 45)—could not have been anticipated. Yet these possibilities not only become imaginable in the aftermath of settlement but also prove to be the very qualities by which this Regime is to be identified.

Ultimately, Pretty Shield's words remind me that my very presence in this country, the very conditions of both my biotic and my political citizenship in it, hinges on precisely this outcome to these events: that this land would be shorn of its Buffalo. Buffalo genocide, along with the prairie ecocide that accompanies it, occurs, then, in my name, among the names of many others who are identified with settlement. I am, then, a sign through my very birth here that this country is no longer to be Buffalo's.

To follow my meditations in this direction and to bring them to this debilitating conclusion perhaps seems histrionic and foolhardy. In confronting the great moral evils through which one has come into one's own place under the sun, one inevitably finds oneself tempted to deplore one's very existence and to repudiate the very world through which one's existence would be affirmed. One might even ask if there were ever a world in which humans were not already haunted by the evil through which that world arose, by the acts of usurpation and displacement through which the world was wrested away from others. Indeed, the memory of one's history inevitably proves so toxic that one is perhaps better cautioned to keep its mayhem at a safe distance, its betrayals in the past tense. The argument can be made that stirring up the memory of Buffalo genocide, precisely through meditation on it, serves only to bring one's own mind into a state of morbidity: indeed, one's heart, one's mind, and one's whole being.

These reflections, then, bring me to a moment not unlike that recounted by Emmanuel Levinas, who, in contemplating the legacy of unfettered violence in the death camps of the Shoah, asks, "Should we insist on bringing into this vertigo a portion of humanity that is not sick from its own memories?" (1996, 120). Pondering how the "chaos and emptiness" of the Shoah, its tohu v'bohu, might in turn be communicated to the generations born in its aftermath, so that it might become a teaching by which one now lives, sets off a crisis for Levinas in which wounds are evidently to be reopened without end, as "nothing is able to fill, or even cover over, the gaping pit" (120). In asking his question, Levinas struggles not only with the precariousness of the human condition, with how difficult it might be to affirm a return to normalcy in the aftermath of times of moral chaos, but also with its treacherousness, with how any affirmation in the time that comes after moments of violence borders on delivering one yet again to that chaos and betraying yet again those who were victims of it.

How, then, might the stench be undone that is entailed in Buffalo genococide? In the very posing of this question, the Montana landscape for me splits asunder. The country into which I was born and through which I was nurtured not only into biological maturity but also into at least the beginnings of philosophical inquiry and religious commitment proves to be harrowingly doubled, a place not only of homecoming and homemaking, of grandeur and fruitfulness, but also of displacement and dispossession, of deanimation and desolation.

To speak of this doubling in particular as "harrowing" requires a moment of exegesis. In one sense, this particular characterization simply provides a correlate for that which might be expressed in either the German *unheimlich* or the English *uncanny*. Either of these terms, both better known to academic philosophy, would be appropriate to name a mode of doubling by which the familiar, intimate, and animate is decentered into the unfamiliar, isolated, and inanimate, in which one trusts oneself to the real and reassuring only to find oneself in the clutches of the abject and ghostly. Each of the more recognizable terms for this condition of doubling has its merits, and each should be kept in mind. But insofar as philosophy might emerge anew in the home grounds of Buffalo genocide, this occurs tellingly in the notion of harrowing. Here a term is employed in which one's country is already speaking, although in another dialect entirely than that understood by those who might insist they are living in God's country.

The harrow that is harrowing: in contemplating the many moments I have spent in my life gazing across the short-grass prairie transformed into wheat fields and grazing land, the plow, both life-giving and ecocidal, comes to mind, and along with it the harrow. An agricultural implement with spiked teeth or upright disks, the harrow is drawn over plowed land to level it, break up clods, and root up growth to prepare soil for planting. And from this concrete act arises in turn the metaphorical sense of disturbing keenly or painfully, of distressing the mind.[9]

Imagine, then, the harrowing circumstances cutting one's mind to the quick, in which the harrows of settlement render land fruitful, even as the latter is submitted in this very gesture to thoroughgoing uprooting and deanimation. Imagine the prairie witnessed by Pretty Shield, in which living kinds are being ripped away wholesale and the stench of Buffalo genocide is overpowering, now transformed into vast and rigorously maintained fields of grain and grazing lands, this country now shaped by practices of serial monoculture that are sustained by regular applications of fertilizer distilled out of the atmosphere by machines, along with pesticides derived from petrochemicals pumped from the depths of the earth. The doubling of the harrowing of this land, that in its very harrowing it is rendered harrowing, turns out to be not simply a metaphor or a poetic trope, a quick turn of phrase; it's also an earthly condition, one with teeth in it, teeth of metal.

To meditate on this is itself harrowed and harrowing. As a strategic intervention, then, let those who read these lines refer to this state of being in a state, this State of Montana, God's country, where vast congregations of Buffalo once roamed the prairie and now wheat fields stretch out in every direction, as the State of Harrowing. In fact, let one say, the Regime of Harrowing.

AM I NOT THEN ASHAMED?

I would ask leave, then, to become thoughtful in the company of the reader about the plight of those who find themselves not only to have been born into the Regime of Harrowing but also to have led lives that have been sustained by it. In doing so, I am mindful of how the very inception of philosophy as a way of life is to be traced back to a defense of the philosopher's life, a defense in which words are offered on behalf of how that life might have come to be lived without shame. Indeed, the very thought that a life is possible that might be lived without shame is arguably the inaugural project of the philosophical tradition. In it, a human life is provided a means to its nobility.

Yet should I not be ashamed, even in these very words, to be consumed with the prospect of living nobly and to be speaking of a life that might be justified, burdened as I am by so many unfulfilled responsibilities in regard to the legacy of affliction I have inherited and in which now in turn I am entangled? In these circumstances, one rightfully becomes skeptical of whether offering words, any words at all, on behalf of the way one lives one's all-too-human life, functions to do anything other than further the injustice in which one is already implicated. One is led to ask anew whether the very notion of Socratic apologetics, of carefully working out the intelligible shape of a life that would be justified in its having been lived, functions as no more than a species of egodicy, an anthropological correlate to Gottfried Wilhelm Leibniz's notion of theodicy, in which one strains, no matter how deeply entangled one is in the unjust circumstances into which one is born, to break free of these fetters, to look away from the uncanny gesticulation of shadows and search out more enlightened and less bloodstained circumstances in which to conduct one's philosophical practice.

160

JAMES HATLEY

Levinas, in a passage from *Totality and Infinity*, submits to torsion the Socratic notion of apology, or at least that notion of Socratic apology that all too often is ascendant in our world, in which one's reasoning, acting through its own means, would find itself sufficiently endowed with wisdom to mark out clearly the difference between its having lived justly or unjustly. In doing so, one would proceed, Levinas fears, as if "reason creates the relations between me and the other," in lieu of attending to how "the Other's teaching me creates reason" (1969, 252). In the former situation, one would retreat to the safety of a mind released from any specific perspective in order to act consistently upon the principles that reason itself has ascertained as worthy of guiding not only one's own life but also every other life. In this way, one would find the gateway to one's integrity and so nobility through the very anonymity of reason, in that it speaks for no one in particular and so fairly of all. Further, as own one's voice becomes synonymous with that of reason, so, too, must the voice of any other who would in turn reason with me. The voice of one's reason then would live apart from the thorny entanglements, rife with misunderstanding and misapprehension, that inevitably cloud one's congress with others.

One would live as if the first lesson offered by reasoning about one's life is to become rigorously consistent in and confident about how one understands the approach of others. This is, indeed, the very point of Immanuel Kant's notion of a Kingdom of Ends. But if the other speaks in a voice that my own reasoning about the other has failed to anticipate, the very assumption of consistency and the confidence it underwrites serves only to subjugate the other to my notion of what that consistency itself would consist in. The question here is not whether some sort of accounting is called for in one's thinking but rather whether that call can be front-loaded simply by demanding that reason follow out the logical unfolding of how its anonymous and faceless terms, shorn from any unique perspective, purportedly guarantee their outcome as being transparent, as without guile. What Levinas fears is that in hearing the voice of the other only as what I have predetermined through working out in reason what must be involved in hearing that voice, I am failing to hear how the other is already giving birth to a manner of being in reason that had not, at least as of yet, registered in my thinking or in the terms by which it is proceeding.

To seek to live justly, then, even in a world of mayhem and wounds, indeed, especially there, is to submit the very manner in which the question of one's acting justly is to be posed to the purview of the other, whose approach of me disrupts the very words by which I would seek to justify my life, even before I could have spoken them. Apology then leads not only to a discourse intent on the recognition of one's former indifference to the suffering of others so that pardon might be sought and perhaps received but also to a discourse intent on how the very recognition of one's indifference in regard to the other has been forestalled or, even worse, has become, through a sleight of hand, surreptitious self-justification. The uncanniness of violence, the fact that it inevitably infects the very attempt to render oneself free of it, cannot be gotten around. That is what makes it uncanny. One is called upon, then, in one's apology to become circumspect about how one's suing for peace with another might be occurring only in those very terms that hide how one remains committed to engaging in war at yet another level.

PROVOCATIONS OF APOLOGY

To resist this outcome, Deborah Bird Rose, in her *Reports from a Wild Country: Ethics for Decolonisation*, calls for cultivating practices of discourse sensitive to divergence, to registering how one's very words, even as one offers them, already have come to be heard otherwise in the ears of another than one could ever have anticipated on one's own (Rose 2004, 31, 177). In such moments, one's speaking, even before it leaves one's mouth, is witnessed as speaking otherwise than one would have spoken in one's own right. There was, it turns out, never a time given in which one might have exercised mastery over the significance of what one is expressing. Instead, one's speaking is aroused or challenged from within its very saying—a doubling of the already twinned senses of calling forth and being called forth expressed in the Latin *pro-vocare*. One finds then that one's very words have become provocative to one's saying of them in their very saying, as they twist in meaning in a manner that is harrowingly disconcerting. This in turn calls for careful discernment in regard to how one is heard by others, not to mention how one hears oneself anew through how one is heard by others.

For example, when the First Peoples Buffalo Jump State Park was to be given its new name (formerly, it was called the Ulm Pushkin State Park), the thought was that it should go by the name First Peoples *Bison* Jump State Park. This was planned by state authorities in order to correct the mistaken assumption on the part of European settlers that the so-called Buffalo indigenous to North America were bovines taxonomically part of the genus *Bubalus*, when, in fact, bison turned out to be in another unique genus of bovine altogether. The thinking went that by using the term *bison*, the authorities were showing respect to First Peoples for whom Buffalo is sacred by not confusing a species endemic to this area with those of other places under the sun. The authorities were, then, intent on correcting the injustice of colonial occupation and enforced settlement on some level.

But when Richard Hopkins, who was to be the first director of the renamed state park, met with a council of tribal elders from across the region, he was surprised to find resistance to this gesture of goodwill. The members of that group asked what the reason exactly for the suggestion was. When he explained that the intent was to be accurate scientifically, the tribal elders, as he put it, responded by wondering, "Why should we care about that? That is your way of naming things. For us, as long as we have known to name the Buffalo in English, we have called them Buffalo. That is the word we would have you use."[10]

One wonders as well if the very thought of the descendants of settlers using another name for Buffalo after two catastrophic centuries of its widespread extirpation and near extinction might not have appeared as a sleight of hand, as a surreptitious mode of distancing oneself from involvement in a legacy that one would rather not have to think about. In rebranding Buffalo as bison, this line of thought might go, one is given leave to think about them in more refined and scientifically delineated terms without unpleasant ghosts arising. Indeed, if one attends carefully to the manner in which settler Americans generally bring Buffalo into discourse and so into mind, it becomes quickly apparent that a panoply of diversion tactics are marshaled to keep unpleasant truths at a safe distance.

A disquieting example of this tendency, as well as a provocation in regard to it, can be found in a pair of murals located in Great Falls, Montana, just a dozen miles from the First Peoples Buffalo Jump State Park. Covering two opposing concrete walls of the First Avenue North underpass, a busy street channeling traffic toward a nearby bridge crossing the Missouri River, the paired artworks provide an uneasy testament on behalf of settlement culture in regard to the place to be held by Buffalo in it. The underpass allows trains to travel on a railway running overhead so that traffic can move underneath unimpeded. The murals were designed and painted in the main by two local artists, Deeling C. Gregory and Kelli Rochelle Lawson, in 2012–2013, under the aegis of the Great Falls Business Improvement District (BID).[11] The remarks that follow focus on Gregory's contributions to this project, which prove exemplary in regard to the struggle of settlement culture to recognize the uncanniness of the violence, as well as the duplicity of the justice, by which it sustains itself.

163

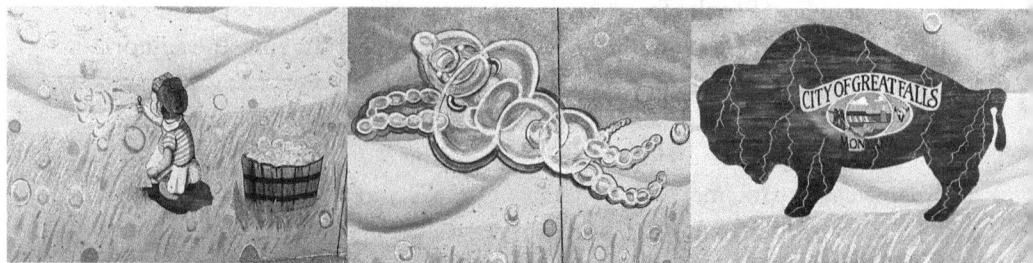

8.1 Deeling C. Gregory, selection of images from the *Great Falls Underpass Mural*, 2014.
PHOTOGRAPHS BY JAMES HATLEY. USED WITH PERMISSION OF THE BUSINESS
IMPROVEMENT DISTRICT OF GREAT FALLS, MONTANA.

Stretching along both the southern and northern sides of the underpass, the mural records a growth in Gregory's understanding of the task she had taken on. The southern side (figure 8.1), which was painted first, is, in Gregory's own words, "a light-hearted affair."[12] Its theme was originally suggested by a local student after a call for public input by the BID, which in turn approved and funded its painting.[13] The images are centered on a young boy and girl, both fair-skinned Europeans, positioned in relation to a barnyard fence and dressed traditionally in ranching garb. Their faces are turned away from view (to render them, at least to a degree, anonymous), and each blows strings of bubbles into the air. The circular frame used for blowing these bubbles in the case of the boy is a lasso. Whimsically, as the bubbles move downwind and agglomerate with one another, they become increasingly Buffalo-like—what Gregory came to call "bubbleoes"—until they are magically transformed more or less into bison.

But in actuality, if that word makes any sense here, the transformation involves the emergence of bison not so much into flesh-and-blood animals as into self-consciously wrought pictorial representations whose three-dimensional elements are immediately flattened or hollowed out. This occurs so that the bison in their outlines can in turn serve as a series of stages for a collection of images representing diverse cultural themes within what can be understood as the contemporary instantiation of the Regime of Harrowing. What is disturbing about this state of affairs, at least to this particular set of eyes, is how the mural encourages its audience to reframe the reality of Buffalo genocide within a purportedly Edenic scene of what might be termed, in counterpoint to the tradition of magical realism, nostalgic profanation. Nonchalantly usurping the place of the biblical Creator, the children

164

8.2 Deeling C. Gregory, selection of images from the *Great Falls Underpass Mural*, 2014. PHOTOGRAPHS BY JAMES HATLEY. USED WITH PERMISSION OF THE BUSINESS IMPROVEMENT DISTRICT OF GREAT FALLS, MONTANA.

of settlement, through the power of their breath, restore to country the very living kind through whose extirpation settlement culture itself had become possible. The strangeness of this tableau, as one considers that those who reanimate Buffalo are the representatives of precisely the culture that most explicitly undid bison, is not just awkward but, as one considers its full implications, harrowing. In this activity, bison are brought back to life but only in the insubstantial image, in an icon rendered as a fetish, an object that one fastens one's eyes on in order to celebrate one's occupancy of one's place under the sun at the terrible expense of the very creature that once was at home here.

Gregory reports that in the process of completing the mural on the south side of the underpass, she began to have "vivid dreams about bison."[14] In one, she stood at the edge of a waterfall (keeping in mind the series of waterfalls stretching across the Missouri for which Great Falls is named) while a young white bison faced her from the other bank. In yet another dream, she saw "an infinite herd of bison, pale gold in color, snaking their way across an almost desert-like prairie." Increasingly she was disturbed by the memory of Buffalo genocide and began to sketch out, at first privately and then, with the approval of the administrator of the BID, in public, another vision altogether for the second wall of the mural. Composed in part with Pablo Picasso's *Guernica* in mind, in which a white dove overlooks the slaughter of innocents, the tableau also incorporates aspects of a gigantomachia. Here a steam locomotive, one of the major instruments of Buffalo, as well as Native

165

American, dispossession and displacement, charges into a herd of a more-than-human living kind, crushing them into the earth, even as they struggle with the locomotive in their plight (figure 8.2). The result is difficult to look at, as the violence of Buffalo genocide is untethered in images that do not let a regrettable past fade away but in fact confront the citizens of the Regime of Harrowing with it.

In the first mural, images emerge to tell a story addressed by settlement culture to itself, as bison, as well as those peoples who in times heretofore honored and sustained the presence of Buffalo in their midst, become the playthings of settlement culture and offer in this way a facile justification for settlement culture's hegemony. In the second, the images emerge from beyond the story settlement would tell of itself in such a way as to instruct the Regime of its violence precisely by attending to how Buffalo resists becoming a plaything, both through its vulnerability to suffering and through its own manners of agency.

LITURGICAL WITNESS AND SETTLEMENT BLASPHEMY

What Gregory accomplishes in her second mural, as do the words of Pretty Shield displayed prominently on the entry wall at the interpretive exhibit of the First Peoples Buffalo Jump State Park, is to express—one through images, the other in words—an openness toward how one is already under the burden of another's address, even as one would express in one's own response (whether this be spoken or envisioned) one's faithfulness to that other. In this movement, a manner in which one's expression is always already a doing or acting not only on behalf of others but also under the burden of those others comes into the foreground. As already noted, one is provoked, one is called forth, by the divergence in how one's expressiveness, the significance of the very words emerging from one's mouth or the very image from one's brush, is altered in its hearing and seeing by others. This is particularly the case in regard to those others who have been submitted to the Regime of Harrowing, such that the very capacity to speak one's victimization, to even appear in a discourse in which one's claims for justice might even be heard, is systematically repressed and denied. Or, indeed, is punished.

This movement toward the other in one's very speaking is what Levinas comes to characterize in his essay "The Humanism of the Other" as liturgy. *Liturgy* in its Greek coining is literally the "people's (*leitos*) work (*ergos*)" (Levinas 2006, 28). For Levinas, the crucial aspect of this work is to accomplish "a movement of the Same towards the Other which never returns to the Same"

(26). Liturgy, then, is that mode of expression, at various levels of public sociality and polity, in which one would speak "for another," not in the sense of
speaking in place of the other but rather in the sense of speaking as a mode
of service to the other.

In a 1997 essay, "Liturgy: Divine and Human Service," Michael Purcell identifies several elements crucial to a Levinasian account of liturgy. The first involves how the significance of the work to be accomplished through liturgy
moves from the French *travail*, which is to say effort that is effectual on behalf
of the one who applies it, to *oeuvre*, which is to say effort as an offering or
service, in which the one who applies her or his effort lets go of her or his
own interest in that labor. Here one might also think of a Hebrew term that
is surely in Levinas's mind as he formulates a notion of liturgy, namely,
that of *avodat*, of service that is also understood as elevation of the one to
whom that service is rendered. Liturgy, then, is inevitably a work of offering
that elevates another or, at the very least, is in debt to that which one finds to
have been elevated. As Purcell puts it, "At the core of the offering of liturgy
is always a debt and indebtedness, a sense of repayment, a sense of 'what return can I make?'" (1997, 147, quoting Psalms 115:12). In this way, the work of
liturgy, Purcell argues, becomes heteronomous, no longer concerned about
how one's own ability to effect something under the sun sustains one's autonomy, one's hold on the place in which one abides, but rather about how
the movement in one's doing that is open to the elevation of another exposes
one to an anarchical submission to others. As Purcell puts it, "In opening
on to heteronomy, oeuvre/work ceases to be a transformative activity of a
subject, who, through technical skill and expertise converts the foreign into
the familiar" (148).

The activity of European settlement of the Americas, among many other
places under the sun, was precisely one of a subject who through technical
skill and scientific expertise converted the foreign into the familiar. This is arguably the story that the sunny, eternally blissful landscape of the first mural
would tell. And while there is nothing objectionable prima facie in human
activity that would convert the foreign into the familiar through techne or,
for that matter, through establishing relationships with others that are eco-
nomical in nature, engaging in a tit for tat, rather than being immediately oriented toward the gift, one's confusing of these latter notions of relationship
with liturgy is. Or to put this in another, more provocative manner, a liturgy
fixed upon converting the other into the same involves the degradation of
liturgy into the blasphemy of fascism, into a mode of speaking and doing in
which the very notion of being indebted to others for one's own place under

the sun is rejected with a thoroughgoing relentlessness that proves horrifying. Here is enacted a violence that glorifies itself as holy in its own right and so gives itself leave to proclaim its very suppression of the other not as violence but as justice, even as inspiration. One acts in a self-induced delusion, in which the very alterity of the other is lost to oneself and to the world one would sustain by one's activities.

This re-jection of the other, which is to say that movement in which the other is thrown out or away, if one thinks for a moment of the Latin etymology, is not only spatial but also temporal. For liturgy leads the same toward the other precisely in the manner in which the very reach of my own time is chastened and humbled by its issue into the time of another. Liturgy leads me, then, beyond my own birth and death, which is to say beyond how I am confidently rooted in a time that is discernibly and discretely my own. As Purcell puts it, the movement of the liturgical in Levinas is ultimately "*for* a time without me, *for* a time after [and, I would add, *before*] my time, *for* the time of the other" (1997, 157). Or as Levinas, calling on the thought of Leon Blum, puts it, in liturgy "we work *in* the present, not *for* the present" (2006, 28). The emptying out of the self, then, that is the work of liturgy—its kenosis—involves one's becoming a witness to how one's very efforts thought of as travail (labor) ultimately become oeuvres (works) that are assigned to others through one's death or that have been assigned to one by others through one's having been born from out of their deaths. In this movement across generations of time, one moves or is moved beyond one's capacity to determine the significance of that movement in regard to those others who are its provocation. One's works, one's liturgies, end up in the hands of others.

And so, in rejecting not only the other before oneself here and now, but also the very time by which the other exceeds one's own time, the settler would colonize modes of alterity emerging not only in the place in which they would abide but also in all its pasts and futures as well. Deborah Bird Rose (2004, 57–61) discusses how one of the most powerful and violent tools of settlement culture is the deployment of the Year Zero, which is to say, the institution of a point in time before which the world is understood to have been old, failing, and even debased and after which the world has been transformed, renewed, and elevated. The world of After the Zero is consecrated to and celebrates the interests of those who proclaim as their very birthright their temporal as well as spatial hegemony over those others still entwined in the times Before the Zero. The Year Zero, then, in its very declaration functions as a dark liturgy, one that is intent on swallowing up the other in the same rather than finding its same being exceeded for the sake of the other. Unlike a declaration of war, in which the other is to be coerced but remains in possession of the right to sue for peace, and the basic dignity that right accords its holder, the declaration of the Year Zero is honed so that those whose world here and now emerges from and is inspired by the time before settlement are to be left in shameful circumstances, in debasement and mayhem, even after peace is sued for. Policies of dispossession and displacement, of broken treaties and forged documents, of forced marches and mass conversion, and finally of enforced enculturation in which one's very language is ripped from out of one's mouth all emerge as ways of inflicting mayhem on the lives of the other who is sentenced without end to arrive here and now from the back side of the Year Zero. The intent here is to reduce or deanimate the very expressiveness of the voices of another's time to mere hissing and babbling. In this way, not only is the space in which the Regime of Harrowing exists colonized by European settlement but also the very timing of its time is wrested away from those stemming from Before the Zero and made solely the property of one's own occupation of this space here and now. It is as if nothing else exists under the sun but the settler's own time and place.

The almost universal extirpation of the Buffalo consciously wrought by settlement culture was a key event in its declaration of the Year Zero. In a renewed resistance to this moment both genocidal and ecocidal, Gregory's second version of her mural pointedly attends to and witnesses the divergence of the Buffalo's view of the Regime of Harrowing from that of the European settlers who instituted and continue to sustain it. In doing so, Gregory's expressiveness as it emerges in her artwork's attention to another's plight inaugurates a mode of Levinasian liturgy such that the work of expressiveness not only elevates another but also resists those modes of blaspheming the other, of debasing her or him, that are ingrained in a Regime of Harrowing. In doing so, it resists the declaration of the Year Zero even as it offers a pictorial document of its arrival.

But Gregory's mural does all of this with this difference—it attends to and elevates not only the humanism of the other, as Levinas would have it, but also the Buffaloism of the other, if the coining of this term is not too violent to the English in which it is being employed. Indeed, both Pretty Shield's words and Gregory's images, as well as the words and images of a host of Native American painters and authors, make clear that liturgical resistance to the Regime of Harrowing must take into account not only one's fraternity with another human but also one's fraternity with a host of other living kinds.[15] The very manner in which Indigenous peoples have been submitted to genocide has inevitably involved ecocide as its necessary ancillary. Dehumanization of the other, then, is not the only question that burdens discourse in such circumstances. One is also called upon to attend to the deanimation of other living kinds, in which their lives are rendered superfluous, in which they are deprived not only of their very place under the sun, of their habitat, and so of their continued presence among us but also of their standing to be significant to other living kinds, including humankind. Gregory's painting reminds us that in cultivating the company of Buffalo, one finds that one's all-too-human expressiveness is articulated, startlingly and arrestingly, otherwise than what one could have ever accomplished in one's own all-too-human manner. Recognizing that the Buffalo's place in the Regime of Harrowing and the ethical order it entails is to be elevated rather than diminished is crucial to the undoing of the dark liturgies characterizing settlement culture that would swallow the other in the same.

CODA: A BLESSING

After a summer cloudburst, white flecks of Buffalo bones, loosened from the soil, sprinkle the ground along a muddy path snaking down from the cliffs of the First Peoples Buffalo Jump State Park. Even as clouds part and the sun reemerges, thunder is still rattling somewhere to the east. Nearby, electric-blue damselflies perch on chokecherry bushes, twigs shaking in the wind. A little farther off, prairie dogs are yipping. Overhead a hawk is circling. In this place where Buffalo was once so fully at home with humankind, the power of that relationship remains palpable, even in a time of prairie ecocide, perhaps especially so. This is a place where, as Kate Wright puts it, "place breathes" (2017, 14).

And speaks. Indeed, even as one walks these paths, these bones are speaking. They have, one realizes, never stopped doing so. "If you're seeing the Land without the Story," writes Margaret Kemarre Turner, "then there's nothing there" (2010, 126). In a variation on this terrible possibility, settlement has been apt to tell the story of its fabled prairie grasslands, as if the Buffalo and the world it sustained have been long departed and so consigned to the unreal. Perhaps no greater violence can be done to a living kind than to remove its voice from its own story. In doing so, humankind tells a story in which no one but oneself is speaking, in which no one but oneself is listening. This has been all too often the practice of settlement in consolidating its hold on its own place under the sun. In her provocative mural on a concrete wall a dozen miles from here, Deeling Gregory has opened up a line of communication, however tenuous and provisional, with Buffalo. For this, one should be thankful. Buffalo, I imagine, is waiting for more.

NOTES

1. Richard Hopkins, interview with author, Great Falls, Montana, July 15, 2012.

2. Richard Manning's *Grassland: The History, Politics and Promise of the American Prairie* (1995) offers trenchant criticism on how Manifest Destiny and the industrialization of the grasslands have led to wave upon wave of environmental catastrophe and economic malaise across the Great Plains since European settlement occurred. In light of this history, he advances a reenvisioning of settlement in which one's very understanding of democracy, as well as the culture and politics it entails, becomes attuned to how humans might be called on to thrive within the ambit of prairie ecosystems rather than at odds with them.

3. Originally known as the Ulm Pushkin, the park's site was transformed into a historical monument in 1972 and then, in 2000, into a state park. It is one of over three hundred locations in Montana where First Peoples were known to have engaged in organized Buffalo kills before European settlement wiped Buffalo off the Great Plains. The Wikipedia article on this historical site offers a helpful overview of its history. See Wikipedia, s.v. "First Peoples Buffalo Jump State Park," last modified April 11, 2021, 4:58 (UTC), https://en.wikipedia.org/wiki/First_Peoples _Buffalo_Jump_State_Park.

4. Hopkins, interview with author, 2012.

5. In formulating this project, I am indebted to the work of Kate Wright, who has probed tellingly the deep ambivalence at work in the stories told by the settlement culture of the New England tablelands of eastern Australia about itself, stories in which "places of memory and warm familiarity" are inevitably intertwined with "colonial violence and dispossession" (2017, 11). Her notion of cultivating a "sentient education" in which the diverse voices of country are no longer silenced by settlement's "monologue" has been particularly helpful in the discussion being developed here.

6. This suggestion is in part inspired by Nimachia Howe's recent work on modes of storying land in the Blackfeet language through which "oblique participants" or "bystanders" are acknowledged even as one is speaking toward yet others: "Participation [in a speech act] . . . can be expressed by listening, being present, acknowledging others' views, and bearing witness—none of which involve the use of words. . . . The degree to which Blackfeet speakers regard grammatical correctness has to do with how well speakers account for non-verbal participants" (2019, 121).

7. To be exact, van Dooren characterizes species extinction as a "dull edge," through which the loss involved "begins long before the death of the last individual and continues to ripple forward long afterward, drawing in living beings in a range of different ways" (2014, 12).

8. This passage from Pretty Shield also emerges as pivotal in two of my other recently published papers, in addition to this one, all of which struggle from the

perspective of settlement with the legacy of Buffalo genocide and prairie ecocide in its various dimensions. See Hatley (2016, 2019).

9. See Dictionary.com, s.v. "harrowing," accessed January 26, 2020, https://www .dictionary.com/browse/harrowing.

10. Hopkins, interview with author, 2012.

11. Joan Redeen, community director of Great Falls Improvement District, interview with author, Great Falls, Montana, June 28, 2018.

12. Deeling C. Gregory, interview with author, Great Falls, Montana, June 29, 2018.

13. Redeen, interview with author, 2018.

14. Deeling C. Gregory, text message to author, August 18, 2017.

15. While many could be spoken of here, one might begin by mentioning the paintings of John Nieto, Monte Yellow Bird, and Ric Gendron, as well as videographer Tasha Hubbard's rich essay, "'The Buffaloes are Gone' or 'Return: Buffalo'?— The Relationship of the Buffalo to Indigenous Creative Expression" (2009), in which she calls on First Peoples of the plains to take seriously anew the maxim "The Buffalo is also our Education."

REFERENCES

Aderhold, Mike, Doug Monger, and M. Jeff Hagener. 2005. *Ulm Pushkin State Park Management Plan: Final.* Helena: Montana Fish, Wildlife and Parks.

Chalier, Catherine. 2017. "Love and Asymmetry." Paper presented at the annual meeting for the Society for Contemporary Jewish Philosophy, Memphis, Tennessee, October 19, 2017.

Davis, Wade. 2018. "On Ecological Amnesia." In *Memory*, edited by Phillippe Tortell, Mark Turin, and Margot Young, 21–29. Vancouver, BC: Peter Wall Institute for Advanced Studies.

Hatley, James. 2016. "Telling Stories in the Company of Buffalo: Wisdom, Fluency and Rough Knowledge." *Environmental Philosophy* 13 (1): 105–122.

Hatley, James. 2019. "There Is Buffalo Ecocide: A Meditation upon Homecoming in Buffalo Country." *Cultural Studies Review* 25 (1): 172–188.

Hillesum, Etty. 1996. *An Interrupted Life: The Diaries, 1941–1943; and, Letters from Westerbork.* Translated by Arnold J. Pomerans. New York: Henry Holt.

Hogan, Linda. 2007. "What Holds the Water, What Holds the Light." In *Dwellings: A Spiritual History of the Living World*, 42–46. New York: W. W. Norton & Company.

Howe, Nimachia. 2019. *Retelling Trickster in Naapi's Language.* Louisville: University Press of Colorado.

Hubbard, Tasha. 2009. "'The Buffaloes Are Gone' or 'Return: Buffalo'?—The Relationship of the Buffalo to Indigenous Creative Expression." *Canadian Journal of Native Studies* 29 (1–2): 65–85.

Levinas, Emmanuel. 1969. *Totality and Infinity.* Translated by Alphonso Lingis. Pittsburgh, PA: Duquesne University Press.

Levinas, Emmanuel. 1996. *Proper Names*. Translated by Michael B. Smith. Stanford, CA: Stanford University Press.

Levinas, Emmanuel. 2006. *Humanism of the Other*. Translated by Nidra Poller. Chicago: University of Illinois Press.

Linderman, Frank B. 1974. *Pretty-Shield: Medicine Woman of the Crows*. Lincoln: University of Nebraska Press.

Manning, Richard. 1995. *Grassland: The History, Biology, Politics and Promise of the American Prairie*. New York: Penguin Books.

Purcell, Michael. 1997. "Liturgy: Divine and Human Service." *Heythrop Journal* 38 (2): 144–164.

Rose, Deborah Bird. 2004. *Reports from a Wild Country: Ethics for Decolonisation*. Sydney: University of New South Wales Press.

Stauffer, Jill. 2015. *Ethical Loneliness: The Injustice of Not Being Heard*. New York: Columbia University Press.

Turner, Margaret Kemarre. 2010. *Iwenhe Tyerrtye—What It Means to Be an Aboriginal Person*. Alice Springs, NT: IAD Press.

van Dooren, Thom. 2014. *Flight Ways: Life and Loss at the Edge of Extinction*. New York: Columbia University Press.

van Dooren, Thom, and Deborah Bird Rose. 2016. "Lively Ethography: Storying Animist Worlds." *Environmental Humanities* 8 (3): 77–94.

Wright, Kate. 2017. *Transdisciplinary Journeys in the Anthropocene: More-Than-Human Encounters*. New York: Routledge.

ENDING WITH THE WIND, CRYING THE DAWN

BAWAKA COUNTRY including SANDIE SUCHET-PEARSON, KATE
LLOYD, SARAH WRIGHT, LAKLAK BURARRWANGA, RITJILILI
GANAMBARR, MERRKIYAWUY GANAMBARR-STUBBS, BANBAPUY
GANAMBARR, AND DJAWUNDIL MAYMURU

FROM THE WATER THAT DROPS TO THE SOIL and molds in with the pieces of sticks and clay that are picked up on the way, to its journey as it sinks into the soil, to the particles of the soil, those tiny pieces of sticks and leaves and grass and sands, as they become huge rocks. We see them, we see them as we go down, inside the soil and then deep in; we see the roots of the trees as we pass through. We fall in between; we seep into the soil, down past the roots, past worms in the soil, the creatures and bugs; together we travel down to the underground water and travel with the flood, out to the river, into the currents, down to the sea (adapted from Burarrwanga et al. 2019, 257–258). When Yolŋu women cry milkarri, they keen their songspirals; they bring the world to life with language and keep it alive. They keen for their ancestors, with their ancestors, as our ancestors, and through this tremulous voice, they live and nourish Yolŋu time, space, and place—Country. For Yolŋu people, even though someone may have passed away a long time ago, they are still alive. Why? When they sing through milkarri, they always think about that person. It doesn't matter if they passed away twenty, thirty years ago, they still keen for that person so they are with them; they feel their motion, their presence. They feel their help. Milkarri keeps them alive. Through milkarri, the song tells the story of each particular person's journey. In this chapter we relish the opportunity to harmonize with Debbie as part of our ever-spiraling song, as part of our journey out into the currents and the sea. Debbie has ever been a part of our story, our song, nurturing and guiding its early unsure warblings and helping to form its braver chords. Through her dialogues, unruliness, and becomings, Debbie has become intimately woven into Bawaka Country's work. So here we celebrate and honor Debbie and how she contributes to our ongoing journeys, bringing us together through space and time yet honoring our particular and always changing songs. Our waters and currents speak to each other; in order not to harm each other, they flow out into the sea and then go back into the land, giving and taking. "Don't collide with me," we might say. "I am just passing through" (Burarrwanga et al. 2019, 258).

When Yolŋu women cry milkarri, they sing Country through their tears. They become Country, every particle, every being that is sung and spoken. As Yolŋu women cry milkarri for/as the rain, they are the raindrops. And as raindrops, they see everything around them as they fall. As the raindrops sink into the soil, they see the particles of soil, the tiny pieces, passing by the tree roots, picking up particles—clay, sticks, grass, and sands—moving along together. The water is moving out to the rivers, down to the sea: they co-become, unfold, spiral, emerge in and through togetherness.

Bawaka Country is the authorship team of this chapter and is also known as the Bawaka Collective, an Indigenous–non-Indigenous, more-than-human research group. We understand our collective as co-becoming; our relationships, our work, our beings, emerging together. It is the ebb and flow, the fresh water going out, the salt water coming in, the waters meeting and mixing, the giving and taking. Yolŋu people have Ganma, where the fresh water meets the salt water. And in the middle, there is a balance. Our work and being-together comes about through an iterative process of unfolding, as we see and know and live that nothing exists in isolation: "Connections make us who we are. As we begin gathering the clouds, we walk, yearning for and thinking of our homeland. It is alive in us. It is a matter of belonging, but it is more. It is our being and our longing. We yearn for our homelands, we are connected to them through gurruṯu, through kinship. Gurruṯu is the way we are related to one another and to everything" (Burarrwanga et al. 2019, 79). These connectivities spiral over time and space, through time and space, and as time and space, enabling us to emerge together, not as one undifferentiated mass, but through relationships, relationships that honor our difference as Yolŋu and ŋäpaki (non-Indigenous people), as salt and fresh waters, as gurruṯu, kin. Gurruṯu is how we are related, our place in and as Country. Gurruṯu positions us, but it does not suggest a conflation of difference, does not let mother become daughter; rather, it honors our connected kinship as it lives the cyclical relationality of our existence. This is our universe, from before, the present and into the future.

As the Yolŋu sisters and daughter of the Bawaka Collective—Laklak Burarrwanga, Ritjilili Ganambarr, Merrkiyawuy Ganambarr-Stubbs, Banbapuy Ganambarr, and Djawundil Maymuru—cry milkarri of the songspirals, they sing themselves into Country; they sing all members of the collective into Country; they sing those who listen into Country; they sing our connections through the spirals of our being-emerging-becoming together:

> Songspirals are often called songlines or song cycles. In this book, we call them songspirals as they spiral out and spiral in, they go up and down, round and round, forever. They are a line within a cycle. They are infinite. They spiral, connecting and remaking. They twist and turn, they move and loop. This is like all our songs. Our songs are not a straight line. They do not move in one direction through time and space. They are a map we follow through Country as they connect to other clans. Everything is connected, layered with beauty and pride. Each time we sing our songspirals we learn more, go deeper, spiral in and spiral out. (adapted from Burarrwanga et al. 2019, xvi)

Spiraling means there is no single direction, no thing that is entirely new, nor ever separate from other things. Yolŋu histories, ŋäpaki histories, histories of colonization, the harm and hurt, the survivances, the Yolŋu ceremonial songs, the lineages of concepts, the situated engagements, our ancestors, the Countries in which we live (Yolŋu people on Yolŋu Country, ŋäpaki migrant colonizers on stolen land), spiral, emerge, connect. And as we work together, share together, share with Yolŋu and with ŋäpaki, we are not breaking new ground; rather, we spiral, we dha yutakum, we make it new again, starting again, onward together with myriad other conversations and relationships and teachings, underpinned by the foundation of Rom, by Yolŋu Law, yet always emerging in place (Bawaka Country 2019a). The Rom, the Law, along

176

with its language, has always been there; it never changes. And yet it is always emerging in and with and as place, so that while it is always there, has been there all along, it allows new things to be communicated or seen in new ways; it emerges again, anew, because there's always a new context. We spiral.

Deborah Bird Rose, her work and her being and her life and her death, have been an important part of this spiraling and co-becoming. Sandie Suchet-Pearson, Sarah Wright, and Kate Lloyd, the three ŋäpaki academics of the collective, have been deeply influenced by Debbie's inspiring work, which has been part of their spirals as they come to the collective with their own histories and positionalities. From there, Debbie's generous thoughts and inspiration have resonated, harmonized, fed into discussions, suggested pathways, opened avenues, and provided guidance. As Kate Wright (this volume) shares through her reflections of Debbie, "Life is a woven basket of relations, and each earthly creature emerges from this fabric as a dense knot of embodied multispecies time."

As we spiral together now, allowing thoughts and conversations to unfold, we relish the opportunity to continue to harmonize with Debbie as part of our ever-spiraling song, as part of our journey out into the currents and the sea, and from the sea back in to the brackish water. And we do this by attending to how Debbie has connected with and come into our co-becomings, our more-than-human dialogues. As she says, and we use the tense purposefully, we co-become together: "Bearing the burden of our histories of harm, and going gently into encounters that are both situated and open, we shake our capacity for connection loose from the bondage of monologue. Only then will we be able to start the work of becoming human in connection with others, negotiating forms of neighbourly kinship in the on-going project of life" (Rose 2015a, 131).

IN 2008 ALL FOUR SISTERS—Laklak, a D̲äṯiwuy Elder, Caretaker for Gumatj, Yunupiŋu mother clan and eldest sister; her younger sisters, Ritjilili, Merrki-yawuy, and Banbapuy; and their daughter, Djawundil—came to Sydney for the launch of our first book, *Weaving Lives Together at Bawaka* (Burarrwanga et al. 2008). Debbie was at the book launch and was identified by the Yolŋu who saw her as Bayini, a saltwater woman. Bayini came to Bawaka long ago; a Macassan princess with long hair, she came on the wind from Makassar. She lives in the land- and seascapes of Bawaka, protecting the land with her millions of eyes. As Laklak says, "If you have been invited to our country, she'll protect and watch over you too" (Burarrwanga et al. 2008).

As Banbapuy and Sarah talked together about Debbie, crafting some thoughts to share in this piece, Banbapuy, as the main spokesperson for the family and an author, artist, weaver, and dedicated teacher, pointed out the meanings that flow from Debbie as one of many Bayinis—Debbie is part of the songspirals now. Banbapuy explains that the work the Bawaka Collective does together "is coming from the land. Debbie/Bayini comes from salt water; she came here by boat, and she has got that foundation. She is ŋäpaki, but she had a reason to come. She came to this world for a reason. So she could inspire other women, miyalk mala. She had that knowledge to pass on. She was in between. She balanced Western society and Indigenous people" (pers. com., June 17, 2019).

Debbie has that openness, that respect, that knowledge to see other knowledges. She is well respected, for her understanding, for her patience, for her commitment as well, and she has that power and wisdom in herself for doing those things, helping people who don't know about Indigenous people to understand. She does that in a different way, writing books, meeting people, being patient, respecting other peoples' values and cultures and differences. She helped create a flourishing present, not suggesting settler-migrants could become Yolŋu or find salvation in Indigenous ways of knowing and being from the guilt and violences of colonialism, but creating two-way learning, supporting our difference through dialogue and relationship (see Haraway, this volume).

It is the salt water meeting the water from the land. They interact and together make the brackish water, and this is the knowledge. The waters come into conversation; they dialogue together. They refuse the monologues that Debbie identified as critical to the justifications of colonizing processes; they reject the narcissism, arrogance, and selfishness (Rose 1999). The waters make themselves available to each other, they communicate, they open themselves up to being surprised, and they entwine in productive embraces. Then balance comes.

And these productive dialogues are always situated. They are real, and they are embodied in real places. We see Ganma, the salt and the fresh water mixing together, at Biranybirany Homeland, Laklak and her sisters' motherland, in North East Arnhem Land. And that mixing is the knowledges too. And Rorruwuy is another place where the waters mix. We call it mel'bon, as the water is so muddy, and it is the territory for shark. The water flows from Dhalinbuy, another homeland that is our motherland. There is the yothu-and-yindi relationship, the child-and-mother relationship, between the two places that meet. Yothu and yindi, the child and the mother, hold the balance, as manifested by the salt and fresh water. Yothu and yindi make up everything; they are always in relationship, cycling and passing down and up through the generations, spiraling, yet never the same. And when the mother's water runs from inland, from Dhalinbuy, the fresh water mixes in with the muddy water, and it makes it clear; it takes out that muddy water, that bon water. It takes out the mud as it takes out the anger when someone is angry; it takes out the anger and soothes it down, makes it calm.

The Rom, Law, is there to ensure that the mixing, the conversations, the dialogues, occur in the right way, in the right order with a foundation that does not change (Bawaka Country 2019a). But the meeting is also always situated, always in place, always anew, spiraling, and able to respond with openness, wonder, and surprise (akin to the snail stories of mystery and wonder that Thom van Dooren shares in this volume). Merrkiyawuy reminds us that a healthy person has a mind full of wonder. A mind full of wonder is wondrous, and a wondrous mind learns so much more than a mind that is sick and narrow-minded. Living our responsibilities means opening ourselves up to being surprised and transformed, to changing what we do and to trying to do things that make a positive difference. In this volume Donna J. Haraway speaks to living well as "part of the obligation of taking care of unexpected country." Our relationships and engagements are not static and certainly not stuck in the past. They continue to unfold. But beneath that is Rom, Law. Rom ensures that the salt water will not harm the fresh water, and the fresh water will not harm the salt. They entwine together. The knowledge is respected. Respected and celebrated. Our waters and currents speak to each other; in order not to harm each other, they flow out into the sea and then go back into the land, giving and taking. "'Don't collide with me,' we might say, 'I am just passing through'" (Burarrwanga et al. 2019, 258).

YOLŊU WOMEN CRY MILKARRI; they keen their songspirals; they bring the world to life and keep it alive. As we describe in our book on songspirals, "Milkarri is an ancient song, an ancient poem, a map, a ceremony and a guide, but it is more than all this too. Milkarri is a very powerful thing in Yolŋu life" (Burarrwanga et al. 2019, xvi). Yolŋu women keen for their ancestors, with their ancestors, as their ancestors, and through this tremulous

179

voice, they live and nourish Yolŋu time and place, Country: "We let that feeling flow through us. Let our body be that body of water of which we sing. Let our singing and crying milkarri be that body and our body, and know that we and Country are one, that we are Country, that we must do milkarri, name Country, harmonise with Country so that our knowledge, our sound, the vibration inside us brings Country alive, makes it sacred again and again and again. Of that body of water we sing. And that water sings us" (Burarrwanga et al. 2019, 16–17). Only Yolŋu women can keen milkarri. Country is female, and we are looking after our motherland. We children look after Country because it is our mother. Women give life and are the first teachers, are the first educators even as a child enters and grows in the womb. All humans go through the same journey, even as the journey itself is so different. Debbie, as a woman, miyalk, she understands well. She understands not only the important role women have to play but, as also described by Linda Payi Ford in this volume, the processes that are needed to bring back balance. We need to counter the deep colonizing processes that mean that more attention has been paid to men's side of things, including the way there are so many more recordings of Yolŋu men singing songspirals, as well as books by male academics about this. "We need to bring back the balance. Women's part of songspirals is vital. Without women's milkarri the songspirals, life itself, won't be whole" (Burarrwanga et al. 2019, 197).

And women's role in songspirals, women's milkarri, is fundamental. It holds the emotions and the balance. Milkarri does not merely reflect Country, milkarri makes it. Yolŋu women cry the dawn, greet the dawn; as the sun rises, they bring the new day into being. They cry milkarri for the mist and through the mist; they keen milkarri for the spiders making their web. When they keen the spider, they help it along, they make it exist, they sing it building its home and help it build that home so that it can get food, so it can live, be truly alive. This is not made up, it is not a metaphor, it is real, it is true. And Dhuwa songspirals always end with the wind, to close the day, cleansing, cleansing the footprints from the sand, smoothing the sand ready for a new day, ready to cry the dawn again, cycling, spiraling, making always. Whatever Yolŋu women cry, whenever they keen milkarri, they bring that being to life: the animals, the sun, the winds, a person. Country exists when they do milkarri.

And humans are not the only beings who milkarri; they are only one part of Country. Animals, plants, trees, the winds, they sing too; they are also singing the songspirals into existence:

The whale, the guwak (koel bird), they have songspirals. So do the wind and the sand. It is all in Country, the songspirals, more than we can know. Animals, plants and other beings have understandings through each other, such as from whales to turtles to birds, to anything that makes a sound; any living thing that makes a sound communicates with each other. They have that knowledge, their own laws.

They sing to us too. Animals, plants, trees—in the morning they give the wake-up call. When you hear that bird, they are singing the songspirals into existence. . . . They sing and we sing the winds; the songs talk about how soft the wind is, where it's coming from, what time of year it is, what food we can collect. Yes, the trees they sing too. That is in the songs too. We listen to the djomula trees, the casuarina. Songspirals make things live. (Burarrwanga et al. 2019, 44)

And we honor this connection in our work by authoring as Bawaka Country, decentering human authority. This academic shift, something seen as obvious for the Yolŋu authors, was enabled in part by Debbie and the spaces she opens within academia to challenge dominant knowledge systems and conventions. Indeed, when we talk about Country, we talk about the mutual co-becoming of life and place, of waters, elements, processes and dreams, story, ceremony and song and feeling.

It is difficult, impossible, to talk about Country in English, even in Yolŋu Matha, as Country is more than human. Country knows and communicates beyond words, beyond human understanding, even as we come into relationship with it, and we know and are Country through songspirals. Debbie helps find ways to speak about what cannot be spoken of just in words. As she wrote so eloquently in *Nourishing Terrains*:

Country in Aboriginal English is not only a common noun but also a proper noun. People talk about country in the same way that they would talk about a person: they speak to country, sing to country, visit country, worry about country, feel sorry for country, and long for country. People say that country knows, hears, smells, takes notice, takes care, is sorry or happy. Country is not a generalised or undifferentiated type of place, such as one might indicate with terms like "spending a day in the country" or "going up the country". Rather, country is a living entity with a yesterday, today and tomorrow, with a consciousness, and a will toward life. Because of this richness, country is home, and peace; nourishment for body, mind, and spirit; heart's ease. (Rose 1996, 7)

Country, beyond words, is "heart's ease": Yolŋu feel it, sing it, are it, through emotions, connections, embodied beings, and vibrations. Country is all that Yolŋu feel, all the deep connections, the patterns and relationships, the profound meanings that women cry, and remake, as they milkarri. Milkarri comes from deep inside, from feeling a song and letting it flow. Milkarri is rich with emotion, with grief and joy and more. As we say, "We all bring our resonance, our heart, our love and sorrow, our vibrations. When we do milkarri, it is to make something exist, that land in all its beauty and pain and connections" (Burarrwanga et al. 2019, 110). Emotions are Country; they are our memory. And memories are released through milkarri as Country is sung. We don't keep our emotions bottled up. With milkarri, we let our emotions flow, let them into the open. In this way, we help the emotions flow for men and boys, too, as tears may run down their faces as they listen to women keening their milkarri. Milkarri is driven by our emotions; it holds emotions. This is the meaning of milkarri. It is how Country heals us, and we heal it.

In these more-than-human dialogues that we engage in, and indeed nourish through connections of kinship, of gurruṯu, including through relationships of yothu yindi, child and mother, with all living and indeed "nonliving" things, we attend to Country's messages and heed them as we can. In doing so, we, as Debbie beautifully suggests, attempt to "include all of the living world within the domain of 'neighbors.'" In doing so, we "embrace noisy and unruly processes capable of finding dialogue not only with other people but equally with the world itself" (Rose 2015a, 131). For Yolŋu, these processes may be complex, even messy, but they should not be muddled or too unruly. They are held, in deep and rich ways, through relationships of kinship. In this way, we work not to embrace "unruly" processes so much as processes guided by different kinds of rules—of Country, of kinship, of Rom (Bawaka Country 2019a).

AS OUR SONGS SPIRAL ONWARD, we invite you to feel Debbie, to connect with her through emotion, through your connections, through her life that continues onward. For Yolŋu, even though people may have passed away a long time ago, they are still alive.

When women sing milkarri, they think about those that have passed away, even if that person passed away many, many years ago. Yolŋu women still keen milkarri for that person so their presence can be felt, to keep them here, to feel their motion and their emotion, to feel their help. Milkarri keeps them alive. As we say in our book, "From there, we feel emotion. We feel like the spirit is ready to hop on that boat. Honest, sometimes we cry, we feel our brothers or sisters who have passed away on that boat, on that same journey. They're dancing with us. We feel the motion, their presence. We feel their help. Then we start crying milkarri. We think about that person, when they were alive, what they saw, seeing the fire. We don't keep that to ourselves, we express it through milkarri. It's healing" (Burarrwanga et al. 2019, 227). Yolŋu women's crying of songspirals remembers and respects the passing of loved ones. As Yolŋu people remember, as Laklak, Ritjilili, Merr-kiyawuy, Banbapuy, and Djawundil keen, they keep alive their connections to loved ones. It is a happy ending. Those people are there, waiting for all of us who connect to them. These connections are connections that Debbie understands. Through ongoing connections, we respect and revive, we care, we heal, we co-become. As Debbie says, "We reach to each other because no singular self can mend the world, and because regaining an inter-subjectivity of mutually active care must be a step towards deconstructing the pitiless isolation and regimes of violence that have both dominated and seduced us" (1999, 184). For the Bawaka Collective, this intersubjectivity underpins all through co-becoming. Intersubjectivity becomes intrasubjectivity as we care for ourselves, care for others, care for Country, are cared for by Country, as part of Country itself (Bawaka Country 2019b).

Yolŋu songspirals are the story of each particular person's journey and of their co-becomings, their gurruṯu, their relationships and the care that holds them. As Yolŋu women's keening milkarri of the songspirals tells these stories, sings and cries with rich emotion, milkarri keeps them alive: alive in memory, alive in Country, alive and sentient through the complex past/present/future of coexisting Yolŋu time (Bawaka Country 2017). Yolŋu know a person was a good hunter, a good gatherer, a good mother, a good grandmother. They know the place they come from. They know them, and they know Country:

> Through milkarri the women are taking us back to a place, to Country, to a person, to everything that lives there and that lived there. It touches our soul. They know that Country. When people die, when a person dies, we sing about that person's life. We sing about going hunting, finding a tree, gathering under it; about a person going down to the beach, looking out to the horizon, making a fire. That is what women sing through the tears of milkarri, what we do in our songspirals. We are singing a picture but

that picture is alive, that Country is alive, that person's being is linked to that Country, it can't be separated from that Country. Every songspiral is a song, a ceremony, a picture, a story, a person, a place, a mapping, some things that we did, that we do and that we will always do, and it is all of those things together because those things are really the same. And it is more, much more. It is knowledge and language and Law. (Burarrwanga et al. 2019, xxiv–xxv)

So, for Yolŋu people, our lives and our deaths keep the songspirals alive. And the songspirals keep us alive too. Learning and singing and keening and crying—these keep Country alive too. For people *are* Country. Yolŋu cry the smells of Country, the specifics of season, the drying mud, the wind that comes, the emotions we feel as we gather the water lily; we smell the mud as we did before, as our ancestors did, as those in the future will do, now. We hear the laughter, the feeling in our hearts: being on the land, walking quickly across hot sand, starting the fire. It makes Yolŋu alive and, after they have passed, keeps them alive still. It keeps the moment living, now, and the place too. As Debbie says, "The people who belonged to country in life continue to belong to it in death" (Rose 1996, 71). When Yolŋu keen and see a cloud, that is the person who has passed away seeing that cloud. They are not there to see it, so "we keen and sing to make the person and the cloud alive together" (Burarrwanga et al. 2019, 229). As Yolŋu sing the clouds gathering and the rain falling, so Yolŋu keep the rains falling and the clouds gathering. Yolŋu practice it, they do not lose it, they keep it awake. This keeps the balance.

As we honor Debbie, as we recall her life, her sharings, her stories, she becomes part of the spiral, part of bringing the world into existence. Debbie is moving, as we all do, to a place of greater more-than-human agency. As with her namesake Bayini, she is becoming ancestor now; "her spirit is still living and protecting the land" (Burarrwanga et al. 2013, 10). But this does not make her any less real, far from it. As we describe, the songspiral is

the story of us as we spiral through the generations. The generations of our ancestors, those who have come before, as well as the generations yet to come. When we cry milkarri or sing at a funeral, it is the deceased person who is alive. They are seeing, they are looking, feeling, walking, breathing and smelling. All senses are there and all things, the talking, doing, hunting, in the songspiral. We go together with that person, guiding them, with their spirit. We are taking them back to where they started, back to that same spot where they were conceived. It is the journey back, guiding them back to that place. (Burarrwanga et al. 2019, 207)

Debbie is living and dying, her "relational ethics" still calling for us to "assume ever greater mutuality and accountability as intra-dependent members of the suffering family of life on Earth" (Rose 2015b, 89). She is still inspiring us to care, care for what is here, care for what is not. Even if something has been damaged or destroyed, if something hasn't been visited or connected with for a while, the imperative is to sing it still, make it alive, feel Country with us, and us with and as Country: "When that person was alive they have given to the family, the grandchildren, the land, the Country, and in return we have to respect that person through manikay including milkarri. Even if we don't know that person, we still go to the ceremony to sit down and be with our gurruṯu, our kin relations. We are connected through kin, through the land, through the songs" (Burarrwanga et al. 2019, 245). Milkarri tells a story; it is a healing for everyone, a celebration, too, for a being's life, a celebration and a way of saying thank you and respecting that being, their knowledge and actions. So here we celebrate Debbie and how she contributes to our ongoing journeys, bringing us together through space and time yet honoring our particular and always changing songs:

> The Law and the songspirals like the clouds that gather and separate, tell us to live life to the fullest. Life is precious [was the message that our mother gave before she went to another world], and we must do what we have to do before we go so that later on, when we are gone, others will respect us. We don't have a word for thank you exactly, but we say buku-wekam or buku-wurrpan. These mean to give back, saying a type of thank you. It is a matter of honouring a person for what they have done, honouring them for looking after the land or for how they helped us in the past, in the days when they lived, when they were alive. (Burarrwanga et al. 2019, 108)

NOTE

Section break art: Manala Marika Gulurunja (our brother's daughter), *Rulyapa*, 2018. Buku-Larrŋgay Mulka Centre archives. Used with permission.

REFERENCES

Bawaka Country including Sandie Suchet-Pearson, Sarah L. Wright, Kate Lloyd, Laklak Burarrwanga, Ritjilili Ganambarr, Merrkiyawuy Ganambarr-Stubbs, Banbapuy Ganambarr, Djawundil Maymuru, and Jill Sweeney. 2017. "Co-becoming Time/s: Time/s-as-Telling-as-Time/s." In *Experiments with Methods in*

Nature-Culture-History Research, edited by Jocelyn Thorpe, Stephanie Rutherford, and L. Anders Sandberg, 81–92. London: Routledge.

Bawaka Country, including Sandie Suchet-Pearson, Sarah Wright, Kate Lloyd, Matalena Tofa, Laklak Burarrwanga, Ritjilili Ganambarr, Merrkiyawuy Ganambarr-Stubbs, Banbapuy Ganambarr, and Djawundil Maymuru. 2019a. "Bunbum ga dhä-yutagum: To Make It Right Again, to Remake." *Social and Cultural Geography* 21 (7): 985–1001.

Bawaka Country, including Sarah L. Wright, Sandie Suchet-Pearson, Kate Lloyd, Laklak Burarrwanga, Ritjilili Ganambarr, Merrkiyawuy Ganambarr-Stubbs, Banbapuy Ganambarr, Djawundil Maymuru, and Marnie Graham. 2019b. "Everything Is Love: Mobilising Knowledges, Identities and Places as Bawaka." In *Indigenous Place and Colonial Spaces: The Politics of Intertwined Relations*, edited by Nicole Gombay and Marcela Palomino-Schalscha, 51–71. London: Routledge.

Burarrwanga, Laklak, Ritjilili Ganambarr, Merrkiyawuy Ganambarr-Stubbs, Banbapuy Ganambarr, Djawundil Maymuru, Sarah Wright, Sandie Suchet-Pearson, and Kate Lloyd. 2013. *Welcome to My Country*. Sydney: Allen and Unwin.

Burarrwanga, Laklak, Ritjilili Ganambarr, Merrkiyawuy Ganambarr-Stubbs, Banbapuy Ganambarr, Djawundil Maymuru, Sarah Wright, Sandie Suchet-Pearson, and Kate Lloyd. 2019. *Songspirals: Sharing Women's Wisdom of Country through Songlines*. Sydney: Allen and Unwin.

Burarrwanga, Laklak, Djawundil Maymuru, Ritjilili Ganambarr, Banbapuy Ganambarr, Sarah Wright, Sandie Suchet-Pearson, and Kate Lloyd. 2008. *Weaving Lives Together at Bawaka: North East Arnhem Land*. Callaghan, NSW: Centre for Urban and Regional Studies.

Rose, Deborah Bird. 1996. *Nourishing Terrains: Australian Aboriginal Views of Landscape and Wilderness*. Canberra: Australian Heritage Commission.

Rose, Deborah Bird. 1999. "Indigenous Ecologies and an Ethic of Connection." In *Global Ethics and Environment*, edited by Nicholas Low, 175–187. London: Routledge.

Rose, Deborah Bird. 2015a. "Dialogue." In *Manifesto for Living in the Anthropocene*, edited by Katherine Gibson, Deborah Bird Rose, and Ruth Fincher, 127–131. Brooklyn, NY: Punctum Books.

Rose, Deborah Bird. 2015b. "Flying Foxes in Sydney." In *Manifesto for Living in the Anthropocene*, edited by Katherine Gibson, Deborah Bird Rose, and Ruth Fincher, 83–89. Brooklyn, NY: Punctum Books.

ANIMALITY AND
THE LIFE OF THE SPIRIT TEN

COLIN DAYAN

That which endures is not ordinary.
—DEBORAH BIRD ROSE, *Reports from a Wild Country* (2004)

DOGS SET THE TERMS for how we might talk about creaturely experience
that upsets the sensible or reasonable—and the mean and monopolizing
spirit such legitimacy masks. They experience pain and suffering. They remember. They grieve. They also think, which has a great deal to do with sentience and emotions as well as with reason or with rationality. The stakes are
clear. If sentience is the stuff of personhood, then animals are nonhuman
persons with rights to be free from harm. But instead of opposing humans
and animals, we need to question the boundaries of humanity.

No one understood this questioning better and more intensely than
Deborah Bird Rose. She sought a more nuanced vocabulary for the feel and

texture of violation. In the process, she articulated a unique form of ethics that prompts us to move beyond dehumanization and the anthropocentric worldview that supports it. What, she asks, might it mean to reorient our ethical and conceptual assumptions to the perspective of other creatures? In eschewing standard liberal approaches to human and nonhuman relations—such as animal rights or animal welfare—she asks for an alternative, riskier, bracing way of being in the world. Indeed, she prompts another way of thinking, and of loving.

Perhaps *animality* is what we should be thinking about rather than claims to humanity. We need to interrogate the status of the human as a problem and see that if it is a kind of privilege, it remains ambiguous at best. Dogs live on the track between the mental and the physical and seem to enact a near-mystical disintegration of the bounds between them. Their form of knowing (as if *thought thinking itself through*) has everything to do with perception, an attentiveness that unleashes another kind of intelligibility beyond the world of the human.

What about dogs? Are they persons? Of course they are. But I'll add a caveat here. Although I'm keen for animal rights lawyers to succeed in their struggle to recognize the *legal personhood* of animals, even dogs, I also recognize the dangers in using human terminology when dealing with non-humans. To say that dogs are *persons* is to attribute to them the kind of conscious intentionality that defines subjectivity, as we understand it, and giving dogs what we think they need in terms of human conceptions of right and wrong or capacity and incapacity is part of the top-down judgment that always fails those we speak for. So instead of opposing them to humans, perhaps we need to question the limits of humanity and start defining ourselves from the ground up, alongside and through dogs.

Can we push beyond the residual humanism that lurks in considerations of the rights of personhood? To amplify the lure of animality, I attend to the sentience that matters more than abstract moralizing. We need to think along with our dogs and apprehend them as the basis for human sensibility and cognition, not the other way around. In the materiality of such a terrain, perhaps the word *human* can be redeemed. That renewed political life is laid out in Rose's work, from *Dingo Makes Us Human: Life and Land in an Aboriginal Australian Culture* (2000) to *Reports from a Wild Country: Ethics for Decolonisation* (2004) and on, finally, to the extraordinary *Wild Dog Dreaming: Love and Extinction* (2011), a work so wrenching that I have found it for a long time hard to write about.

COLIN DAYAN

Wild Dog Dreaming urges me on now, both as background and as goad for these thoughts on animals as nothing less than thermometers of extinction. They signal what is most wrong with the society that destroys them. And their destruction always goes along with the annihilation of those humans labeled as "extraneous" or "dangers" or "threats."

The war against dingoes in the Aboriginal lands of the Northern Territory—which Rose focused on—like the war against pit bulls or American Staffordshire terriers in the United States, or any dog thought too feral to be in the presence of a certain kind of human being, remains a war against the land, against all things that live beyond the greed and consumption of that most cunning of predators, the human animal. As Rose writes, "Dingo deaths are one ripple in the larger pattern of destruction that calls us to ask: Is eco-reconciliation nothing more than a wild and crazy dream? Is it necessary that all animals become either pets or enemies? Is there no room for the companionability of others who share with us the glories of life without being directly beholden to us in any particular way?" (2011, 69). What I have come to see as Rose's "broken eulogy" or "aesthetic of a piecemeal grief" bears in its fragments the traces of everyday racism, careless slaughter, and commonplace servitude.

In her hands, all elements of nature, human and nonhuman, are revved up into something that cannot be described as *supernatural* in the way we usually mean the term. Indeed, even in what she calls "stories of wager and willful death" (Job's grief; Rose 2011, 71), our experience is always corporeal—a piling up of matter so extreme that it becomes utterly mystical. In death and during funerals, the spirit of the dead person finds its way back to earth through the grief of the living. In haunting words, Rose describes a ritual of reciprocity that surrounded the death of an Aboriginal man in a community she lived and worked in, centering on the "real work of singing him home" (75): "All this grieving reaches out into the death space, and if life is truly finished, then all this grieving sought a response from the living, sought voices that howl in sympathy and assure us all that neither the living nor the dying have been abandoned. This was a sharing of grief so as to soothe the throbbing emptiness left in the country, and in the family, and in the world more widely. Shared grief brought death into the world of life" (74).

In the time of Donald Trump, we must turn to Rose's attempt to understand the limits and extent of human cruelty when placed alongside the lives of those "animals and plants, life forms that for long had been held to be outside the bounds of ethical consideration" (61). When her writing most strains, comes apart, seems least intelligible, it engages the heart, penetrating and fracturing any utopian dream of perfection, ideal of progress, or instrumental moralism. Reading her now, I get chills, I have to stop reading, for what she prophesied concerning the onward trek of human gluttony now comes to pass, whether we look to Jair Bolsonaro's assault on the Amazon or Trump's attack on wildlife, trees, and the laws that protect them, most recently in the Arctic National Wildlife Refuge as he opens it to oil and gas drilling.

STELLA'S FACE, MY LOVE

Early one morning, I walked my dog, Stella, down the main street of my Nashville neighborhood. She's a black American Staffordshire terrier with front paws of white fur and a tail that has always been crooked. A man in a pickup truck was waiting in a drive. She ran up to him, as she sometimes does when white men in trucks, those I grew up knowing as *crackers* or *rednecks*, look out at her—a ritual I've never understood. She jumped, one paw on the man's seat and another on his leg, and began to greet him with licks, sniffs, and nudges. He welcomed her, as I looked on in wonder. Then he explained, "She knows I'm sick, and that's why she's trying to help me. I'm dying." Then he gently beat his chest, adding, "She can smell it. She wants to give me some relief."

I have been suffering with an undiagnosed illness, a wasting away, for the past year. I lived through Stella. No matter her health—in spite of the tumor on her rump, the pancreatitis in her gut, the white hairs on her jowls—she remains game for all kinds of fun. She lives through all manner of things, with a focus on what she loves—until she can't. Stella knows that I am in trouble. She stays by my side. Sometimes I catch her gazing fixedly at me. Even when I acknowledge her glance, she stays with her stare, never looking away.

Now Stella has died. I can no longer look into her eyes and know a faith more palpable than the divine. Can you find God in the least likely of places? Stella answered the question. Utterly Pauline in her consecration of matter—no matter how foul—she led me on the surest road to the spirit. That tough faith relies on paradox, since the stuff of spiritual life is never anything if not radically material. By watching Stella, I learned about faith—and its difference from abstract vagaries of belief. She looked for faith, as Herman Melville put it in *Moby-Dick*, among the jackals, in an earth of rot and stink (1952, 36).

In her eyes, any bone discarded could become sacred. I learned of her transformative powers by watching how instead of chewing and devouring the bones I gave her, she wandered purposefully inside the house or outside in the backyard, looking for a suitable place to bury them. And no mere burial did she intend. Rather, in a studied performance of care, she sniffed the dirt, moved it aside with her paws, and then fiercely dug the hole into which she would lay the bone with a delicacy that astonished.

By watching her, I learned to know feeling that is nothing other than knowing: an exhilaration that braces the mind. This knowing has nothing to do with our assumptions and everything to do with ways of seeing. It demands an unprecedented attentiveness that summons another way of being in the world. What would it mean to reorient our ethical and conceptual assumptions by taking on the perspective of dogs? Remaining in touch with the matter of daily life, we, too, might begin to travel across space and into other bodies—a state of dogs. This *condition of being dog* is not the precondition for uniqueness but rather an imperative to seek a more voracious if always provisional communion.

We might compare it to the communion shared by the psychoanalyst and the patient: equivocal, risky, transformative, what Sigmund Freud understood as a kind of knowing without knowing. He identified this relation more fully in *Group Psychology and the Analysis of the Ego* (1921) as *Einfühlung*, or empathy. It became essential to *transference*, the wondrous relation that alone made analysis possible. In "The Dynamics of Transference" (1912), "Remembering, Repeating, and Working Through" (1914), and "Observations on Transference-Love" (1915), Freud found his method in the redirection of a patient's past emotions onto the present relation with the analyst. The very "peculiarities of the transference to the doctor," Freud wrote, exceed, "both in amount and nature, anything that could be justified on sensible or rational grounds" (1912, 99). It is not surprising that at the end of his life Freud turned to dogs as his companions. They alone know pure love, a love beyond convenience or comfort. They also bite. As Freud famously said, though no one is quite sure where, "Dogs love their friends and bite their enemies, quite unlike people, who are incapable of pure love and always have to mix love and hate in their object relations."

Such love has little to do with romance, or the frills that go along with it. It remains visceral, as physical as a punch to the gut. So, then, what does it mean to become more like a dog? Lucy protests to David Lurie in J. M. Coetzee's *Disgrace* (1999) that she has no property, no this, no that, just "like a dog." To be like a dog is something more akin to plenitude than nothing, as Lurie learns when he, too, gives up what he holds on to most dearly. He surrenders the crippled dog whom he loves and who loves him to the lethal injection endured by all the stray and abandoned dogs around him.

191

Living with Stella helped me to reconsider my priorities. I have lost friendships and nearly a marriage because of that reconsideration. Her sense of ethics was spot-on. What I mean by *ethics* here is relatedness, *a being with others* that depends on proximity, a closeness that demands an experience quite distinct from something as abstract as morality. So, if you happen to live with a human who has firm ideas about dirt and cleanliness, right and wrong ways to be—on or off the bed—a dog like Stella, by luring you into her rowdy antics, gives you the chance to be another kind of person.

WILD ECOLOGIES, A NEW SACRAMENT

In Rose's writings, humanity remains a position marked by relativity and uncertainty, and nonhumans—whether animals, plants, artifacts, or celestial bodies—also possess an animist essence or power like a demonic underbelly. (Or does that force reside under the skin?) This does not mean that humans, for example, are not animals but rather that everything we grant to that privileged status of human must be suspect if it is not shared. Defeating hierarchy everywhere she found it, Rose presses hard on what divides in order to rank. She dissolves distinctions between all kinds of things; incorporeal and physical are put into relation, as are other dichotomies such as the living and the dead, just like the human and the nonhuman. Not only do humans in their souls have various roles that share qualities with the objects they possess or destroy, but also, like their bodies, their souls, too, have bones and blood and skin, and they take their representational cues (and the limits and extent of their existence) from their material connections with animals.

What is most striking about the method in Rose's imprecision and fragmentations is her emphatic denial of a supernaturalism emptied of what harrows: the wounds, the wear and tear of daily life. Her argument— her tenuous but exacting perturbation of civility and privilege—depends on a radical way of looking at the natural. She offers another rendition of creaturely experience that upsets the reliable, reasonable, moral order of things. Consider with me again what it might mean to feel sufficiently, not sentimentally. It is another life she envisions, one that finds its expression through a reorientation of our ways of seeing and thinking.

What kind of world is this? It is not easy to write this cosmos into being. Not only will she use her craft to project a radical questioning of society and nature, but she will also unveil the modes of thought and language that work to mask what remains alive and unsettling in the terrain of the coerced and exploited. Rose's persistent attentiveness promises to give creatures not just our consideration but also our love. In a time of impoverishment and extinction, she explores and affirms what is inextinguishable, in order to ask: What constitutes a life worth living? For her, the answers constitute nothing less than an embodied ethics and a new sense of the political.

How can we shed the mantle of civility, consensus, and rationality just long enough to question the claims of the Western world? We are living in a time of extinctions: a systematic disposal of creatures deemed threatening or unfit. How easy it is for fear and dogma to allow us to demonize others, to deny them a common humanity, to do unspeakable things to them. In a morally disenchanted world, daily cruelty and casual violence accompany the call for order, the need for security. But what might we feel if we could feel what we experience? Reading Rose demands a radical change in perspective. She sets out to test the limits of decency and common sense. Words no longer mean what we assume. Further, the feeling she demands is not sympathy or sentiment. Instead, it remains much less comforting, more acute and unsettling.

In *Wild Dog Dreaming*, her most haunting book, she writes a lament for "a system of cross-species kinship . . . in dreadful peril at this time" (2011, 3). But she goes further. She answers the call for immediacy and captures the gist of a very corporeal life of the spirit that I have longed for in much of my work, early and late. What she calls "an ecological erotics" in her chapter "The Beginning Law" examines how the divide between what we call *spiritual* and what we call *secular* is far more permeable than enlightened claims and their emphatic reasonableness would have us believe. The stories she tells about Old Tim's stories on a hot afternoon lead us to that place where the dead do not die but live on in stories thought, remembered, and performed. As she writes:

> Such stories constitute more-than-human genealogies that enmesh people in cross-species transformations. I came to learn that everyone had a history that told how their life came across through other species. Hobbles Danaiyarri, another of my great teachers, was a barramundi before he became a human. . . .
>
> Old Tim's stories on that hot, tense afternoon offered a philosophy of connectivity not through abstractions but through engagement. Words and events became a contrapuntal performance. (133)

In writing from within the terrain of whatever is not human, Rose finds "The Beginning Law." Positioning herself before spirits, humans, dogs, and ghosts, she finds a respite from the mania for money, the illusion of progress, the devastation of lands, and the obliteration of lives.

What does it mean to find a politics in this alternative treatment and understanding of law? With us, it is the "real" world that seems the immediate thing, and the "supernatural" world is something above and beyond. But once in the precincts of wild dogs and the episodes of massive harm she depicts, the immediate thing is as if the supernatural (for which, of course, *super*natural would thus be an inappropriate term) and what we call the "real" (where injury is obvious and its meaning clear) are no more than a symbolization of events in the world of ritual. There, what is most bizarre, most incorporeal, is recast as reasonable. A relentless acceptance of unreality is a necessary part of life in the wreckage of human history. Yet what at first seems fantastic is locked into nature continuously undergoing transformation: "Life is always in a state of metamorphosis, across death into more life, crossing bodies, species, and generations" (137).

Her writing gives to the color, shape, feel, and smell of matter—dead or alive—the claims of the spirit. The management of what is deemed society's refuse—what I call *fecal motives*—draws distinctions between the free and the bound, the familiar and the strange, the privileged and the stigmatized. This ongoing cultivation of human waste materials asks us to recast interpretation itself. In this visceral philosophy lie the radiance and persistence of "the Beginning Law." As Old Tim put it, "From beginning Dreaming, White man, Blackfella, Indian, any one, they're all born from that Beginning Law" (137).

The annihilation of dingoes, the disposal of their bodies once dead, must alert us to what is more than another "dog story." It is not a call for sympathy or sentiment but rather a recognition of conscience, in the oldest sense of the word. As I have suggested (in *With Dogs at the Edge of Life* [Dayan 2015]), this is not feeling as we understand it but, rather, knowing what it means to know and to share the knowledge together, a collective recognition not just of wrong done but of the casual force of cruelty. For those who adhere to a myth of progress or faith in reason, the continuum between past and present, human and nonhuman, natural and unnatural, living and dead, must be deeply felt. This deep feeling is what Rose's suggestive and evocative writing strives both to arouse and to engage, while also leading into an inclusive ethics, in Rose's words: "Connectivity ethics are open, uncertain, attentive, participatory, contingent" (143).

Such an ethics does not invoke any concept of relativism but instead, as I suggested, casts doubt on the robustness and transportability of the ontological partitions that we so easily assume. This is admittedly a personal bias, since I have long tried to address, even if tentatively, the seepage between entities assumed to be distinct, whether dead or living, animate or inanimate, human or nonhuman.

Fear is a vice that takes root. Fear and the brutality that accompanies it can be recognized only when the human and the animal are brought together, when what yokes us together as *creatures* puts us in the proverbial same boat. The language of threat, removal, and loss has become both medium and prompt for the ongoing intimidation, control, and debasement of humans in their turn. As I said, we are living in a time of extinctions. And the disposal of the Aboriginal wild dingoes helps us to understand why.

REFERENCES

Coetzee, J. M. 1999. *Disgrace*. London: Secker and Warburg.

Dayan, Colin. 2015. *With Dogs at the Edge of Life*. New York: Columbia University Press.

Freud, Sigmund. 1912 [1958]. "The Dynamics of Transference." In Freud, *The Standard Edition of the Complete Psychological Works of Sigmund Freud*, Vol. XII, 97–108.

Freud, Sigmund. 1914 [1958]. "Remembering, Repeating, and Working Through." In Freud, *The Standard Edition of the Complete Psychological Works of Sigmund Freud*, Vol. XII, 145–157.

Freud, Sigmund. 1915a [1958]. "Observations on Transference-Love." In Freud, *The Standard Edition of the Complete Psychological Works of Sigmund Freud*, Vol. XII, 159–171.

Freud, Sigmund. 1915b [1958]. *The Standard Edition of the Complete Psychological Works of Sigmund Freud. Volume XII (1911–1913): The Case of Schreber, Papers on Technique and Other Works*. Edited by James Strachey, Anna Freud, Alix Strachey, and Alan Tyson. London: The Hogarth Press and Institute of Psychoanalysis.

Freud, Sigmund. 1921 [1955]. "Group Psychology and the Analysis of the Ego." In *The Standard Edition of the Complete Psychological Works of Sigmund Freud. Volume XVIII (1920–1922): Beyond the Pleasure Principle, Group Psychology and Other Works*, 65–144. Edited by James Strachey, Anna Freud, Alix Strachey, and Alan Tyson. London: The Hogarth Press and Institute of Psychoanalysis.

Melville, Herman. 1952. *Moby-Dick, or, The Whale*. New York: Hendricks House.

Rose, Deborah Bird. 2000. *Dingo Makes Us Human: Life and Land in an Aboriginal Australian Culture*. Cambridge: Cambridge University Press.

Rose, Deborah Bird. 2004. *Reports from a Wild Country: Ethics for Decolonisation*. Sydney: University of New South Wales Press.

Rose, Deborah Bird. 2011. *Wild Dog Dreaming: Love and Extinction*. Charlottesville: University of Virginia Press.

LIFE IS A WOVEN BASKET
OF RELATIONS

ELEVEN

KATE WRIGHT

EVERYTHING ON EARTH can be wonderfully made and wonderfully undone.[1] Life is a woven basket of relations, each of us threaded through
the other, knotted to creaturely futures and patterned by a coevolutionary
past.

The country that grew me up is the gorge country that splits coastal northeastern Australia from the red dirt of its center. I remember bellowing into
the cavernous escarpment and hearing echoes of my childhood voice carried
back to me by multispecies memories of erosion. At this granite precipice,
traces of the past are felt through absence, where rocky strata stripped bare
sculpt an immense landscape of loss.

As an adult I learned that the rugged escarpment and distant blue hills
that resound with my earliest memories of belonging and connection were
some of the last places Anaiwan people could find brief refuge from colonial terror. The ancient cliffs of my youth are awash with blood. Anaiwan

language revivalist Callum Clayton-Dixon explains, "By the late 1830s, stations sprawled right across the mostly undulating, lightly wooded, and well-watered terrain of the New England plateau. As the invaders tightened their control over the district's prized grazing lands, stations on the Tableland's more rugged fringes became the primary target of resistance efforts. These runs occupied or backed onto very rough country, and this kind of environment was a place of safe harbour" (2019, 40). While colonization can be read in planetary archives of rock—inextricable from the emergence of the Anthropocene and its stratigraphic record of environmental devastation and mass death—colonialism and its violences are not confined to history. Colonization is not a contained event but a generative one, a tsunami of terror that ripples out through interconnected biological, social, and ecological systems in recursive waves of damage and destruction.

James Hatley argues that genocide is not only the obliteration of existing lives and cultures but an attack on the intergenerational multitemporal webs that sustain life. He terms this *aenocide*—"a murdering of the generations" (2000, 30). "The great Australian holocaust known as colonisation" (Rose 1992, 2) cannot be situated in one historical epoch because it is a targeted attack on Aboriginal people's futures that works to erase their past.

My teacher, colleague, and friend Deborah Bird Rose observed that life on Earth is constituted and sustained by "dense knots of embodied time." Every individual of every species "is both itself in the present, and the history of its forebears and mutualists" (Rose 2012b, 136). We carry in our bodies an intricate pattern of creaturely gifts of life and time. Colonial aenocide, then, is an attack on the gift of life as it is shared across generations and between species—a "murder of ethical time" (Hatley 2000, 219).

Now a woman in my mid-thirties, I find myself again at a precipice in the gorge country of my youth, struggling to reconcile the creaturely gifts I embody and so am responsible for with the violence I have inherited—the colonial spoils that have blessed my life with gifts born of suffering. Gazing at the rocky strata of the so-called New England tablelands, I think of the multitemporal horizons that have demarcated my privileged, yet harshly situated, position as a settler-descendant in a settler-colonial state—a stratigraphy composed of tens of thousands of years of Indigenous custodianship in Anaiwan Country, all the multispecies nourishment that has fed and sustained me; the care and love of my mother, my father, the house they built on stolen land; the pervading silence surrounding massacres; and the ongoing waves of cultural genocide, ecocide, and transgenerational trauma that reverberate through this troubled land.[2]

LIFE IS A WOVEN BASKET OF RELATIONS

11.1 The strata of my youth at Gara Gorge in Oxley Wild Rivers National Park, New England, New South Wales, Australia, 2016. PHOTOGRAPH BY KATE WRIGHT.

Like a child bellowing into a vastness they cannot comprehend, hearing their voice returned, at once a narcissistic echo and at the same time a dialogue with the deepest and most ancient of rhythms, I write this chapter in a struggle to find an ethical voice in the world.

I am guided in this endeavor by the profoundly thoughtful and emotionally rich scholarship of Debbie Rose, my PhD supervisor who became my dear friend. Underneath the beautiful cadence of her writing and the poetic hope she expressed through her ideas, Debbie carried a deep sadness for the injustices of this country. Refusing complicity with ongoing colonizing forces, Debbie advocated for "recuperative work": material and intellectual labors that "trawl the past and the present, searching out the hidden histories and the local possibilities that illuminate alternatives to our embeddedness in violence" (2004, 25).

During my PhD research, I interviewed Aboriginal Elders about their connection to place in the region where I spent the first eighteen years of my life.

KATE WRIGHT

As Elders shared with me intimate accounts of their childhoods filled with devastating experiences of racism and dispossession, this forced me to confront the deeply uncomfortable fact that my places of intimate habitation, the places where I grew to understand myself and the world, are, as James Hatley writes in this collection, "permeated by currents of ecological diminishment and cultural displacement that continue to haunt all those who would call themselves at home in this place." While I had read and learned about colonization for many years, this situated account of trauma called me into a new relationship of responsibility. I felt for the first time that I had lived my life on stolen land. I had known that for a long time, but now I *felt* it.[3]

After I had completed my PhD, I returned to Armidale to work with the community whose violent dispossession had created the privileged conditions of my childhood. In collaboration with Anaiwan Elder Uncle Steve Widders, I helped to create the Armidale Aboriginal Community Garden, a grassroots community-driven site for recuperative work. In alliance with the more-than-human world, the community garden works to reinscribe Aboriginal presence, fighting the settler-colonial state's "violent practices of occupation, erasure and colonial resignification" (Pugliese 2015, 31). As Elders use the community garden to share their survivor testimony of living through colonial oppression and to work with younger generations to revive native plants, cultural practices, and ancestral languages, they reclaim repressed histories and activate the rhythms of deep ancestral aeonic time held enduring in Country and culture.

One of the regular cultural revival activities taking place in the community garden is monthly weaving workshops, hosted by Anaiwan and Gumbaynggirr weaver and artist Gabi Briggs. These workshops are open to Aboriginal women and use lomandra grasses harvested from nearby gorge country to weave pieces of material culture while also weaving circles of togetherness by creating what Briggs describes as "safe and autonomous spaces for Black women."[4]

Running my fingers along tightly bound lomandra grasses, I cannot help but feel that a woven basket is one of the most tangible and eloquent examples of what Debbie termed "multispecies knots of ethical time." In its intricate pattern, each piece of weaving is an interface where "time, species, and nourishment become densely knotted up in ethics of gift, motion, death, life, and desire" (Rose 2012b, 127).

My hope for this chapter is that it weaves Debbie's poetic and profound insights into the eloquent form of a woven lomandra basket. My intention is not to exploit weaving to articulate one of Debbie's concepts, or to use the tools of Western thought and thinkers to unravel a woven basket as an act of dissection and interrogation; rather, I aim to reveal how weaving can be understood as a performative practice of cultural resurgence that crafts multispecies knots of ethical time. Debbie wrote so beautifully of connection, of relationship, of the wonders of a living planet. Her work, though complex and scholarly, seemed to hover at the edge of language, frequently drifting into poetry, as she traced the lyrical utterances of biological life on Earth. Pieces of weaving, too, are material texts that trace intricate, life-sustaining webs of mutuality, while also helping to nurture those webs. My central argument in this chapter is that the revival of weaving, a multispecies relational practice that becomes-with ancestral rhythms drawn from a deep Indigenous past, is a form of material and intellectual recuperative labor that resists colonial aenocide and the murder of ethical time.

EMBODIED KNOTS OF TIME

Yolngu Elder Laklak Burarrwanga from Bawaka Country, North East Arnhem Land, explains the way patterns of intergenerational time are woven into a basket: "The spiral shows the life cycle—tells us how babies grow, their arteries and their selves, both in the womb and as a baby grows into a child and on through the generations. It starts as a small baby girl and then as the basket grows so the baby girl grows up until she's a young mother and she'll learn and have babies and the knowledge and growth keeps spiralling. It cycles through the generations, the woman becomes a grandmother with the ongoing cycles and it keeps going. There's no actual death, life keeps spiralling on through the generations" (Burarrwanga et al. 2008, 33). Burarrwanga's poetic meditation on passages of gestation and continuity woven into the spiral of a basket is both allegorical and material. Biology and culture become deeply entwined through the embodied and performative knowledge practice of weaving that knots generations together. While Burarrwanga's quote here deals primarily with sequential, intergenerational temporality, Debbie emphasized that "life depends both on the sequential processes of generational time . . . and on the synchronous processes of multispecies nourishment. These processes and patterns intersect to form dense knots of embodied time" (Rose 2012b, 131).

Debbie adopted Hatley's concept of the gift to explain the way connective patterns of sequence and synchrony emerge against the entropic arrow of time that tends toward dissolution. While the second law of thermodynamics—the law of entropy—ensures that "the randomness of

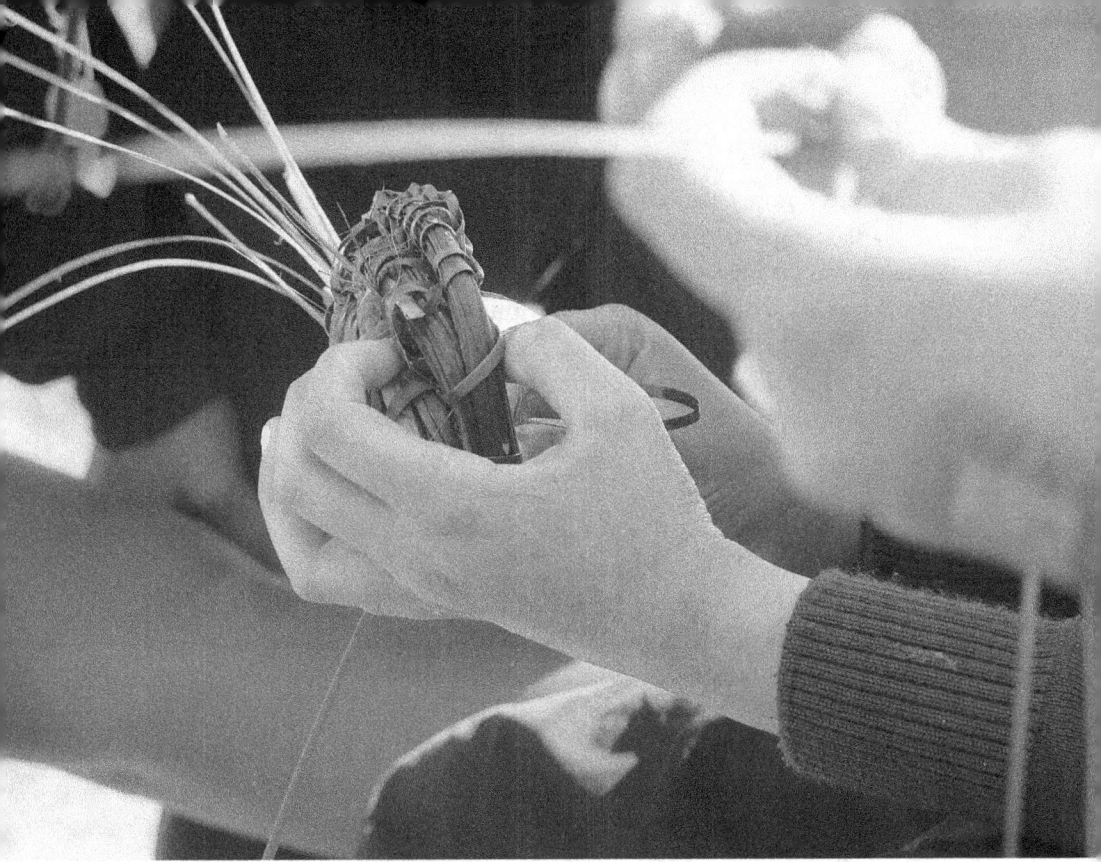

11.2 Young hands weaving lomandra grasses at one of Gabi Briggs's weaving workshops at the Armidale Aboriginal Community Garden, 2015. PHOTOGRAPH BY KATE WRIGHT.

probability will always eat up order and pattern in the world" (Bateson 1972, 176), life, "the biological order on earth" (Harries-Jones 1995, 107), draws order out of disorder and organization out of disorganization (Rose 2012b, 135) as it weaves patterns of mutuality where "energy is channelled into renewal, or, into order emerging against entropy" (136). Life resists entropy because living organisms are open systems, exchanging heat and matter with other living systems. In other words, life is a woven basket of relations, and each earthly creature emerges from this fabric as a dense knot of embodied multispecies time.

Just as living organisms are emergent products of sequential and synchronous time, interwoven by relational encounters that create and nurture us until we once again disperse at the moment of death, pieces of weaving emerge from ongoing iterative environmental, biological, and cultural processes. Anthropologist Tim Ingold argues that weaving is akin to autopoiesis because the human weaver is one component within a communicative more-than-human field "caught up in a reciprocal and quite muscular dialogue with the [weaving] material" (2000, 342). He writes that since the weaver "is involved in the same system as the material with which he works, so his activity does not transform that system but is—like the growth of plants and animals—part and parcel of the system's transformation of itself . . . [as] the temporal rhythms of life are gradually built into the structural properties of things" (345). Ingold poetically observes that in this autopoietic becoming, "weaving . . . continues for as long as life goes on— punctuated but not terminated by the appearance of the pieces that it successively brings into being" (348). Like Burarrwanga's ecology of life, in weaving there is no "actual" death, because in immanent relational systems life is held enduring in synchronous and sequential patterns rather than in the fleeting (but vital) actualizations (or embodied knots) of those patterns.

Anaiwan and Gumbaynggirr weaver Gabi Briggs commented to me that lomandra grasses that are woven into a basket never truly die. The grasses always stay green, Briggs explained, and they continue to be part of the web of life as nourishing interfaces, such as dilly bags to collect berries, or eel traps.[5] Weaving is a process in which organic beings and environments become entangled in very real and direct ways, articulating the cosmology of connectivity Debbie wrote so eloquently about and for.

As an object and practice of material culture that connects species in relationships of nourishment and death and that spans generations, pieces of weaving have much to teach us about life as a verb rather than a noun—life as a process that "repairs, maintains, re-creates, and outdoes itself" (Margulis and Sagan 2000, 16). Lynn Margulis and Dorion Sagan explain the way life weaves increasingly complex knots of embodied time: "Preserving the past, making a difference between past and present, life binds time, expanding complexity and creating new problems for itself" (86). Thom van Dooren observes that what is tied together in embodied knots of time "is not 'the past' and 'the future' as abstract temporal horizons, but real embodied generations—ancestors and descendants—in rich but imperfect relationships of inheritance, nourishment and care" (2014, 27–29). Van Dooren emphasizes that on this precarious planet, each embodied knot of time is an intergenerational and multispecies achievement. In its intricate enfolding of places and organisms, weaving poetically reflects the delicate labors involved in threading patterns of time through fragile webs of life and death.

Hatley uses the concept of "ethical time" to articulate time "as a differentiation across which and by means of which responsibilities are born" (2000, 61). In Hatley's analysis, drawing closely on the work of Emmanuel Levinas, ethics is not an afterthought but what sustains and enables life, where relationships of responsibility to others in a time-binding world are "the very articulation of the 'real'" (61). Debbie's profound contribution to Hatley's sophisticated discussion of ethical time is to note that in a world of multispecies mutualisms, we are not born only from the womb of our mothers—and not gifted only the time of our ancestors—but emerge from the womb of living Country, our bodies archives of planetary becomings that stretch to the coevolutionary beginnings of life on Earth.

RIVERS

My homeland—the unceded Anaiwan Country now commonly known as the New England tableland region of New South Wales—is crisscrossed by rivers that flow from inland Australia, south to the sea. In the midst of this country of rivers is a dramatic dividing escarpment. When they reach the unforgiving chasms of gorge country, gentle river currents become thunderous waterfalls, and the land reverberates with the sound of oceans thrashing against Archean rock.

Traveling these vibrant transitive watercourses are long-finned river eels (*Anguilla reinhardtii*) that follow a migratory path from the coastal currents of the Pacific Ocean to the meandering rivers and tributaries of the tablelands and the western slopes and plains.[6] One of the main ancestral products woven from lomandra grasses was eel traps. In the form of nets, traps, and food containers, lomandra grasses carry "great patterns of life, death, sustenance and renewal that intersect across species and generations to form flows of life-giving life" (Rose 2012b, 139).

Eels are catadromous—migrating from inland freshwater rivers to the salty sea to spawn. After spawning, the eels perish, and their young return inland to continue to trace a watery pattern of life and death that has existed for millennia. Debbie explains that the life cycles of sexually reproductive creatures tell us that sex and death are inextricably entangled—"within the ecology of life, death is a necessary partner" (Rose 2012b, 127).

The metamorphosis of the long-finned river eel that ensures the continuation of the species is carried on the tide: Adult eels migrate to the Coral Sea to spawn (Aoyama et al. 1999; Gooley et al. 1999). During the larval stage individuals are transported via the East Australian Current to near shore waters where they metamorphose into unpigmented "glass eels" (Shiao et al. 2001; Beumer 1992). Glass eels then move upstream to grow and develop through a small, pigmented "elver" stage into the large but still immature "adult" eels. When adults reach sexual maturity they undergo marked changes in their appearance and become silvery. Anatomy and physiology also alter at sexual maturity and eels undertake a once only downstream migration to the spawning grounds, where it is believed they spawn and subsequently die (Queensland Eel Fishery 2009, 5). Long-finned eels can live as long as fifty-two years (Lintermans 2009, 34), but, like all reproductive creatures, individual deaths are gifts to subsequent generations, as "continual dying makes way for and makes possible new forms of life" (Parkin 2017, 461).

The eel's own life cycle—its aeonic intergenerational pattern of embodied gifts of time and life—intersects with human nourishment. Over tens of thousands of years, synchronous encounters become part of the sequential lifeway of a species and a culture, as species live and die well together (Haraway 2016) in transitive patterns of coevolutionary becoming. Woven lomandra grasses emerge at the interface of violence and nourishment, sex and death, the renewal of birth and the deep death narratives of ancestral Country.

Hatley uses the term *death narrative* to describe sequential patterns of generational time, where each group or population "can be seen as a wave of memory, insight, and expectation coursing through time, a wave that lifts up and sustains the individuals of each succeeding generation, even as those individuals make their own particular contributions to or modifications of that wave" (2000, 60–61). The long-finned river eel reminds us that in a "world of ecological death, gifts and flows" (Rose 2012b, 135), rivers and waves are not merely metaphors but nourishing interfaces where matter binds time in webs of ethical and ecological connectivity.

ANCESTRAL WAVES

I attended Debbie's last public lecture, at the Australian Museum in Sydney in 2018. I remember her saying that "the gift of life is a gift that must keep moving" (Rose 2018). The gift moves on ancestral tides as if they were currents in a river carrying gestational generations of eels to their birthing place in the sea. And this gift moves because we die, and the rivers and waves of our lives carry our death into the future.

Lynn Margulis and Dorion Sagan observe that Cartesian separations of mind and body, human and nonhuman, have constructed a particularly finite understanding of death that does not match the multitemporal enfolding of biological life on Earth: "We moderns accept that a caterpillar 'metamorphoses' into a butterfly, yet we employ the term 'death' for what happens to grandfather's body. Nevertheless, with both the metamorphosing insect and the dying grandparent, the fresh body of youth reappears. . . . [A] parent contributing to the flesh of a child is a prolongation, not an abrupt end, to biological continuity. The 'individual' is not so complete, in time, as we have been taught" (2000, 228). I have been told that I have my grandmother's blue eyes, a reminder that my body is inextricably interwoven with the bodies of my human ancestors. But a human face is also a nest of multispecies relations—an embodied knot of multispecies time. You have your grandmother's blue eyes, they say, to the face born out of the faces of others, a chain of faces stretching back over ancient rivers before blue eyes even existed, before human beings were even human.

Hatley observes that in the Jewish liturgy there is a special blessing for rain that links its fall to the resurrection of the dead, to the "revivifying of the human face by its creator" (Genesis Rabbah 13:6; cited in Hatley 2002, 16). Rain calls deceased faces forth and rebirths them—faces that carry the pattern of rivers and tributaries, of waves and currents, of birds of prey circling overhead. In an ecological system where the "condition of being-birthed is a gift, and every interface that nourishes and promotes life is another gift" (Rose 2012b, 137), newborn faces carry memories of the world before they have even seen the sun. The meandering gully can be found in a gurgling smile, the billowing cloud in the furrowed brow.

When I look at woven lomandra baskets, I think of the rivers of my homeland, their currents and courses patterned across my life as if wrinkles around my eyes. I think of standing with my two-year-old son on the stones of the Bellinger River in the coastal hinterland between my homeland and the sea—the ice-cold water so clear you almost cannot see it. I think of the murky waters of the Gara River I swam in as a child, my feet sinking into the mud, the nip of a yabby, the smell of earth. All these rivers that flow in my memory carry me like a tide of creaturely amniotic fluid into the maternal womb of Country.

THE MURDER OF ETHICAL TIME

Recently, dead eels have been collecting in pools throughout the river catchments of the tablelands. This is believed to be a result of algal blooms and a lack of oxygen caused by prolonged drought conditions.[7] Hilaire Drouineau and colleagues (2018, 914) note that the past forty years of anthropogenic

environmental change has begun to unravel over 50 million years of coevolutionary adaptation for the *Anguilla* species, threatening the survival of eels
across the world. This is part of a much broader assault on the nourishing
interfaces and situated sets of multispecies relations that protect and nurture
the future of multiple earthly species, including our own. Drawing Hatley's
discussion of aenocide into a biosocial context, Debbie emphasized that the
degradation of multispecies ecologies that has ushered in the Earth's sixth
mass extinction event can also be characterized as the murder of ethical time:
"the irreparable loss not only of the living but of the multiplicity of forms of
life and of the capacity of evolutionary processes to regenerate life" (Chrulew
2011, 149, cited in Rose 2012b). As Thom van Dooren observes in this collection, the extinction of a species dispossesses the world of "a diversity of potentialities, left hovering just beyond the edge of the real"—an aeonic attack
on coevolutionary futures: "all of those other incredible . . . species that don't
yet quite exist, not to mention the other plants and animals that might have
emerged in relationship with them."

The unraveling of multispecies webs of ethical time that we witness in
the era of the Anthropocene has "direct roots in the epistemic violences of
discovery, dispossession, extraction, and the horrific capture of life, bodies,
and worlds" that began with colonization (Davis and Todd 2017, 772). In
September 1818 surveyor general John Oxley traversed the ancestral rivers
of Anaiwan lands, a "reconnaissance mission [that] laid the foundations for
the sweeping colonization of the New England Tableland and its peoples"
(Clayton-Dixon 2019, 11). Anaiwan language revivalist and scholar Callum
Clayton-Dixon observes, "Colonial invasion and occupation of the New
England Tableland region of New South Wales was especially rapid and
intense, the first few decades of upheaval (1830s–1860s) having absolutely
catastrophic ramifications for the autochthonous population, thoroughly
devastating all aspects of Aboriginal society" (2019, 10).

Heather Davis and Zoe Todd describe the way colonization enacted a
"quickening of space-time in a seismic sense," "laying waste to legal orders,
languages, place-story in quick succession" (2017, 772). As violent colonial
processes "compressed space and time in terrifying and unpredictable ways,"
they brought about the end of Indigenous worlds (773). Debbie Rose
observed that this Earth-shattering violence involved both genocide and
ecocide: "It is well known that settlers cleared the land of both native people
and native ecologies in order to establish what they took to be civilisation. . . .
The violence wrought on indigenous Australian ecosystems . . . is both long-
standing and ongoing. Much of the past can be known in the present as

KATE WRIGHT

absence—the mammals that are no longer here, the plants that are gone; or as danger—all those species that are on a trajectory towards extinction" (2004, 35–36).

Interlinked genocide and ecocide can be understood as a murder of ethical time—an unraveling of the intricately woven threads that tie generations and species together. Hatley writes that aenocide occurs when "humans conspire to repress, to destroy the future of . . . groups. In doing so, humans show the reprehensible capacity to turn their history, their remembrance of time across the aeons, the generations, into a sort of narcissistic mirror. . . . One writes the past and future as a mode of colonisation. All the other times are resources for one's own" (2000, 63).

In the so-called New England tablelands, deep creaturely and ancestral reservoirs have been both materially and discursively exploited as a resource by occupying colonial powers—a form of temporal extractivism where time is ripped from bodies and environments, and the embodied knots of ethical time that sustain diverse lifeways are unraveled. Clayton-Dixon points to the links between capitalist extractivism and rapid colonial occupation and Aboriginal dispossession operating in early nineteenth-century New England:

> New England was deemed one of the most desirable destinations for pastoral investment, a focus for intense economic exploitation and settler-colonial expansion, and unimpeded access to land was vital to successful colonization of the region. The presence of autochthonous communities represented a significant obstacle to capitalist exploitation of the Tableland's natural resources, and "settler society required the practical elimination of the natives in order to establish itself on their territory" (Wolfe, 2016 pp. 388–389). Rapid outpopulation accelerated the rate at which local Aboriginal people were conquered, dispossessed and assimilated, helping to make way for so-called "progress" and "civilisation." (2019, 42–43)

In her sophisticated analysis of the way settler-colonial cultures use time to reproduce ecologies of erasure, Debbie observed that settlers viewed themselves as "agents of disjunction" and that their intention to create new societies and leave the old behind is signaled by their terminology of "new worlds," such as the name New England (Rose 2004, 57).

Debbie wrote powerfully of the tragedy at the heart of this disjunction—"a vision of progress continuously wrested from this country through torture and crucifixion" as "Indigenous people and the land, waters, soils, plants and animals are sacrificed" (2004, 65) in the name of illusory ideals of modern civilization. She argued that through disjunction, erasure, and a focus on re-demptive futures, "new world" settler societies become detached from the moral accountability produced by continuities with both time and place and begin to generate violence, moral deprivation, and social and environmen-tal catastrophe. The ancient gorge country where I spent many childhood hours, and where Gabi Briggs now harvests lomandra grasses for weaving, is named after surveyor John Oxley: Oxley Wild Rivers National Park—further testament to colonial appropriation of Anaiwan lands, resources, and history. This disjunctive naming points to the way cartographies of time and place become interwoven with the violent extraction of time from bodies and places in what Hatley (this volume) terms a colonial "Regime of Harrowing" that works to erase Aboriginal pasts, presents, and futures.

RECUPERATIVE WORK

As a process of becoming-with "ancestral spirits, stories and knowledge developed over countless generations" (Bawaka Country, 2015, 466), Indige-nous weaving revival resists colonial aenocide and the murder of ethical time by calling forth an enduring ancestral presence that exists beyond and out-side of the violent extractive temporality of colonial invasion and ongoing settler-colonial occupation. In doing so, weaving enacts what Debbie termed *recuperative work*: "Recuperative work takes an ethical stance in opposition to the temporal and monological practices that cause suffering and damage and that exclude or deny the reality of that suffering and damage. Breaking up the linearity of the past → present → future, recuperative work imagines all accessible time as rich with possibility" (Rose 2004, 25).

Weaving revival figures a deep Indigenous past not as something that has been obliterated by an inevitable tide of progress but as an embodied source of strength that can be rethreaded through cultural practices into the lives and bodies of Aboriginal people. Gabi Briggs explains how weaving is a pro-cess of connecting to aeonic, ancestral rhythms:

> I think it's just so incredibly beautiful and humbling that you're . . . doing the same movements, you're weaving the same thing—or weaving a product—that your people used for thousands of years. . . . And you're thinking, "Is this the mindset? Is this the state of being?" and it's not even "if." You know that you are sharing the same experience as your ancestors thousands of years ago . . . and it's just so powerful and so incredible to be in that moment. It makes me stronger, I know that for sure, culturally

stronger, personally a lot stronger—my confidence, and how I navigate myself throughout this world. And it makes me want to be home, to be on Country, and to do this here.[8]

Weaving creates time knots, in the products that emerge from weavers' rhythmic motions and in the practice itself. Briggs describes being "in that moment," and the moment she describes is dense with multiple temporalities—an immanent enfolding of ancestral, abiding time with the present. As her fingers delicately fold lomandra grasses into a patterned basket, those grasses themselves carrying morphogenetic material histories of tens of thousands of years of Aboriginal custodianship of this continent, Briggs folds time into space, past into present, and ancestral waves of strength, resistance, and becoming into her own body.

Because dispossession is not a singular historical event but the ongoing apparatus of settler-colonial occupation of Aboriginal Country, weaving can also be considered a version of what Christina Sharpe calls "wake work," a form of labor and healing that takes place "in an ongoing present of subjection and resistance" (2016, 20). As a radical form of decolonial resurgence that "roots resistance in the spirit, knowledge, and laws . . . of ancestors" (Alfred 2018), weaving is a practice that manifests embodied knots of time that also craft embodied lines of flight from the imaginative and territorial bounds of the colonial world (Martineau and Ritskes 2014). Through multitemporal ancestral becoming, weaving enacts what Jarrett Martineau and Eric Ritskes describe as a fugitive escape from colonialism, pushing "against the limits of colonial knowing and sensing . . . [seeking] to limn the margins of land, culture and consciousness for . . . creative spaces of departure and renewal" (2014, iv).

On January 28, 2013, Gabi Briggs was involved in a protest in Westfield's Eastgardens Shopping Centre on Eora land that mobilized weaving as a form of performative wake work to rupture structural silences (Sharpe 2016, 22) through a silent demonstration of sovereignty. Briggs was part of a group of members and supporters of Idle No More Sydney who formed a weaving circle in the middle of Westfield plaza to demonstrate solidarity with the Idle No More movement in Canada and global Indigenous resistance to colonial-capitalist extractivism and dispossession. The group explain:

A week prior to the event we harvested the native grass lomandra traditionally used for weaving. We stripped, dried, and soaked the lomandra in preparation for the protest. During the weaving circle we made dilly bags using the traditional weaving techniques passed down to us from

209

our Elders in NSW. After 30 minutes Westfield Centre management cautioned us to vacate the shopping centre. Our spokesperson discussed with management and all interested onlookers what it meant for us to weave as our ancestors had for thousands of years before the Centre had been built. We did not vacate and continued to weave in silence for an hour and fifteen minutes. (Idle No More Sydney 2013)

In this protest the weaving circle produces an aesthetic of what Gerald Vizenor (1999) has termed *survivance*, asserting Indigenous presences against the continued erasures wrought by settler colonialism. In a space of fast-paced consumerism, weaving becomes hypervisible as a form of radical alterity, irrecuperable to the corporate logics of the shopping plaza. Anthropologist Marc Augé (1995) used the term *nonplace* to capture the homogeneity of a shopping plaza, the consumerist heart of late capitalism that appears to lack grounding in time or history. In the air-conditioned fluorescent buzz of a Westfield plaza in Sydney's east, consumers were forced into an unexpected confrontation with the Eora lands that underlie capitalist and settler-colonial structures, encountering unceded Aboriginal sovereignty, Indigenous solidarity across the globe, the deep time of Country, and the ongoing immanence of ancestral strength and resistance in the bodies of the weaving women.

As the Aboriginal women wove silently and slowly, puncturing the fast-paced transactional rhythms with decolonial movements drawn from ancestral time, the protest enacted what Martineau and Ritskes describe as a "strategic motion of refusal" that works "to evade capture, resist co-option, and renew Indigenous life-ways through the creative negation of reductive colonial demarcations of being and sensing . . . [a form of] decolonization [that disrupts] colonialism's linear ordering of the world and its conditioning of possibility" (2014, v). The linear coordinates of settler-colonial history incarcerate Indigenous weaving in the prisons of Western modernity. Not only have pieces of Aboriginal weaving been literally stolen by imperial powers, who display them in museums as evidence of a "primitive" and "ancient" culture, weaving is discursively incarcerated by linear temporal orders that enclave it to a premodern past that can no longer speak or compel action. But Aboriginal concepts of temporality have no such finitude.

Based on decades of research with Aboriginal people in the Victoria River District of Australia, Debbie explained that rhythm and pattern are vital time concepts in Aboriginal ecocosmologies that speak to the complex relationship between the ephemeral actions of mortal beings and the abiding, enduring time of ancestors, Dreaming, and Country. Debbie wrote, "Dreaming life continues to unfold into the world as ephemeral life precisely through the patterned actions of the ephemeral." She explains that "in place of the abstracted, disembedded, disembodied absolute time posited by Newton" (Rose 2012b, 128), Aboriginal temporality is embodied and embedded in the patterns of living Country. "Patterns form across numerous scales and domains, so that the web of life can be understood as the complex interactions of sequence and synchrony, as these patterns play out across the lives of individuals, species, country, climate, and years" (129).

In contrast to linear temporality oriented toward progress, where the past seems to disappear with the tide of history, in Aboriginal cosmologies "presence can be held in place, enduring" (Muecke 2004, 16). Abiding, ancestral time exists within Country and can be brought into the living present through what Tony Swain (1993, 19) termed *rhythmed events*. Debbie described these rhythmed events as a kind of porous becoming-with multispecies ancestral time. She writes, "Time, rather than being rendered static or absent, becomes experientially and overwhelmingly focused, present and shared. The person flips from being an actor in time to becoming a heartbeat of time, and the whole on-going systole and diastole of life/time pours into and through persons, places and other living things. Perhaps time itself is a sound, a wave, a call that is pulled into specific places, social groups and ecosystems as it flows from the source through waves of generations of the ephemeral whose actions invigorate this outpouring" (Rose 2000, 295).

In a synchronous manner, Gabi Briggs identifies rhythm to be fundamental to her weaving practice. She describes the way weaving patterns unfold through the ongoing flow of life, punctuated by intervals and pauses in the weaving process:

> I will only weave when I'm in the right space, and then I'll stop, and then I'll pick it back up when I feel like I can do it again. . . . There's a real rhythm to it, and I won't work on something until I feel that I'm in the right space. . . . So, it's a continuous thing. It tells my story, it tells my journey, through what it looks like, where it's at—what stage it's at, where I stopped, and when I'm going to pick it back up. . . . It's not about having an end product, it's about the whole journey. Because you weave that journey into whatever you're making.[9]

Tim Ingold observes that whereas "making" regards "the object as the expression of an idea," weaving regards objects as "the embodiment of a rhythmic movement" (2000, 346). To embody a rhythm that allows for weaving requires

11.3 Aboriginal Elder's hands weaving lomandra grasses at one of Gabi Briggs's weaving workshops at the Armidale Aboriginal Community Garden, 2013. PHOTOGRAPH BY KATE WRIGHT.

a particular way of being in the world. Briggs describes it as a "meditative state" connected to ancestral time. "You're constantly thinking about the old fellas, how they did this practice, and why they did it the way they did."

Mohawk scholar Taiaiake Alfred describes cultural resurgence and regeneration as ways to "power-surge against the empire with integrity" (2005, 24). Rather than *reacting* to ongoing colonial oppression, weaving re*activates* the power of ancestral waves to embolden subsequent generations through aeonic rhythms. The embodiment of these meditative rhythms draws weavers into immanent relation with the practices of ancestors and so manifests a lived, embodied resistance to aenocide—to the colonial murder of ethical time—as "the past that is not past reappears . . . to rupture the present" (Sharpe 2016, 9).

KATE WRIGHT

Dipesh Chakrabarty observed that subaltern minority pasts are "stubborn knots" that break up "the otherwise evenly woven surface of the fabric" of Western historical time (2000, 15). Entangling past with present through reactivating the strength of ancestral practices targeted for annihilation, a woven lomandra basket appears as a "stubborn knot" in the "empty homogenous time" (Benjamin [1936] 1968) of settler-colonial history and the violent disjunctions that work to separate the present from the past. A piece of weaving, whether produced in the middle of a Westfield plaza or in a weaving circle at a little community garden in regional Australia, is "a becoming breaking through into history" (Deleuze 1995, 153). In rhythmic multitemporal pleats and folds, weaving reactivates an ancestral decolonial web of abiding, enduring time alive in place that "makes the continuum of history explode" (Benjamin [1936] 1968, 69–70).

Gilles Deleuze writes of becomings, and microbecomings, "which don't even have the same rhythm as our 'history,'" becomings that belong to "another politics, another time, another individuation" (Deleuze and Parnet 1977, 124). As a process that follows the rhythmic patterns of life—the embodied knots of multispecies time that sustain creaturely existence—weaving activates parts of the self, parts of the grasses, and parts of the connected living world in a series of relational happenings that become-with the past. If colonization is a kind of death work that murders the future, the present, and the past, weaving is a resurgent practice that works to rebuild life-sustaining webs that enliven the ancestral death narratives of Country.

STRATA

I began this chapter contemplating the gorge country where I was raised and the complex entanglements of ethics, time, and colonization in Anaiwan lands. I want to return now to geological strata to think through the creative powers of rhythmed becoming in the midst of so much ongoing violence.

Bushwalking through the volcanic ruins of my youth, amid granite crevices of time that cannot be relived yet never disappear, I often find myself slipping into the rhythms of my childhood. My eyes wander across rocks becoming blue-tongued lizards, and my hands unconsciously collect sticks and stones and absentmindedly drop them again. Debbie wrote, "The great rhythms of the earth are built on motion and on the intervals or pauses. We are tuned to life before we even come into the world: the heartbeat is part of these patterns" (Rose 2000, 287). The etymological origins of the English word *text* can be traced back to the Latin *texere*, meaning "to weave," and our bodies, too, are living woven texts, carrying not only the biological narratives of our creaturely lives but the rhythms of a deep coevolutionary past that resonate at the periphery of our consciousness.

Time marks itself in all of us, not only in wrinkles and scars, but in patterns of synchronous and sequential time stretching back to the beginning of the universe. The temporal strata of the planet are woven within us as if they were grasses woven into a basket. Each woven thread builds on and follows the next. Epigenetic and morphological histories can be read in the color of our eyes, the mitochondria in our cells, the bacteria in our guts. We are legion and polyrhythmic all the way down.

Debbie's concept of multispecies knots of ethical time is a poetic framework in which to make sense of our ancestral, multispecies enfolding as an ethics sustained by connectivity: "To be for one's self one must always, also, be for others" (2012a, 110). In this chapter I have sought to bring Debbie's notion of embodied knots of time as multispecies ethics into dialogue with her own call for recuperative work in dark times. Drawing on encounters and dialogues with Anaiwan communities, practices, and environments, experiences that Debbie's mentorship and work inspired, I hope I have helped to articulate that a knot of multispecies ethical time is not merely a poetic tool for understanding biological life on Earth but can also be materially and discursively mobilized as a tactic of resistance to colonial violence and death work. Weaving reveals one of the many ways embodied knots of multispecies time can be rethreaded through recuperative practices at a time when the delicate connections that nurture life are being unraveled.

Debbie wrote, "The moral burden of the past in the present includes the work of sustaining the heterogeneous gifts of time" (Rose 2004, 27). As creatures of memory and story, we are woven from the presences of the past. In a world that is sustained by multispecies knots of ethical time, "weaving our journey into whatever we are making" is a process of weaving gifts of time into the matter of the world—not the time of a single isolated life but the legion times of the living, connected, multispecies planet that we carry within us.[10]

If life is sustained by gifts of time, each gift is both a blessing from the past and a responsibility for the future. I carry the gifts of Debbie's insight, mentorship, and friendship with me as if they were a woven basket. This nourishing interface, made of poetry and thought, holds and nurtures knowledges and, if handled with commitment and care, can knot together times, lives, and worlds.

KATE WRIGHT

NOTES

1. This echoes a line from A. R. Ammons's poem "Embedded Storms," cited in Hatley (2002, 7). The line is "and we, too, are wonderfully made and wonderfully undone," in which Ammons appeals for humans to come to grips with their mortality and temporal finitude.

2. Rose (2004) argues that decolonization depends on ethical dialogue, which in turn depends on our acknowledgment and understanding of our own "harshly situated presence" in damaged places and within a history of conquest and violence (21–22).

3. Parts of these interviews and my reflections on encounter as a decolonizing process have been published in Wright (2017, 2018).

4. Briggs, personal communication, Armidale, New South Wales, Australia, November 30, 2018.

5. Briggs, personal communication, 2018.

6. Gabi Briggs was the first to inform me about the significance of the eels' migratory journey and its relationship to lomandra weaving.

7. Patrick Lupica, ranger, New England Area—National Parks and Wildlife, personal communication, January 10, 2019.

8. Briggs, personal communication, Armidale, New South Wales, Australia, August 17, 2015.

9. Briggs, personal communication, 2018.

10. The quotation is from Briggs, personal communication, 2018.

REFERENCES

Alfred, Taiaiake. 2005. *Wasáse: Indigenous Pathways of Action and Freedom*. Toronto: University of Toronto Press.

Alfred, Taiaiake. 2018. "Don't Just Resist. Return to Who You Are." In "The Decolonize Issue." Special issue, *YES! Magazine*, Spring 2018. https://www.yesmagazine.org/issues/decolonize/dont-just-resist-return-to-who-you-are-20180409.

Aoyama, Jun, Noritaka Mochioka, Tsuguo Otake, Satoshi Ishikawa, Yutaka Kawakami, Peter Castle, Mutsumi Nishida, and Katsumi Tsukamoto. 1999. "Distribution and Dispersal of Anguillid Leptocephali in the Western Pacific Ocean Revealed by Molecular Analysis." *Marine Ecology Progress Series*, no. 188: 193–200.

Augé, Marc. 1995. *Non-places: Introduction to an Anthropology of Supermodernity*. Translated by John Howe. London: Verso.

Bateson, Gregory. 1972. *Steps to an Ecology of Mind*. San Francisco: Chandler.

Bawaka Country, Sarah Wright, Sandie Suchet-Pearson, Kate Lloyd, LakLak Burarrwanga, Ritjilili Ganambarr, Merrkiyawuy Ganambarr-Stubbs, Banbapuy Ganambarr, Djawundil Maymuru, Jill Sweeney. 2015. "Co-Becoming Bawaka: Towards a Relational Understanding of Place/Space." *Progress in Human Geography* 40 (4): 455–475.

Benjamin, Walter. [1936] 1968. *Illuminations*. Edited and translated by Hannah Arendt. London: Fontana.

Beumer, John P. 1992. "Eels: Biology, Control, and Culture." Fisheries Information Leaflet QL92006. Brisbane: Queensland Department of Primary Industries.

Burarrwanga, Laklak, Ritjilili Ganambarr, Merrkiyawuy Ganambarr-Stubbs, Banbapuy Ganambarr, Djawundil Maymuru, Sarah Wright, Sandie Suchet-Pearson, and Kate Lloyd. 2008. *Weaving Lives Together at Bawaka, North East Arnhem Land*. Newcastle: Centre for Urban and Regional Studies, University of Newcastle.

Chakrabarty, Dipesh. 2000. *Provincializing Europe: Postcolonial Thought and Historical Difference*. Princeton, NJ: Princeton University Press.

Chrulew, Matthew. 2011. "Managing Love and Death at the Zoo: The Biopolitics of Endangered Species Preservation." *Australian Humanities Review*, no. 50, 137–157.

Clayton-Dixon, Callum. 2019. "Reclaiming Our Story: Resistance, Survival and the New England Linguicide." Master's thesis, University of New England.

Davis, Heather, and Zoe Todd. 2017. "On the Importance of a Date, or, Decolonizing the Anthropocene." *ACME: An International Journal for Critical Geographies* 16 (4): 761–780.

Deleuze, Gilles. 1995. *Negotiations 1972–1990*. Edited by Constantin Boundas. Translated by Mark Lester with Charles Stivale. New York: Columbia University Press.

Deleuze, Gilles, and Clare Parnet. 1977. *Dialogues*. Translated by Hugh Tomlinson and Barbara Habberjam. New York: Columbia University Press.

Drouineau, Hilaire, Caroline Durif, Martin Castonguay, Maria Mateo, Eric Rochard, Guy Verreault, Kazuki Yokouchi, and Patrick Lambert. 2018. "Freshwater Eels: A Symbol of the Effects of Global Change." *Fish and Fisheries* 9 (5): 903–930.

Gooley, Geoffrey J., Lachlan J. McKinnon, Brett A. Ingram, Brendan Larkin, R. O. Collins, and Sena De Silva. 1999. "Assessment of Juvenile Eel Resources in South Eastern Australia and Associated Development of Intensive Eel Farming for Local Production." Final Report FRDC Project No. 94/067. Queenscliff, VIC: Marine and Freshwater Resources Institute.

Haraway, Donna. 2016. *Staying with the Trouble: Making Kin in the Chthulucene*. Durham, NC: Duke University Press.

Harries-Jones, Peter. 1995. *A Recursive Vision: Ecological Understanding and Gregory Bateson*. Toronto: University of Toronto Press.

Hatley, James. 2000. *Suffering Witness: The Quandary of Responsibility after the Irreparable*. Albany: State University of New York Press.

Hatley, James. 2002. "The Virtue of Temporal Discernment: Rethinking the Extent and Coherence of the Good in a Time of Mass Species Extinction." *Environmental Philosophy* 9 (1): 1–22.

Idle No More Sydney. 2013. "Idle No More Sydney International Day of Action— 28th January, 2013." YouTube video, 4:17. https://www.youtube.com/watch?v =ei7woE1pdDc&fbclid=IwAR2OEqQldHUM31iMp5etRczkASu1ahlSvzbwXj M1Dt49UrTEyQ4n8yL5NpY.

Ingold, Tim. 2000. *The Perception of the Environment: Essays on Livelihood, Dwelling and Skill*. London: Routledge.

Lintermans, Mark. 2009. *Fishes of the Murray Darling Basin: An Introductory Guide.* Canberra: Murray Darling Basin Authority.

Margulis, Lynn, and Dorion Sagan. 2000. *What Is Life?* Berkeley: University of California Press.

Martineau, Jarrett, and Eric Ritskes. 2014. "Fugitive Indigeneity: Reclaiming the Terrain of Decolonial Struggle through Indigenous Art." *Decolonization: Indigeneity, Education and Society* 3 (1): i–xii.

Muecke, Stephen. 2004. *Ancient and Modern: Time, Culture and Indigenous Philosophy.* Sydney: University of New South Wales Press.

Parkin, Justine. 2017. "Fecundity." *Environmental Humanities* 9 (2): 460–463.

Pugliese, Joseph. 2015. "Forensic Ecologies of Occupied Zones and Geographies of Dispossession: Gaza and Occupied East Jerusalem." *Borderlands* 14 (1): 1–37.

Queensland Eel Fishery. 2009. *Annual Status Report 2009—Queensland Eel Fishery.* Brisbane: Queensland Primary Industries and Fisheries.

Rose, Deborah Bird. 1992. *Dingo Makes Us Human: Life and Land in an Aboriginal Australian Culture.* Cambridge: Cambridge University Press.

Rose, Deborah Bird. 2000. "To Dance with Time: A Victoria River Aboriginal Study." *Australian Journal of Anthropology* 11 (3): 287–296.

Rose, Deborah Bird. 2004. *Reports from a Wild Country: Ethics for Decolonisation,* Sydney: University of New South Wales Press.

Rose, Deborah Bird. 2012a. "Cosmopolitics: The Kiss of Life." *New Formations,* no. 76, 101–113.

Rose, Deborah Bird. 2012b. "Multispecies Knots of Ethical Time." *Environmental Philosophy* 9 (1): 127–140.

Rose, Deborah Bird. 2018. "Gifts of Life in the Shadow of Death." HumanNature Sydney Environmental Humanities Lecture Series, Australian Museum, Sydney, March 8, 2018.

Sharpe, Christina. 2016. *In the Wake: On Blackness and Being.* Durham, NC: Duke University Press.

Shiao, Jen-Chieh, Wan-Nian Tzeng, Adrian Collins, and D. J. Jellyman. 2001. "Dispersal Pattern of Glass Eel Stage of Anguilla Australis Revealed by Otolith Growth Increments." *Marine Ecology Progress Series,* no. 219: 241–250.

Swain, Tony. 1993. *A Place for Strangers: Towards a History of Australian Aboriginal Being.* Cambridge: Cambridge University Press.

van Dooren, Thom. 2014. *Flight Ways: Life and Loss at the Edge of Extinction.* New York: Columbia University Press.

Vizenor, Gerald. 1999. *Manifest Manners: Narratives on Postindian Survivance.* Lincoln: University of Nebraska Press.

Wolfe, Patrick. 2006. "Settler Colonialism and the Elimination of the Native." *Journal of Genocide Research* 8 (4): 387–409.

Wright, Kate. 2017. *Transdisciplinary Journeys in the Anthropocene: More-Than-Human Encounters.* London: Routledge.

Wright, Kate. 2018. "In the Shadow of a Willow Tree: A Community Garden Experiment in Decolonising, Multispecies Research." *Cultural Studies Review* 24 (1): 74–101.

AFTERWORD

Memories with Deborah Rose

LINDA PAYI FORD

IT HAS BEEN A LONG JOURNEY since Deborah Bird Rose and I first met for the Wagait Dispute Hearing in 1993 in the town of Batchelor in the Northern Territory. We met under a huge rainbow that had filled my biological mother, Ala Nancy Ngulilkang Daiyi, and me with hope. Ala Daiyi hoped that this female anthropologist named Deborah Bird Rose would better serve Aboriginal social justice and have the capacity to support her and her Mak Marranunggu family to be recognized as Traditional Owners of the lands covered by the Delissaville, Wagait, Larrakia Aboriginal Land Trust.

Another group had been recognized as the Traditional Owners of these lands in 1981 in the Finniss River Land Claim. But in 1991 that decision was overturned by the Federal Court, opening the way for new hearings of claims from the five competing clans. It was, and still is, the Mak Marranunggu or Mak Mak family's claim that the Northern Land Council had not appropriately examined all the evidence provided to them by our old people and had made the wrong decision in 1981.[1]

I tell my stories of the struggle for social justice and what was created by this moment in my family's shared histories. My reality today offers a pathway for Aboriginal people and their future for justice to honor my mothers.

In this story I share how Deborah Bird Rose, Debbie, was adopted into my clan by my Ala Nancy Ngulilkang Daiyi as her sister Tyaemaen. *Ala* in the Marranunggu language and kinship system refers to a "mother." This relationship extends through the deeply interconnected kinship system to other mothers. Hence, Daiyi is my Ala—mother. When my Ala Daiyi adopted Debbie as her sister, she bestowed on her the name Tyaemaen. Tyaemaen is a Mak Mak Marranunggu name and the name of my Ala Nancy Ngulilkang Daiyi's sister. Therefore, through kinship, Debbie became my Ala Tyaemaen—a significant milestone for an outsider to achieve. Ala Tyaemaen is Mangali or grandmother to my two children, Chloe and Emily Ford, and mother-in-law to my husband, Mark Ford. These are my key family members who support my research and celebrate in our success.

Debbie is always there for us Mak Mak mob. She will always be with me in spirit.

As a young Aboriginal woman, I moved with my husband, Mark, from Batchelor in the Northern Territory so that I could attend the Aboriginal Teacher Education Program at Townsville Teachers College in 1981. After twelve months we relocated to Warrnambool in Victoria, and I transferred my undergraduate studies. I successfully completed the course and graduated from Warrnambool College of Advanced Education (now known as Deakin University) in 1985 with a diploma of teaching (primary). This was a significant milestone nationally, with a thousand Aboriginal and Torres Strait Islander teachers graduating by 1990. In 1985 twenty-five Indigenous teachers graduated nationally, and I was one of very few Aboriginal teachers to graduate in the state of Victoria.

I worked in the Western District of Victoria as a primary schoolteacher until 1991, teaching in Portland, Narrawong, and Heywood. Mark and I had a shared-farm arrangement with his siblings near the town of Heywood in the southwestern district, raising beef cattle and lambs for the domestic and live export market.

In 1991 Mark and I returned to Batchelor in the Northern Territory. I started work at Batchelor College as a lecturer. In 1993 I completed my graduate diploma in special education and was granted my testamur at Batchelor

219

College's graduation ceremony. Pat Varley traveled to Batchelor to deliver my testamur at my graduation ceremony, where my Wangga and Wali ceremony family from Wagait and Daly River danced me up to receive my testamur. I never imagined my life as an Aboriginal scholar.

It was later that year that Ala Debbie Tyaemaen was invited to meet the Mak Mak Marranunggu family in Batchelor at our White Eagle office at the Outdoor Education Village. Debbie spoke to all of us and wanted to assess what we thought the land claim meant to us in preparation for giving evidence to the Wagait Dispute Hearing proceedings.

Over the next two years, Ala Debbie Tyaemaen worked closely with us. I recall having numerous discussions with her about the discourse of pedagogy and what this meant for Aboriginal people, especially since I was now working as an academic at Batchelor College (now called Batchelor Institute of Indigenous Tertiary Education). Those discussions opened my mind's eye to the endless possibilities for Aboriginal people and for me. I was teaching in the education programs applying the "Both Ways Philosophy" developed by Aboriginal people and colleagues at this time. It was an exciting place to be. Both Ala Daiyi and Ala Debbie Tyaemaen always gave me 100 percent support and encouraged me to continue to further my education. Ala Daiyi would say, "If you don't do it, no one else will!" Ala Debbie Tyaemaen reinforced this philosophy.

Ala Debbie Tyaemaen had continued to stay in close contact with Ala Daiyi regarding the Wagait Dispute Hearing to hear their decision. In 1995 (by which time I had enrolled in my master of education at Deakin University), Dad and I were having a yarn about Ala Debbie Tyaemaen, and he mentioned how she had taken an interest in my career and had taken me under her wing. I agreed and confirmed that I would be respectful of our relationship and that I would approach Ala Debbie Tyaemaen to discuss career options with her.

My father, Maurice (aka Max) Sargent, was very unwell. He passed on June 24, 1995, just before the Dispute Hearing Committee handed down its decision that recognized Mak Mak Marranunggu as Traditional Owners of E2 of the Delissaville, Wagait, Larrakia Aboriginal Land Trust.

Ala Debbie Tyaemaen encouraged me to apply for the Inaugural Stanner Scholarship at the Australian National University, which I was awarded later in 1995. Owing to personal reasons, I ceased my scholarship in early 1996—I had become pregnant with Chloe Ngelebe. Three years later, I graduated with my master of education from Deakin University in 1998. This was the year Emily Tyaemaen, my second daughter, was born. Mark and I were truly blessed.

In 1998 I enrolled part-time in a doctoral degree at Northern Territory University. I later transferred to Deakin University in 2001. I resigned from Batchelor and accepted an academic lecturing position at the Northern Territory University in the Faculty of Science, Information Technology and Education. Northern Territory University became Charles Darwin University in 2003.

Throughout this period Ala Tyaemaen had been drafting the book *Country of the Heart: An Indigenous Australian Homeland* with us (Rose et al. 2002). She arranged for the photographer Sharon D'Amico to visit and take photos for the book and later organized slide nights in Batchelor at our place or at her place in Tiwi, a suburb of Darwin. The first edition of the book was published in 2002 by the Aboriginal Studies Press.

We all celebrated the amazing event of becoming coauthors with Deborah Bird Rose.

Ala Debbie Tyaemaen had indeed opened my eyes to scholarly work, and she shared her knowledge. I felt there was honor and integrity in her approach to working with Australia's First Peoples. This was illuminated when she shared authorship with us for the publication of *Country of the Heart* in 2002. This unprecedented reciprocation of the Western "treasures" in this way with us was nothing short of brilliant.

From that moment, my view of higher education and knowledge changed.

Ala Debbie Tyaemaen had ignited the metaphorical fire within me to address Indigenous knowledge and intellectual property and shared ownership. Publishing research changed the way I thought about publishing our stories—and for Ala Daiyi. She would often say, "If only I could read and write, I would write my own book!" She said this often when outsiders would visit our Mak Mak community, and they couldn't understand what Ala Daiyi was expressing. The cultural barriers were and still are present. This would frustrate her no end. The relationship that Ala Debbie Tyaemaen had with her sister Ala Daiyi was unique. They could understand each other's standpoint.

I realized then how much Ala Daiyi really wanted to know more about writing, reading, and multiple literacies. She was hungry to obtain knowledge and to share her knowledge. Ala Daiyi, Mark and I, and later Chloe and Emily traveled as a family unit across the Country to places where Ala Debbie Tyaemaen had organized book launches. We went to the Sydney Writers Festival, the University of Melbourne, and the Australian National University, as well as to Scotland and America. Then, for the second edition of the book, we went to the Brisbane Writers Festival in 2010. Her sister Tyaemaen and I made Ala Daiyi's dream of a book a reality.

Debbie certainly looked after us.

In the late 1990s, Ala Tyaemaen relocated to Canberra, so we did not see each other as often as we would have liked. She invited me and family members to do guest lectures at the Australian National University on a regular basis. She also organized an installation at the Australian National Museum of the Mak Mak Marranunggu in the "Tangled Destinies" exhibition in 2002. This had a huge impact on my views on what museums and archives were and how they housed historical records and influenced the people who visited them to check out their collections.

In October 2006 I completed my doctoral dissertation "Narratives and Landscapes: Their Capacity to Serve Indigenous Knowledge Interests" (Ford 2005). My Ala Daiyi and Ala Debbie Tyaemaen were very proud. I was proud of both my Alas. At the time Ala Daiyi was unwell. She passed on April 4, 2007. I, as well as loved ones and others, was dealt such a huge blow. Ala Debbie Tyaemaen attended the ceremonies on Country on the Wagait.

Ala Debbie continued to work on projects that she was passionate about. She loved the environment and the plants and animals. Ala Debbie's use of words to portray her worldview was profound. Our book, *Country of the Heart*, and her own *Dingo Makes Us Human* captured the moods of the Country's spirit.

Ala Debbie's anthropological studies were amazing. In her later years of academia, her focus was the anthropology of the environment, how land and animals were tied up with people.

Ala Debbie Tyaemaen supported my Australian Research Council grants and other research projects. I felt blessed to have someone of her standing in academia working alongside me. When Ala Debbie informed me that she was unwell, my family and I were devastated. We often visited her when we were traveling to Sydney University to work at the "Con" (Sydney Conservatorium of Music).

Ala Debbie Tyaemaen passed away. What a great loss to the Australian academy.

Both my Alas' spirits continue to influence my research and are powerful drivers in what I do today. They have supported my research spiritually, and their presence continues to manifest in my research. My Alas Daiyi and Debbie Tyaemaen had taught me about the benefits of historical files in museums and archive collections to the extent that I have led the development of a repository with the Pacific and Regional Archive for Digital Sources in Endangered Cultures. This was a collaborative effort with Linda Barwick, Allan Marett, Jodie Kell, Mark Ford, Emily Ford, Chloe Ford, Nicole

Thompson, Ruth Wallace, Michael Christie, Ngandi Kathy Guthadjaka, and the Mak Mak Marranunggu and Warramiri family.

My research has taken me, my family, other Mak Mak Marranunggu, and colleagues to museums and archives, both private and public. There are amazing amounts of information stored in the archive collections waiting to be read.

My Alas have transferred their knowledges about the information that is important. Honoring my Alas' knowledge about history provides an account of the past to right the wrongs and to include an Aboriginal perspective. This practice is formalizing an alternative historical narrative to forge a better future for generations of Australians.

It is with honor that I have known the great works produced by Ala Tyaemaen Deborah Rose.

This is my story of how Ala Tyaemaen Deborah Rose shared her sweat on our Country Kurrindju.

NOTE

1. The Delissaville, Wagait, Larrakia Aboriginal Land Trust was identified as an Aboriginal Reserve by South Australia's colonial surveyor George Goyder in 1869. During the 1976–1981 Finniss River Land Claim, several groups disputed ownership. The Northern Land Council recognized other peoples as the Traditional Owners, a decision that the competing clans disputed. The Federal Court heard the case in 1991. Justice Olney overturned the Northern Land Council's decision as to their recognition of Traditional Aboriginal Owners. The Wagait Dispute Hearings were set for 1993–1995 to hear the five competing clans who were disputing ownership. This hearing was chaired by Dr. David Richie and overseen by Justice Michael Maurice with panel members representing the Full Council of the Northern Land Council.

REFERENCES

Rose, Deborah Bird. 2000. *Dingo Makes Us Human: Life and Land in an Australian Aboriginal Culture*. Cambridge: Cambridge University Press.

Rose, Deborah Bird, Sharon D'Amico, Nancy Daiyi, Kathy Deveraux, Margaret Daiyi, Linda Ford, and April Bright. 2002. *Country of the Heart: An Indigenous Australian Homeland*. Canberra: Aboriginal Studies Press.

Ford, Linda M. 2005. "Narratives and Landscapes: Their Capacity to Serve Indigenous Knowledge Interests." PhD dissertation, Deakin University, Geelong, Victoria, Australia.

CONTRIBUTORS

BAWAKA COUNTRY including SANDIE SUCHET-PEARSON, SARAH WRIGHT, KATE LLOYD, LAKLAK BURARRWANGA, RITJILILI GANAMBARR, MERRKIYAWUY GANAMBARR-STUBBS, BANBAPUY GANAMBARR, AND DJAWUNDIL MAYMURU is an Indigenous and non-Indigenous, more-than-human research collective. Bawaka Country is the diverse land, water, human and nonhuman animals (including the human authors of this chapter), plants, rocks, thoughts, and songs that make up the Yolŋu homeland of Bawaka in North East Arnhem Land, Australia. Laklak, Ritjilili, Merrkiyawuy, and Banbapuy are four Yolŋu sisters, elders, and caretakers for Bawaka Country, together with their daughter, Djawundil. Kate, Sarah, and Sandie are three non-Indigenous human geographers from Newcastle and Macquarie Universities who have been adopted into the family as granddaughter, sister, and daughter. The authorship team is also known as the Bawaka Collective. They have worked together since 2006 and have established an international reputation for being on the forefront of innovative and ethical research.

MATTHEW CHRULEW is senior research fellow in the School of Media, Creative Arts and Social Inquiry at Curtin University. His essays have appeared in *Angelaki*, *SubStance*, *Parallax*, and *Biosemiotics* and his short stories in *Cosmos* and *Westerly*. He is coeditor of *Foucault and Animals* (2016) and *Extinction Studies: Stories of Time, Death, and Generations* (2017), was a founding associate editor of *Environmental Humanities* journal, and is series editor of the Edinburgh University Press book series Animalities.

COLIN DAYAN is professor of law and professor of English at Vanderbilt University. She has just published two memoirs that form a diptych: *In the Belly of Her Ghost* (2019) and *Animal Quintet* (2020). Her other books include *The Law Is a*

White Dog (2011) and *With Dogs at the Edge of Life* (2015). A member of the American Academy of Arts and Sciences, she has received fellowships from the National Endowment for the Humanities, the American Council of Learned Societies, and the Guggenheim Foundation.

LINDA PAYI FORD is a Traditional Owner Rak Mak Mak Marranunggu woman from Kurrindju in the Finniss River and Reynold River regions southwest of Darwin in the Northern Territory, Australia. Associate Professor Ford is a principal research fellow in the Northern Institute in the College of Indigenous Futures, Arts and Society, located in Darwin, Northern Territory, Australia. She applies her Mirrwana and Wurrkama methodology to her Indigenous research practice and theory across multiple disciplinary fields. Ford balances her academic research career, teaching and learning in higher education, family, and caring for country and culture.

DONNA J. HARAWAY is distinguished professor emerita in the History of Consciousness Department at the University of California, Santa Cruz. Attending to the implosions of biology, culture, and politics, Haraway's work explores string figures composed by science fact, science fiction, speculative feminism, speculative fabulation, science and technology studies, and multispecies worlding. Her books include *Staying with the Trouble: Making Kin in the Chthulucene* (2016) and *When Species Meet* (2008). With Adele Clarke she coedited *Making Kin Not Population* (2018), which addresses questions of human numbers, feminist antiracist reproductive and environmental justice, and multispecies flourishing.

JAMES HATLEY is an emeritus professor in both philosophy and environmental studies at Salisbury University in Maryland. He is the author of *Suffering Witness: The Quandary of Responsibility after the Irreparable* (2000) and numerous other essays and collections in, and at the intersections of, Holocaust and genocide studies, extinction studies, and environmental philosophy.

OWAIN JONES is a cultural geographer and became the first professor of environmental humanities in the United Kingdom in 2014 at Bath Spa University, where he was deputy director of the Research Centre for the Environmental Humanities (2016–2019). He has published over eighty scholarly articles on various aspects of nature-society relations and four books (coedited/authored): *Visual Culture in the Northern British Archipelago: Imagining Islands* (2018), *Participatory Research in More-Than-Human Worlds* (2017), *Geography and Memory: Identity, Place and Becoming* (2012), and *Tree Cultures: Places of Trees* (2002).

STEPHEN MUECKE is professor of creative writing in the College of Humanities, Arts and Social Sciences at Flinders University, South Australia, and is a fellow of the Australian Academy of the Humanities. His recent books are *Latour and the Humanities* (2020), edited with Rita Felski, and *The Children's Country: Creation of a Goolarabooloo Future in North-West Australia*, coauthored with Paddy Roe (2020).

KATE RIGBY, FAHA, is director of the Research Centre for Environmental Humanities at Bath Spa University and adjunct professor of literary studies at Monash University. She was the founding president of the Australia–New Zealand Association for the Study of Literature, Environment and Culture and founding coeditor of PAN (*Philosophy Activism Nature*). Her books include *Dancing with Disaster: Environmental Histories, Narratives and Ethics for Perilous Times* (2015) and *Reclaiming Romanticism: Towards an Ecopoetics of Decolonization* (2020).

CATRIONA SANDILANDS is professor in the Faculty of Environmental and Urban Change at York University. Her recent and upcoming publications on plant-human relations include contributions to *Catalyst: Feminism, Theory, Technoscience* and *The Cambridge Companion to the Environmental Humanities*. This writing will be collected in a book, "Plantasmagoria: Botanical Encounters in the [M]Anthropocene." Other recent publications include the edited creative writing collection *Rising Tides: Reflections for Climate Changing Times* (2019). She divides her time between Toronto and Galiano Island, British Columbia.

ISABELLE STENGERS is professor emerita at the Université Libre de Bruxelles. She has written numerous books, including *Thinking with Whitehead* (2014), *Cosmopolitics I* (2010), *Cosmopolitics II* (2011), *In Catastrophic Times* (2015), and *Another Science Is Possible* (2015). She has developed a speculative constructionist concept of "ecology of practices" in connection with the philosophy of Gilles Deleuze, Alfred N. Whitehead, and William James and the anthropology of Bruno Latour.

ANNA LOWENHAUPT TSING teaches anthropology at the University of California, Santa Cruz. Her most recent project, with many collaborators, is *Feral Atlas: The More-Than-Human Anthropocene* (2021; feralatlas.org). She is the author of numerous books, including *The Mushroom at the End of the World* (2015) and *Friction: An Ethnography of Global Connection* (2005).

THOM VAN DOOREN is associate professor in the Department of Gender and Cultural Studies and the Sydney Environment Institute, University of Sydney, and professor II in the Oslo School of Environmental Humanities, University of Oslo. His research and writing focus on some of the many philosophical, ethical, cultural, and political issues that arise in the context of species extinctions and human entanglements with threatened species and places. He is the author of *Flight Ways: Life and Loss at the Edge of Extinction* (2014) and *The Wake of Crows: Living and Dying in Shared Worlds* (2019) and coeditor of *Extinction Studies: Stories of Time, Death, and Generations* (2017).

KATE WRIGHT works at the interface of community-based social and environmental activism and environmental humanities research. Her first book, *Transdisciplinary Journeys in the Anthropocene: More-than-Human Encounters*, was published in the Routledge Environmental Humanities series in 2017. She is currently completing her second book, an experimental environmental history of the Armidale Aboriginal Community Garden, coauthored with Anaiwan Elder Steve Widders.

231

INDEX

233

Lloyd, Kate, 177
lomandra grasses, 199, 201–205, 208, 209, 212
long-finned river eels (*Anguilla reinhardtii*), 203–204, 206
Lopez, Barry, 124
Lupinus argenteus, 157
Lupinus siriceus, 157

magic of state, 139
Mak Mak Marranunggu, 218–223
mammalian extinction, 119
Manambu people, New Guinea, 139
Manning, Richard, 171n1
Manucodia ater (glossy-mantled manucodes), 22
Marett, Allan, 222
Margulis, Lynn, 56–57, 202, 204
Martineau, Jarrett, 209–210
Marx, Karl, 59
matrilineal identity. *See ngurlu*
Mauro, Iwein, 23–24
Maymuru, Djawundil, 176–177, 183
Megapodius freycinet (dusky megapodes), 24
Melville, Herman, 190
microbecoming, 213
Micropsitta keiensis (yellow-capped pygmy parrot), 26–27
milkarri, 174–176, 179–180, 182–185
Millner, Jacquelyn, 76
Mimesis and Alterity (Taussig), 146
Moby Dick (Melville), 190
Moderns, 205; beliefs of, 143–144; extraction colonialism and, 145; modernist iconoclasm, 135; totemism and, 135–136
Monahan, Linda, 121–123
monologue, 171n5; bondage of, 177; critical, 178
Monsanto, 37
Muecke, Stephen, 55
multiple ways of knowing, 26
multispecies: attention, 16, 200; dialogues, 47; ethnography, 137; knots, 214; life, 46, 205; openness, 48; studies, 3

multiverses, 138–140
mystery of world complexity, 107–108

narcissism, 178
Nathan, Tobie, 138
National Museum of Australia, 114, 222
naturalcultural restoration, 91
naturalism, 136
naturaltechnical worlds, 70–71
Nature's Little Helpers (Piccinini), 75, 77–78, 80, 82, 91
Nazi genocide, 156, 158–159
Nazi Holocaust survivors, 53–54, 156–157
Neale, Timothy, 43
neighbors, 43, 122, 181
Nest (Piccinini), 71, 73
Newsome, A. E., 143
ngargulala, 143
ngurlu (matrilineal identity), 146
Nogelmeier, Puakea, 107
Noh, Pak, 26
nonplace, 210
Nourishing Terrains (Rose), 3, 181

ŋäpaki histories, 176
objectivity: challenge to, 144; science and, 57, 59–62
"Observations on Transference-Love" (Freud), 191
Ogden, Laura, 37–39, 46
'Ohu Gon, Sam, 106
'ōhi'a, 94
openness, 82, 166; multispecies, 48; Rose on, 46, 178–179
Orang Rimba people, 121
Other, the: dehumanization of, 170; Levinas on, 122, 166–167; rejection of, 168
Oxley, John, 206, 208
Oxley Wild Rivers National Park, 198, 208

Pacific and Regional Archive for Digital Sources in Endangered Cultures, 222
Palikea snail exclosure, 95, 97, 99–100, 106–107
Palmer, Sue, 116–117
Paradisaea rubra (red bird of paradise), 17

235

INDEX

238

239

www.ingramcontent.com/pod-product-compliance
Lightning Source LLC
Chambersburg PA
CBHW071737270326
41928CB00013B/2715